DATE DUE

MY 2 6 '01			

DEMCO 38-296

DATE DUE

ELDERLEARNING

New Frontier in an

Aging Society

by
Lois Lamdin
with
Mary Fugate

AMERICAN COUNCIL ON EDUCATION ★
ORYX PRESS ★
Series on Higher Education
1997

The rare Arabian oryx is believed to have inspired the myth of the unicorn. This desert antelope became virtually extinct in the early 1960s. At that time several groups of international conservationists arranged to have 9 animals sent to the Phoenix Zoo to be the nucleus of a captive breeding herd. Today the oryx population is over 1,000 and over 500 have been returned to the Middle East.

© 1997 by the American Council on Education and The Oryx Press
Published by The Oryx Press
4041 North Central at Indian School Road
Phoenix, Arizona 85012-3397

Published simultaneously in Canada
Printed and bound in the United States of America

∞ The paper used in this publication meets the minimum requirements of the American National Standard for Information Sciences—Permanence of Paper for Printed Library Materials, ANSI Z39.48-1984.

Library of Congress Cataloging-in-Publication Data

Lamdin, Lois S.
  Elderlearning: new frontier in an aging society / by Lois Lamdin
with Mary Fugate
        p.   cm. — (American Council on Education/Oryx Press series on
  higher education)
  Includes bibliographical references and index.
  ISBN 0-89774-959-6 (cloth : alk. paper)
  1. Aged—Education—United States.   2. Continuing education—
United States.   3. Adult education—United States   I. Fugate,
Mary.   II. Title.   III. Series.
LC5471.L36   1997
374'.01—dc21   96-29843
                                                                    CIP

To Edie and Lou,
who didn't live long enough
to become elderlearners
but who taught me to value
learning at all ages.

CONTENTS

Preface *vii*

CHAPTER 1   Living in the Age Age   1

CHAPTER 2   Defining "Old" in the Age Age   15

CHAPTER 3   Life Stage and Development Theory: Implications for Learning   27

CHAPTER 4   Confounding the Stereotype: The Cognitive Abilities of Older Learners   36

CHAPTER 5   Use It or Lose It   52

CHAPTER 6   A Profile of Elderlearners   66

CHAPTER 7   Older Adult Learning in Colleges and Universities   88

CHAPTER 8   Other Sources of Formal Learning   101

CHAPTER 9   Older Adults' Self-Directed Learning   117

CHAPTER 10   Modes of Learning for Older Adults   130

CHAPTER 11   Socially Constructive Aging: Work, Retirement, Volunteerism, and Leisure Activities   143

CHAPTER 12   An Agenda for the Age Age   161

Appendix A: Elderlearning Survey Questionnaire   179

Appendix B: Resources for Elderlearners   182

Bibliography   185

Index   195

PREFACE

The following three poems are the first ever written by Paul Lohmeyer, a retired marketing manager I met on an Elderhostel in Italy in 1996. He showed them to me with great diffidence, saying apologetically, "They aren't much, but they were something I had to get out."

Crossing the Tiber

Columbia, Sacramento, Rio Grande, Colorado, Mississippi,
Ohio, Hudson, Thames, Seine, Rhine, Danube, Volga—

We cross the Tiber
But not casually . . . not without thought.

The Stones of Assisi

Smaller, slower steps, we strive ascending.
The site attained, the view possessed,
enlightened pause.

Longer, livelier, liquid steps descending.
Watch the color, texture blend with ivy, pot, door,
weathered tile, soft wind moan.

The stones have entered my bone.

What Francis Saw

Francis saw no more than we, but somewhat differently,
the flowers, birds, the land, the vine,
But never said, "this must be mine."
God created all and each as one,
Brother, Sister, Father, Mother Earth,
Not by man's grasping to be undone.

Another member of the same Elderhostel group, a retired Lutheran minister, responded in writing to a question I posed at dinner one evening about what he was learning and what the connection between travel and learning was for him. The next morning at breakfast he handed me a scrap of notebook paper containing the following thoughts:

> I always thought travel, especially to the lands of my roots (Germany, Great Britain, Norway, Sweden, Denmark, Finland, Iceland) would help me understand my heritage, my priorities, my prejudices. . . . [then later] I decided to go back to [France, Greece, Rome, and] the Renaissance to get beneath or behind the Nordic heritage.

> During the 60s, 70s, and 80s, my platform began to crumble; the kids took off for Canada and France, abandoned my cultural preferences and priorities and my faith, which by the 70s began to be more inclusive (Pope John XXIII and the ecumenical movement). Another son bummed around the world, spent some months in India, checked out Yoga, became a vegetarian, and actually reconsidered Christianity(??).

> After making Luther, Bach, and Schweitzer excuses for trips to Europe in '82, '85, '91 and '93, we decided to get back to Italy and Assisi, to Francis, the communities . . . .

> The human race must figure out how to live together peacefully without raping the earth and its other inhabitants. I still believe Jesus had (and has) the best clues to this quest. The church was originally on this track, but it's been wandering since Constantine institutionalized it in the 4-5th centuries. The spirit seems to be calling many back to this community, and I want to be a partner in this second (or third or fourth or tenth) renaissance.

> Thank you for asking me to write this down. Shalom.

>   John Gerberding

Two men, both in their seventies, with disparate backgrounds in commerce and religion, met as strangers and became fellow travelers in an Elderhostel group. These men, both profoundly moved by their learning experiences, symbolize for me the meaning of elderlearning. One expressed himself in a creative mode he had never before attempted, and one found growth and change in the new learning he absorbed.

This book has been a personal journey through a world for which I was already chronologically eligible but in which I had not yet acknowledged my own participation. Like those I am writing about, I am an elderlearner, surveying territory I have never traversed before. The discoveries I've made about older adult learning have immediate resonance for my own life. I have no role models in my family; my parents died too young to become elderlearners. My older friends, who are avid learners, choose not to recognize themselves as blazing new trails. To them it goes without saying that one keeps on learning until the light goes out, and they think it remarkable that I think them remarkable.

PURPOSE AND AUDIENCE

The purpose of this book is to take a comprehensive look at this relatively new phenomenon of elderlearning, to, in effect, map the territory. With the aid of data from the Elderlearning Survey (ES) (developed as a critical component of research for this book), we have taken a wide-angle snapshot of elderlearners: who they are, why they are learning, what they are learning, where they are learning, and how they are learning. We have trained our camera on informal or self-directed learning as well as on formal or classroom learning, and we have tried to deal with the troubling issue of how far elderlearning extends beyond those who are white, middle class, and well educated. We have explored the survey statistics and our own research to examine the relative power of such factors as age, health, income, and previous education to predispose someone towards further learning. We hope also to share our conviction that elderlearning has profound meaning not only for the quality of the learners' individual lives but for the whole of society's well-being.

By exposing negative stereotypes about learning in old age and by suggesting the possibilities for a new paradigm for the learning system, we hope to encourage elderlearners to value their own learning and take pride in their own achievements; to persuade institutions, both academic and governmental, to fully participate in and support this unique late twentieth-century movement; to deepen public understanding of the potential richness of the later years; and to move the current debate on resource allocation to a new level of awareness of the positive contributions older adults can make to society.

This book will primarily appeal to the following professional groups: academic administrators and educators who have compelling demographic and social reasons to adjust their institutions' responses to the learning needs of older people; policy makers and legislators who must deal with the enormous implications for redirecting social policy and financial resources; and program providers (schools, libraries, social agencies, businesses, religious and community groups, travel agencies, retirement centers) who need a guide to creating better services for their older clients.

The book also has a much wider audience of general readers who are interested in the profound changes in individual and cultural human experience that are occurring as the lifespan lengthens. Thoughtful men and women of all ages are both intellectually and personally intrigued by the possibilities for social change that emerge as this generation of healthy, productive elders engage in creating an active, learning society.

Finally, the book will appeal to the heroes and heroines described in its pages—the elderlearners themselves. They're proud of their accomplishments and intensely curious about the who, how, what, and why of learning. They want to see how they fit into the learning picture and feel they have a personal stake in the book's success.

ABOUT THE AUTHORS

I had been professionally involved in adult education for over 20 years. In the fall of 1993, I first broached the idea of a book about the explosion of learning among adults over 65 at a meeting of educators. My academic colleagues were dubious. Their comments sounded something like the following:

> So what's the meaning of all this activity, and why do you care?

> Okay, older people are keeping busy by learning. So what?

> Why should we be concerned and why should scarce educational resources be diverted to them?

> What does it matter that a lot of old codgers are still going to class?

> Sounds like social work to me. What's it good for?

Mary Fugate, my friend, colleague, and associate in the preparation of this book, was the first to seize upon the potential significance of elderlearning. Even before we had begun our research, Mary understood intuitively the new world of learning we would discover and the meaning it held for the individual lives of millions of older individuals and for society itself.

Mary has been at the heart of this project from the beginning. Together we have explored issues, challenged assumptions, expanded our thinking, and thrashed out the shape and direction of this book. We both learned how to do research in fields far removed from our own areas of expertise, thus becoming actual participants in elderlearning. We have acted out, unwittingly, the process of intellectual exploration and growth that can and should be a part of the elderlearning experience.

Mary is an imaginative researcher, a fine editor, and a gifted gatherer of resources. She made the contacts that enabled us to meet leaders in the field of older adult education. Her persuasion and persistence got 3,600 copies of the Elderlearning Survey distributed by AARP, Elderhostel, OASIS, and the Institutes for Learning in Retirement. Without her continued involvement, this book would be much diminished in scope and meaning.

ACKNOWLEDGMENTS

Christine Brooks, director of institutional research at Bowdoin College, was critical in expanding the meaning of this book. Christine became interested in the project when replies to the survey began flooding in and I realized to my horror that a simple paper-and-pencil tabulation would be totally inadequate for looking at 450,000 bits of accumulated information. She showed me how to record the data on a spreadsheet and later transferred the data to a social sciences statistical program. She patiently walked Mary and me, total novices in statistical analysis, through a careful examination of the results. She even used the data to answer questions we hadn't thought to ask. Christine's expertise, insight, and creativity in making sense of an extraordinary amount of information on elderlearners have been crucially important to the making of this book.

As always, generous librarians have been at the heart of our research efforts. Sincerest thanks to the keepers of the flame at Bowdoin College Library and the Curtis Memorial Library in Brunswick, Maine, and Pius XIII Library at St. Louis University. Special thanks go to Sherrie Bergman, head librarian at Bowdoin, for extending me special research status, and to Pat Gregory, reference librarian, and Ellen Raben, library assistant at Pius XIII, for their help in locating numerous references.

Special thanks are also due to those who helped Mary and me in the early stages when the book was more a set of amorphous ideas than a fully conceived project. Jim Murray of the American Council on Education (ACE) gave us early encouragement and facilitated contact with Susan Slesinger of Oryx Press, who has also been unfailingly helpful. Sandra Sweeney of AARP; Bill Berkeley of Elderhostel; Jim Verscheuren of Elderhostel's ILR network; Morris T. Keeton, the dean of adult educators; Ronald Manheimer of the North Carolina Center for Creative Retirement; and Jan Carver of Horizons 60 also offered early encouragement, information, and contacts with other people in the field. Anita Lopatin, the wise director of the Pittsburgh OASIS, deserves special mention for the insights she offered. Jane Steinfirst of the University of Cincinnati ILR and Gretchen Lankfort of Carnegie Mellon's Academy of Lifelong Learning helped me understand the power of learner-led classes.

A number of people lent valuable assistance in reviewing the Elderlearning Survey and assisting with its distribution: Karen Safe of OASIS, Michael

Berens of the Research Division at AARP, Bill Berkeley and Mike Zoob at Elderhostel, Mary Linnehan at Elderhostel's ILR Network, and the members of the 1995 Smithsonian Baja trip whose answers to the draft version of the Survey helped us refine our questions and eliminate repetitions.

Special acknowledgment must be made to Dr. Walter M. Bortz, whose 1991 book, *We Live Too Short and Die Too Long*, directed our research toward the connections among learning, health, and exercise. Thanks are also due to Dr. Irwin Rosenberg of Tufts Medical School for raising some interesting questions and answering others.

Thanks also to the elderlearners we've interviewed; their continuing intellectual journeys are an inspiration: Rev. Maurice B. McNamee, S.J., of St. Louis, Shirley Wilson and Sandra Batte of the Santa Fe Trail learning project, Katherine Siegmund on the complementary nature of formal and informal learning, Betty Williams on the persistence of the intellect, John Duley on experiential learning, and all those we met who are charting the territory.

Mary Fugate wishes to thank her mother, Elizabeth McGarr Connolly, for instilling a deep love of learning in her children, and the American Studies Department at St. Louis University for encouraging her own further learning.

My own personal thanks go to those of my friends whose careers as elderlearners preceded mine by a few years and who have served as eloquent role models: Evelyn and David, Jane S., Helen B., Nellie and Paul D., Morris, Avra and Herb, Annette and Will, Betty and Mickey, and many others. And special thanks always to Ezra, whose criticism is like strong medicine, sometimes difficult to take but ultimately healing.

Lois Lamdin

CHAPTER 1

Living in the Age Age

You can't help getting older. But you don't have to get old.

George Burns at 99

Who would ever have thought that we'd live long enough to forget
our first husband's name?

Gail Sheehy

INTRODUCTION

In the waning years of the twentieth century, we are witnessing what may
be the most profound change in human development in history. Indeed,
those of us who are already 60 and above are pioneers in what Walter Bortz
calls "this immense demographic event,"[1] defining, through our own lives, the
revolution that is transforming the expectations and meaning of what it is to
be "old."

The aging society is no longer a prediction; we already live in the first
decades of the Age Age. Not only in the United States but around the world,
changes in fertility and infant mortality rates, better medical care, and better
diet and public health measures are increasing life expectancy and transforming the definition of what is "old." We are rethinking how we will define,
recognize, cope with, and behave toward "old"; what it will mean to our
families, culture, politics, and economy; how it will change the structure of our
lives.

These changes are certain to have major political repercussions, and are
already having substantial effects on the economies and welfare policies of

a number of aging societies. . .[we are seeing] a societal revolution that may prove to be as important in its long-run consequences as any that technological change is likely to produce.[2]

Today's significantly expanded lifespan, in which people remain healthy and functioning well into their eighties and beyond, means continued intellectual growth and development over a longer time span than ever before envisioned. The perennial human search for meaning is intensified as healthy, alert individuals, suddenly thrust into new, seemingly diminished roles by retirement, seek ways to accommodate a new way of life. Most of us have not prepared for these new situations and new transitions: increased leisure, increased opportunities for learning, increased calls for community service, new and uncharted relationships with family and friends, and new and rewarding interests and activities.

The authors have spent most of their professional lives in adult and continuing education. Although our bumper stickers said "learning never ends," we never truly extended our understanding of that saying to include in the learning community people past 60 or 65 years of age. Until recently, educational jargon defined adult learners as those from 25 to 55 or 60 who were preparing for a work or life transition. For data gathering purposes, most colleges usually recorded age only up to 50+, and matriculating grandmothers and graduating grandfathers were exotics, to be trotted out as public relations bonanzas. You could usually get a local headline out of a story of a 68-year-old woman who had gone back to school for a master's degree in education, or a 73-year-old man who had retired from the production line to study international relations. Such elderlearners were admirable, even "cute," but the fact that they made good press meant that they were far out of the mainstream, unworthy of serious consideration as presaging a "trend," let alone a major movement.

We began realizing only a few years ago that our older friends, many of whom had retired from careers similar to ours, were more engaged with learning than they had ever been. Nor was it just people with academic backgrounds who were going to classes, undertaking independent learning projects, traveling with Elderhostel, or seeking further learning experiences in community organizations, museums, galleries, libraries, and various nonprint media. In unprecedented numbers, millions of older adults were extending the meaning of the phrase we had thought we understood—Learning *really* never ends. So far, the phenomenon has received little attention in academic journals. Many institutions have not even begun to think seriously about the significance of this new population of older adult learners or about the changes in access, emphasis, methodology, curriculum, and resources that would enable it to flourish.

In the course of our research, we ourselves have come to understand the profundity of the structural and attitudinal changes that must occur if older adult learning is to take its full and rightful place in the learning society. We *know* that many of these changes are already in progress. Model programs abound. We can learn from them, and we can invent new ones.

AGEISM

Unfortunately, our aging society is also ageist. The old stereotypes keep cropping up in our thinking. Old people are over the hill, out of it mentally, perhaps even senile. They are frail and fearful, poor and dependent. They have old fashioned ideas about morality and are rigid in their political views, rejecting anything new. They are selfish and self-serving, gobbling up more than their share of the national resources, using organizations like the American Association of Retired Persons (AARP) to pursue narrow, generation-specific issues of benefit only to themselves. They are takers from, not contributors to, society.

Ageism, like sexism and racism, sets people apart and turns them into the "other." Ageism is an aberrant form of bigotry because we are all headed toward old age; it reflects a "deep-seated uneasiness on the part of the young and middle-aged—a personal revulsion to and distaste for growing old, disease, disability; and fear of powerlessness, 'uselessness' and death."[3]

Fortunately, few of these stereotypes accord with the realities with which we live; they ignore the vast numbers of our older relatives, friends, and neighbors whom we see leading active, joyful lives while contributing to their families and communities. This new reality is only beginning to make inroads on negative ways of thinking about age, and is in danger of turning into still another stereotype: the grandma with dyed blonde hair and a filofax, running between her jazzercise class and a presentation at the Foreign Policy Association; or the grandpa besting the wilderness on an Outward Bound expedition and getting in touch with his feminine side through a course in gourmet cooking.

There are encouraging signs that advertising has begun to move away from the earlier, demeaning depictions of older persons as helpless, mean, silly, or skirting senility, or, alternatively, the sentimental notion of them as existing solely to dispense consolation and wisdom from the depths of their Barca Loungers. It is a hopeful sign that June Allyson, the relentlessly perky purveyor of adult diapers, who used to be shown in traditionally grandmotherly situations, was, in a recent commercial, extolling the product's ability to keep her dry and unembarrassed in a painting class. Good for Allyson. Incontinence hasn't kept her from learning.

Although advertisers may have begun to approach age as a lucrative new market, open discussion of age still remains taboo, even at a time when the taboos against sex and bodily functions are rapidly disappearing. Negative attitudes make talking about the realities of aging difficult. We still tend to deny that we all, if we're lucky, will get old, and we don't identify with those who have already made the journey. Too many older people, having bought into society's values, devalue their hard-won wisdom and accomplishments and feel ashamed of their thinning hair, wrinkles, and sagging flesh. Youth is in; old age is out. Purveyors of vitamins, hair dyes, skin lotions, passive exercise machines, and undergarments that mold and shape have zeroed in on these would-be Peter Pans; plastic surgeons are busy tucking eyelids and tidying up sagging chin lines; spas and exercise centers are stressing firm abs and butts over healthy hearts and minds. The new seekers of the fountain of youth will settle for its semblance if not its reality.

SOCIAL EFFECTS OF AGEISM

As their numbers grow, older people are increasingly viewed, in social policy terms, as political and fiscal problems. This new form of ageism is not wholly without reason. Our society must take a hard look at resource allocation and outmoded policies that have failed to keep up with the new realities of the population shift. The number of working adults who supply the tax base is decreasing while the proportion of older adults is increasing. The "graying of America" has produced the graying of the federal budget, the perception that a disproportionate amount of funding is going to the older population. This process impacts directly on the beliefs and practices of society. We saw this in the bitter debates in late 1995 on Medicare and Medicaid. We have also seen the beginning of this budgeting impact on support for Social Security, and in discriminatory practices and institutional policies that have failed to keep up with changes in the needs and abilities of older Americans. Those who are loudest in warning against intergenerational conflict are frequently those who are most actively fomenting it.

COUNTERING THE STEREOTYPES

The all-too-common public perception of older people as poor, frail, fearful, lonely, idle, unwanted, and greedy is out of synch with their own evaluations of themselves. Lou Harris and Associates compared the public's expectations of the problems connected with aging to the responses of older people about their actual problems. The results are instructive.[4]

Problems	Public Expectations	Experience of Older People	Net Difference
fear of crime	50%	23%	+27
poor health	51%	21%	+30
not enough money	62%	15%	+47
loneliness	60%	12%	+48
insufficient medical care	44%	10%	+34
not feeling needed	54%	7%	+47
not having enough to do to keep busy	36%	6%	+30

On all these commonly held perceptions about the problems of aging, public expectations were dramatically more negative than the experience reported by the older people themselves. To put the data into positive terms, 77% of older people do not fear crime; 79% consider themselves in good health; 85% have enough money; 88% are not lonely; 93% feel needed; and 94% have enough to do to keep busy. These numbers hardly indicate widespread decline, poverty, or despair.

DEMOGRAPHICS

The startling rise in the number of older Americans has provided demographers with useful statistics about the graying of America. These numbers flood the media and are a staple of our political rhetoric, whether in the service of saving or decimating the social safety net. Dire predictions of a ravenous elderly horde gobbling up the nation's economic resources, or of intergenerational warfare as the working few labor to feed and house the retired many, have focused on the negatives, the needs of the feeble rather than the contributions of the fully functioning older adults we see among us.

Certainly the numbers must give one pause. Life expectancy has increased by 28 years from an average of 47 years in 1900 to 75.5 years (72 for men and 78.9 for women) in the 1990s.[5] Since the turn of the century, the lifetime of the ordinary American has lengthened by 62.3 percent, and the amount of time that one can expect to spend in adulthood has more than doubled. The change in life expectancy in this century is greater than the change in life expectancy over the previous 2,000 years; the increase is 23 times greater than the average for any previous century.[6] In just the past 35 years, the population 65 and over has grown from 8 to 12 percent of the total population and is expected to reach 17 percent in the next 25 years.[7] The number of individuals over 85, relative to the total population, has more than quadrupled. Two Duke University demographers, Kenneth Manton and James Vaupel, writing in the November 1995 *New England Journal of Medicine*, point out that mortality rates here [the U.S.] have declined 1% to 2% per year for the past quarter century, and that the average life expectancy has increased about two years each decade . . . if such trends continue, a girl born today in the U.S. will live, on average, to 96, and a boy, 90. One out of every three newborn girls and one out of every ten boys will live to be 100.[8]

Dr. Robert Butler of the National Institute on Aging says that "we haven't found any biologic reason not to live to 110,"[9] while Walter Bortz would extend the potential lifespan to 120! This added lifespan is not just extra time to kill; it represents potentially vital, productive years in which older people can either contribute to their society or drain its resources.

Many people may live as much as one-third of their lives as senior adults, up to 30 years in retirement. As the baby boomers enter the 65+ age group, the increase among those over 65 between the years 2010 and 2030 will be from 39.7 million to 69.8 million. By 2030, over 20 percent of the population will be 65 and older. The Bureau of the Census projects that life expectancy at birth for whites will have increased by the year 2050 from 75.8 to 82.1, with minor adjustments up or down for other races and ethnic peoples.[10] In 1994, 33.2 million Americans were older than 65,[11] more than the entire population of Canada. Over 14 percent of these people are persons of color whose relative numbers are rapidly growing.

Those 85 years [old] . . . are the most rapidly growing population segment. This group is expected to double from 2.5 million in 1990 to 5 million by the year 2000 and will continue to grow almost exponentially thereafter.[12]

By 2015, the number of older Americans is expected to equal the number of children 18 years and under, and by 2030, the median age will rise from 33 to 42. "The nation then will look like Florida today."[13]

Moreover, this is a world-wide phenomenon. According to the secretary general of the U.N., there were 307 million persons over 60 years of age in the world in 1970; by 2000, that number will grow to nearly 500 million, an increase of nearly 90 percent.[14] By 2020, the world may have a billion older people.[15]

To put all this into graphic perspective, imagine a geometric shape that reflects the number of people in each age from infancy to, say, 100 years. Traditionally, the age progression has been represented as a pyramid. The long base on the bottom represents the number of newborns and the progressive narrowing of the pyramid represents the working of death through childhood, adolescence, and adulthood until the apex is reached at age 80 or 90. Now, however, the pyramid or triangle is losing its traditional shape. As baby boomers reach 65 (between 2010 and 2030), 6 percent of the population will be under five years old, the same percent as will be aged 65-69, thus substantially altering the geometric figure. By the year 2035, every fifth (possibly every fourth) American will be over 65, and the pyramid will have metamorphosed into a rectangle. If Bortz and Butler are correct in saying that we have not yet reached our biological potential to live to 110 or 120, we can expect that at the top of the figure there will be a narrow segment extending beyond age 100. Are we to allow these millions of people to face old age without a script?

Although futurists frequently treat this demographic change as a recent phenomenon, we've actually been growing older in this country since at least 1800, as have most developed countries. England, with its longer history, supplies a longer perspective on the phenomenon of an aging population.

Peter Laslett, a prominent British demographer, has charted average life expectations in England from the year 1000 to 2500. Although the first 500 and the last 500 years represent informed conjectures, there was clearly a long plateau in life expectancy, with only minor bumps up and down, for about 1,800 years. During this period, average life expectancy ranged from 30 to 40 years, and the number of people over 60 ranged consistently between 8 to 11 percent. In 1801, only 8.7 percent of the British population was over 60, but by 1984, in what Laslett terms a "secular shift . . . so fundamental that it can indeed be conveyed only in geological metaphors," those over 60 accounted for 25.7 percent of the population, "making accepted assumptions about age and aging obsolete almost overnight."[16]

Although the latter figures and the projection for the year 2000 are not as high as in the United States, the swift rise in the twentieth century in the number of older British people is roughly analogous to ours. Moreover, the trend holds for most of the rest of Europe as well as for developed countries elsewhere. If this projected growth is added to the Butler and Bortz predictions about the potential lengthening of the lifespan, the resultant figures, and the needed changes they imply, would indeed be awesome.

However, the projected figures should be viewed with a dash of skepticism. Demographers are better at looking at the past and present than in predicting the future. The percentage of older people in the population is not solely dependent upon how many older people will live, how many will die, and at what age. The other part of the equation depends to a large extent upon the vagaries of the birth rate. Will the baby boomers' grandchildren have 2.3 children each, more, or less? Will the children of recent arrivals, heirs to different cultures, create a second major baby boom when they reach their twenties and thirties or will they adopt the less fecund habits of their new country? Will abstinence, birth control, or abortion figures go up or down?

As Robert Butler observes, this revolution in longevity, although an extraordinary human accomplishment, is not a function of biological evolution but of social and technological change.[17] Most of the increase in longevity can be ascribed to improved medical and public health measures rather than to a genetic propensity to live longer. Thus, the gains could possibly be reversed by economically driven cutbacks in health and welfare funding for the elderly, by the emergence of new and terrible diseases against which our present antibiotics are helpless, or by wars, famines, natural catastrophes, or new outbreaks of "ethnic cleansing."

These dire possibilities aside, we should be looking ahead to a future in which the older population will play a more significant role than ever before in history, living fuller lives and making enhanced contributions to society. If this is to occur, creative change is necessary in our policies and institutions as well as in our understanding of the life cycle.

ISSUES RAISED BY THE GRAYING OF THE POPULATION

Clearly there's good news and bad news connected to the graying of the population. The bad news has been amply signaled by those who forecast economy-breaking demands for medical care, nursing homes, and services of all kinds for a dependent, "non-productive" segment of society while children and grandchildren labor ceaselessly to pay taxes for their elders' upkeep, leaving nothing for their own old age. The noted economist, Lester C. Thurow, paints the future in the darkest possible tones.

> A new class of people is being created. For the first time in human history, Western societies will have a large group of affluent, economically inactive, elderly voters who require expensive social services like health care and who depend upon government for much of their income. It is a revolutionary class, one that is bringing down the social welfare state, destroying government finances, altering the distribution of purchasing power and threatening the investments that all societies need to make to have a successful future.[18]

Although one may (and we certainly do) reject Thurow's Armageddon-like vision, serious problems—economic and social—must be addressed. Thurow's prognostications may seem mean spirited, but they are reflections of a reality that we ignore at our peril.

Robert Butler, the dean of American gerontologists, whose humane and sane approach has been a major factor in the attempt to move his profession to a new vision of aging, identifies a somewhat different series of problems, not all of them economic, that society must address.

- involuntary retirement
- housing
- victimization of older adults (by crime, inadequate facilities, family abuse)
- health care issues
- economic problems
- suicide
- ageism

But the new realities of aging also include some good news. The emerging model of aging bears little resemblance to the old myths and stereotypes. First, many older Americans are still actively working, paying taxes, and financing their own retirements. "The U.S. Bureau of Labor Statistics states that there are 3.5 million people over sixty-five employed in the civilian labor force. Millions of others in this age group are engaged in income-earning work or volunteer activity that does not fit the bureau's definitions."[19] The results of the Elderlearning Survey reinforce this point.

Work and Volunteer Activity N = 860 respondents 55 to 95 years old			
Employed:		**Volunteer Activity:**	
full-time	2.4%	full-time	2.6%
part-time	9.9%	part-time	40.5%
self-employed	5.3%	occasional	29.8%
total	17.6%	total	72.9%

Today's older generations are healthier, happier, and less dependent than in the past. Recent research has found that the percentage of old people who are unable to take care of themselves has been dropping 1 to 2 percent a year since 1982 when the survey began. The chronic disease rate among older people is also dropping, so the elderly population may not be the economic drain it was projected to be.[20]

Not only Social Security but improved pension systems and more sophisticated ways of deploying savings have made this generation of older people better able to live on their own resources. Increased financial security has lessened their dependence on their children, often to the benefit of both generations, improved the quality of their lives, and enabled them to expand their interests and activities. Preventive medicine, new drugs that can control chronic conditions, and public health measures that have improved working conditions and assured potable water and breathable air have eliminated many of the causes of early disability, opening the way for older people to engage in activities not even dreamed of by their own grandparents. They swim, hike, bicycle, play tennis and golf, garden, and, in general, enjoy full, active lives well into their seventies, eighties, and even nineties. The "longevity factor" has given them—and us—the greatest gift of all, the gift of time.

Profound changes in the health, financial situation, and abilities of older people have made chronological age obsolete as a basis for life course policy. The new elders not only have Social Security but are the best-pensioned generation we have seen. Their health is way above the norm for previous generations—87.6 percent of all Elderlearning Survey respondents self-rated their health as excellent or good (an astonishing number whose possible meanings will be explored in later chapters). The new elders don't retire to die, but to move on to a new and active developmental stage of life.

Until recently, older adults were perceived as a crushing burden to children, neighbors, and society. Now, in the middle class at least, their children are just as likely to consider grandma and grandpa as a source of assistance with a down payment on a new home or as a safety net for young families in a generation that is generally not doing as well as its parents.

For their neighbors and for society as a whole, the new breed of senior citizen is a source of volunteer labor in the service of social goals. Seniors are also a powerful political force—the voter turnout of older people far exceeds that of younger generations. In 1992, 70.1 percent of people 65 and over voted compared to a 52.5 percent overall voter turnout.[21] Although some may view older citizens' political activism as problematic, others see it as a beacon of hope.

For all the positives that can and do stem from an aging society, we cannot ignore those problems and issues which can, if unsolved, have negative consequences for society, draining its resources and setting generations against one another.

Rising Costs of Medical Care

The most obvious issue is the rising cost of health care and institutionalization. Many recent figures relating to rising medical costs have been driven by specific political agendas. According to Daniel Callahan in *Setting Limits: Medical Goals in an Aging Society*, the U.S. Special Committee on Aging estimated in 1986 that "pension and health programs were 9.6 percent of the GNP and 39.4 percent of the federal budget. Those figures are projected to jump by 2040 to 14.5 percent of the GNP and 60.4 percent of the budget, respectively."[22]

Clearly, such figures are insupportable. No country can afford to allot over 60 percent of its budget to health care and pensions. But it is also clear that not all of the health care included in that figure is paying for Medicare or nursing homes.[23] Furthermore, such projections are suspect in light of recent findings about the health of older Americans. Dr. Kenneth Manton, who analyzed the National Long Term Care Surveys, "calculates that declining disability rates from 1982 to 1995 have saved Medicare $200 billion."[24] Such figures have yet to be factored into older estimates of Medicare's present and future cost.

We *are* a growing population, but not just at one end. More children are being born, too many of them into poverty. More new citizens are arriving from foreign shores. We still don't have a handle on how to provide adequate health care to all without sacrificing quality, and we still haven't devised a cost effective health *system* that can do the job without bankrupting the country.

However, the advancing age of the population should not be used as the sole (or even primary) excuse for the current mess we are in.

Economic Insecurity

Demographers tell us that over the next 25 years, as the baby boomers begin to retire, we will have more people receiving Social Security benefits supported by fewer working Americans. In effect, grandchildren and great grandchildren will be supporting their parents' and grandparents' retirement while running the risk of endangering their own futures. Perhaps. But if the workforce continues to expand as it historically has, many of its members will be first-generation citizens who in their turn will be supported by more first-generation citizens. The great waves of immigration that have made this country rich in diversity have the potential to continue to carry the Social Security burden while preserving the futures of the new entrants into the workforce. The real problem is structural; if great numbers of jobs continue their evolution from high wage to low wage, how can we continue to provide support services to *any* segment of the population?

Enlightened legislation might still lower the pressures on the current working population while preserving the foundations of Social Security. Qualifying for full Social Security benefits at 65 is a nineteenth-century legacy of Bismarck's Germany, when 65 was a ripe old age. Congress has considered raising that age, as it probably should. However, chronological age alone should not be the sole determinant, nor can we conscionably raise the retirement age at a time when so few jobs are available in the economy. Many people are now retiring at 65 not because they cannot or do not want to keep on working, but because they are encouraged to do so by their employers. If staying at work were encouraged, we would not be losing so many productive adults at a time when their skills and experience make them most valuable.

As of early 1996, congressional cost-cutters have not taken on the political landmine of Social Security, but its immunity cannot last indefinitely in isolation from other social issues. One way to "save" Social Security would be to deny or reduce benefits to the relatively affluent, a remedy that has at least as many negatives as positives. The 70-year-old whose income is $75,000 or more thinks, with some justification, that he has "earned" Social Security through years of FICA payments at the high end of the scale, and for the government to break that implied contract now would be unfair if not unethical. Nor can we return to an earlier day when people at the end of their working lives, if they had no pensions or other resources, were at the mercy of their children (if they had families) and of the community (if they did not). Changing the rates at which Social Security benefits are taxed at different income levels might go some way to saving dollars while not penalizing those whose need is greatest.

Intergenerational Tensions

The same scarcity of resources that drives the Social Security debate also sets young against old in the competition for other kinds of resources. Who shall have prime eligibility for employment in a society in which productivity has been gained by a loss of jobs? Who takes priority for high technology health care? How do we balance the allocation of community resources among Headstart, after-school programs for teenagers, and "meals on wheels" for the shut-in elderly? Who has priority for high-tech training for new jobs? Should scarce education dollars be used to pay for elderlearning programs? Should older adults pay lower admissions fees for museums, parks, films, and other educationally desirable experiences when some younger people can't afford to go at all?

Intergenerational competition for resources in a limited economy could lead to a permanent souring of relations between young and old. If, however, scarce resources are thoughtfully allocated, such competition could lead to a healthy intergenerational conversation. While opposing intergenerational claims on resources are and have always been inevitable, tensions arising from such claims can be defused in open dialogue and by fair resolutions. Many of the learning programs we will describe in later chapters have deliberately been structured to promote intergenerational cooperation and teaching and learning strategies that involve old and young in ways that benefit both.

We have raised some tough issues: an expanding elder population with health care needs, the negative effects of early retirement, allocation of scarce resources, and the social changes implicit in changing demographics. We do not pretend to have definitive solutions for these problems, which are not uniquely American, were not unforeseen, and can be solved. Some Americans have begun to question the assumption that the aging of society brings only a series of problems. We may discover that it presents, instead, a bouquet of possibilities.

THE AGE OF LEARNING

Negative assumptions about age and aging have prevented us from seeing that many older people are *inventing* new ways to use their extended lifespan. This generation of older people has the inherent potential to be an asset rather than a liability.

The impassioned pursuit of learning is one surprise the current generation of older adults has for us. By the millions, members of today's 65+ generation are extending the definition of lifelong learning to include themselves. They are using their time and energy to take formal courses, sometimes even working toward degrees; to engage in other structured learning opportunities of all kinds; and to pursue knowledge and skills on their own through independently generated learning projects of incredible variety. In succeeding chapters, we shall detail and document this explosion of learning, discuss who these learners are, and explore where, how, and why they are learning. Most important, we shall argue that this "elderlearning" phenomenon contains the seeds of a new life role for older people and a regenerative force to heal our presently fractured society.

We are convinced that the extension of the concept of lifelong learning to cover adults well into their nineties (and perhaps beyond) holds promise of transforming the meaning of old age. As we shall argue in later chapters, increased learning opportunities for the aging can substantially increase their health and well-being and their mobility and independence, all of which could help conserve scarce resources. Moreover, education for full- or part-time employment would permit them to re-enter the workforce when needed, supplement their income, and help them stay busy and involved. Educational opportunities directed toward training for volunteerism would help fill the gaps in the social safety net left by the millions of women who did yeoman service as volunteers until they moved into paid employment. Keeping the elderly among us as a vital part of society rather than relegating them to its fringes could also help bring stability to young families and lend wisdom and compassion to a violent society.

Achieving all these goals is a tall order for elderlearning, but both statistically and anecdotally we have encountered the makings of this vision among the young-old and the old-old, among rich and poor, and among the well-educated and the less well-educated. Continued learning is an abundant commodity, ubiquitous, color blind, and not necessarily institution-dependent. Its cost is variable, as inexpensive or as costly as the traffic will bear. One can take out a library book, join a bird watching group, or sign on for a study/travel cruise to the Antarctic.

Elderlearning can enable older people to enrich their own lives, enhance their own health and well-being, and give back to their communities. It can also save dollars, increase the range and breadth of our present social services, and substitute the reward of intergenerational cooperation and interdependence for the threat of intergenerational warfare. Each penny spent to encourage elderlearning could be a dollar invested for the enhancement of life for individual older adults and for American society.

NOTES

1. Walter M. Bortz, *We Live Too Short and Die Too Long* (New York: Bantam Press, 1991), p. 307.

2. "The Aging Society," *Daedalus*, 115,1 (Winter 1986), vi.

3. Robert N. Butler and M. Lewis, *Aging and Mental Health: Positive Psychological Approaches* (St. Louis: C.V. Mosby, 1973).

4. These Harris and Associates figures are from a table in Harold Cox, *Later Life: The Realities of Aging* (Englewood Cliffs, NJ: Prentice-Hall, 1984), p. 31.

5. Frank B. Hobbs, *65+ in the United States* (Washington, DC: Bureau of the Census, 1996), p. 3-1.

6. Lydia Bronte, *The Longevity Factor: The New Reality of Long Careers and How It Can Lead to Richer Lives* (New York: HarperCollins, 1993), p. xvi.

7. Alan Pifer and Lydia Bronte, "Introduction: Squaring the Pyramid," *Daedalus*, 115,1,2 (Winter 1986). The authors, writing in 1986, said 35 years; for this book, the number has been changed to 25 years.

8. Quoted in the *University of California at Berkeley Wellness Letter*, 12, 7 (April 1996), 5.

9. Quoted by Bortz, p. 6.

10. Jennifer Cheeseman Day, "Population Projections of the United States by Age, Sex, Race, and Hispanic Origin: 1992-2050," U.S. Department of Commerce, Economics and Statistics Administration (Washington, DC: Bureau of the Census, 1992), pp. vii, ix.

11. Hobbs, pp. 2-4.

12. T. Franklin Williams, "The Undergraduate Curriculum in Geriatrics," *AJA Proceedings* (October 17, 1994), 41S.

13. Joseph F. Quinn, "The Future of Retirement" in *Columbia Retirement Handbook*, edited by Abraham Monk (New York: Columbia University Press, 1994), p. 571.

14. Michel Philibert, "A Philosophy of Aging from a World Perspective" in *Perspectives on Aging: Exploding the Myths*, edited by Priscilla Johnston (Philadelphia: Ballinger Publishing, 1981), p. 240.

15. Susan Champlin Taylor, "The End of Retirement," *Modern Maturity* (October-November 1993), 32.

16. Peter Laslett, *A Fresh Map of Life* (London: George Weidenfeld and Nicolson Ltd., 1989), pp. 66-67.

17. Robert N. Butler, "Cycles, Clocks, and Power Plants," *Geriatric Curriculum Development Conference and Initiative*, *AJA Proceedings* (October 17, 1994), 36S.

18. "The Birth of a Revolutionary Class," *New York Times Magazine* (May 19, 1996), 46.

19. Bronte, p. 10.

20. Gina Kolata, "New Era of Robust Elderly Belies the Fears of Scientists," *New York Times*, February 27, 1996, A1, C3. This article summarizes the results of the National Long Term Care Surveys, annual federal studies that look at health issues in those 65 and older, by surveying 20,000 people from the Medicare population. The article was part of a *NYT* series on older people's health, in itself an indication of the extraordinary interest in this subject over the past few years.

21. Hobbs, pp. 6-23.

22. Quoted by John L. Palmer and Stephanie G. Gould, "The Economic Consequences of an Aging Society," *Daedalus* 115, 1 (Winter 1986), 295-323.

23. Despite the great outcry about how much money is spent on nursing homes, only 5 percent of Americans over 65 are currently in nursing homes, and less than 10 percent ever will be. Betty Friedan, *The Fountain of Age* (New York: Simon and Schuster, 1993), p. 22.

24. Kolata, C3.

CHAPTER 2

Defining "Old" in the Age Age

Perhaps with full span lives the norm, people may need to learn how to be aged as they once had to learn to be adult. . . . To fall into purposelessness is to fall out of all real consideration.

Ronald Blythe, The View in Winter

Two working definitions of "old" have informed our research and thinking. One is chronological. It is limited and does not reflect our thinking about the possibilities of aging, but serves as a definition of convenience for looking at census data and educational statistics. It has enabled us to set limits on our research and parameters for the Elderlearning Survey. Our second and preferred definition is developmental. It takes account of life stages, styles, and attitudes and assumes that people remain capable of growth and change throughout the lifespan. Looking at age from a developmental perspective supports a key tenet of this book—the potential for continued learning as one ages.

CHRONOLOGICAL AGING: HOW OLD IS OLD?

If we all aged predictably or symmetrically in all dimensions—physical, intellectual, attitudinal—we could more easily settle on some number of years that represented an absolute boundary between middle and old age, or, as popular ageist myth would have it, between growth and decline. We might also use the newer terminologies that attempt to distinguish between those who are more or less active, such as the "young-old" (55-65), the "middle-old" (66-75), the "old-old" (76+), and, in some cases, even the "oldest old" for those over 85.

Chronological age is an arbitrary but convenient and occasionally useful basis for deciding when one is old enough to drive, drink, buy cigarettes, or vote. But even in these matters, there is no consensus among the states about exactly when the rewards of maturity should start, when young people are mature enough to get a learner's permit or a gun permit or be tried as adults in courts of law. Various permissions and prohibitions are legislated at anywhere from 12 to 21 years of age, leading one to suppose that adolescence ends at different times in different states.

If using simple chronology as an official criterion is a problem in youth, when developmental growth is somewhat orderly, why should it be applied in old age, when it frequently works against reality? To paraphrase Jane Austen, it is a universal truth that chronological and biological age do not always coincide. Disparities in people's mental and physical abilities tend to widen with age, and are far too disparate to be appropriate criteria for coherent policy making.

Using the magic age of 65 to denote the official beginning of old age has the virtue of simplicity, but it bolsters an age stereotype that penalizes some, empowers others, and costs society a great deal. The choice of 65 as an across-the-board retirement age is a prime example of a policy based on an arbitrary number that is no longer relevant either to the situation of many older Americans or to the policy's original objectives. The policy harks back to 1883 when the radical new Social Security program of Otto von Bismarck, the chancellor of Germany, pegged 65 as elderly. In the 1880s, a person who had lived long enough to retire at 65 could expect, on the average, only two or three more years of life. Today, mandatory retirement is largely illegal, but employers still perpetuate age 65 as the appropriate end of a career by offering retirement bonuses, "golden parachutes," and whatever inducements will allow them to replace older workers with younger, lower salaried employees. Thus, many able and healthy people, who might otherwise be reluctant to make the transition, involuntarily enter a life of enforced leisure. Even before the era of "downsizing," which has depended heavily on coerced retirements, the workplace culture in many companies had assumed that 65 is retirement time. Retirement based on an arbitrary number is costing this country both expertise and money, and is casting many men and women aside when the country could still benefit from their competence and productivity.

Age 65 also denotes full eligibility for Medicare and Social Security benefits, even though today's 65-year-old may look forward to two or three decades of relatively healthy and productive life after retirement. One 85-year-old may be in a wheelchair in Detroit slum housing, while another is on a private golf course in Boca Raton. Should our social legislation treat both in the same way?

But even 65 is not sacrosanct. The Department of Labor, for purposes that include eligibility for retraining, defines "older workers" as those over 40, and industry is notorious for withholding on-the-job training from those in their 50s and above. Some social service and recreation programs use 50 or 55 as the upper limits for their services, ages at which those services might be of most benefit. Chronological age has clearly become a poor predictor of health, work status, interests, needs, and capabilities. Perpetuating policy based on a predetermined age because it is convenient rather than useful diverts resources from essential to nonessential purposes and contributes to the current uneasiness about fairness in resource allocation.

For all these reasons, deciding how to separate the elderlearner from the adult learner was an early and recurring issue in preparing this book. Current adult education literature has dealt mainly with people from age 25 to 55 or 59. Data tracking of adult students in most institutions and on the national level rarely goes beyond 60 or 65. People over 65 have been treated as interesting exceptions, not as constituting a major group. Their numbers, learning styles, preferences, and needs are relatively uncharted territory, and statistics about the numbers of older people who are learning are scarce. Finally, no one is attempting to keep track of, or even take note of, informal learning, a powerful aspect of lifelong learning.

We were, therefore, fully aware of the limitations of chronology for defining age, but we needed a precise number for working with census data, looking at educational statistics, and constructing the Elderlearning Survey. To meet these needs, we settled on age 55. Using the number 55 has enabled us to gather data on the years ignored by most educational institutions and to make provocative age comparisons between the very young-old and later cohorts. We abhor contributing even minimally to a stereotype and know full well the limitations of the number, but found it to be the most useful choice for our statistical needs.

THE MEDICAL DEFINITION OF AGING

The medical definition of aging is primarily pathology-based, focusing on people who are ill or in decline in the latter part of life. Lacking an imagery of healthy aging, most medical literature views old age as a complex of diseases to be treated, a constant battle against the inevitability of death. With blunt concision, English gerontologist Alex Comfort defines aging as "an increased liability to die."[1] Until recently, this medical model was almost the sole focus of basic biomedical and clinical research and health services delivery for the elderly. Geriatric literature is rich in articles on dementia, incontinence, cancers, heart failure, and bedsores; it is poor in work on preventive medicine, wellness, diet, exercise, and the social and environmental factors that can modify aging. Attention to the psychological and sociological context of the individual, to expansion of health services delivery and research, and to ethical considerations in the care of the elderly has been rare in the past 10 or 15 years. Moreover, research tended to concentrate on middle class males, ignoring the special situations of women, minorities, and the poor.

Medical education is still primarily pathology-based and cure-oriented, preoccupied with disease rather than health. Despite the obvious need for a new generation of gerontologists, the field tends to be shunned by the best and brightest who see treating the aged as a dead end. (The pun was unintended but appropriate.) Of the 400,000 members of the American Medical Association, only about 700 devote most of their time to geriatrics.[2] Our early research indicated that the majority of gerontological articles dealt with the degeneration of rat brains and the treatment of liver failure and severe arthritis rather than with illness prevention. The importance of nutrition and exercise is scarcely taught. The primacy of an active life style and positive involvement with a community may be intuited but is rarely in the curriculum. The importance of cognitive workouts to keep the intellect functioning is not even mentioned. The public has adopted this medical model and expects to buy health with pills, operations, and the latest high-tech interventions.

If money talks, it tells us that the "disease" of aging is not receiving support commensurate with the number of elderly. In 1990, the National Institutes of Health committed only about 5.8 percent of all NIH funds to biomedical aspects of aging. Although 27 percent of the people it serves are over 65, the Department of Veterans Affairs devoted only 8.5 percent of its 1990 budget to age-related research or projects.

Even the national foundations were not much interested in the health of the older population. The Foundation Center's 1989 publication, *Grants for the Aged,* states that "from 1986 to 1987, a meager 2.5 percent of the monies given by private and corporate foundations were directed to the general area of aging and less than 1 percent of all foundation philanthropy was for age-related research."[3]

PHYSIOLOGICAL AGING

According to Walter Bortz, we have, for the first time in history, the knowledge base to propose a universal definition of aging: "Age equals the effect of energy on matter over time." Aging is the inescapable process of entropy at the end of which "your molecules are returned to the earth system whence they arose."[4]

Physiological aging, as it has traditionally been graphed in relation to chronological aging, shows a steady upward curve until somewhere in the twenties, a slowly declining curve to somewhere around 65 or 70, and a more sharply declining curve thereafter, "depending, of course, on which functions are being graphed."[5] The declining age curve does not surprise us. We are programmed to think of age as a decline.

However, Bortz says that we have not yet reached the physiological limits of a "natural" lifespan; most of us are not dying of old age, a gradual deterioration of the body's systems, but of specific diseases and malfunctions. Bortz puts the natural limits of the human lifespan at about 120 years. Such an age might seem good to some, but causes others to remember Jonathan Swift's account of the "struldbrugs," who live forever "despised and hated," and whose deformities and physical and mental conditions make immortality far worse than death.[6]

Bortz also reminds us that "to look at aging solely as decay is to deny a fundamental property of life, namely the capacity of self-repair."[7] As we grow older, we should realize that the length of a life is less important than the quality of that life. The best insurance against decline is a sense of participation, of active involvement in society. A study by Stewart Wolfe, the doctor in a Pennsylvania community with a preponderance of such health negatives as obesity and lack of exercise, showed that the population of 1,700 nonetheless exhibited high levels of health. Wolfe proposed that "the unique characteristics of this community were a strong social fabric and respect for and involvement of the older generation."[8]

Thus, physiological aging, while ultimately inevitable, can be slowed, or even for a time halted, by participation in a positive psycho-social environment. Chapters 4 and 5 will explore the effects of continued active learning on health and longevity, but we can present some highly suggestive figures here from the Elderlearning Survey.

Self-Rated Health Status			
	All Respondents	Males	Females
excellent	30.6%	25.4%	33.2%
good	57.0%	59.5%	55.9%
fair	11.5%	13.8%	10.2%
poor	.9%	1.2%	.7%

Only 12.4 percent of respondents to the Elderlearning Survey, including those who are among the "old-old," described their health as fair or poor. These figures confirm what several experts are currently saying about the health benefits of active involvement in learning; the product of learning can be what Robert Butler calls "productive aging," what John Rowe calls "successful aging," and what Walter Bortz calls "useful aging." All these phrases connote a "directed energy flow, ordered and ordering,"[9] which is essential to a preventive model of health.

SOCIOGENIC AGING

Although physical aging has undeniable negative consequences, aging in a youth-oriented society is particularly difficult. Ageism pervades the American culture; it is reflected in our language, our values, our attitudes and prejudices, and our myths about aging. In *A Good Age*, Alex Comfort wrote the following:

> the things which make oldness insupportable in human societies don't at all commonly arise from consequences of the biological process. They arise from sociogenic aging, i.e., from the role which society imposes on people as they reach a certain chronological age. At this age they retire, or, in plain words are rendered unemployed, useless, and in some cases impoverished. After that transition, and in proportion to their chronological age, they are prescribed to be unintelligent, unemployable, crazy and asexual.[10]

More recently, Betty Friedan compared ageism to sexism.

> The mystique of age denies the personhood of people over 65. It denies their unique *emergent* personhood and all the unknown potential of that extra 25 years of life, made possible for all of us by the new longevity. But this mystique is even more insidious than the feminine mystique because it keeps us from seeing what that potential is, what our possibilities are, and even from being able to distinguish *real* chimeras from spurious problems and fraudulent terrors.[11]

Ironically, as Lydia Bronte reminds us, ageism is also sexist. Women are considered to be "old" a full 10 years earlier than men,[12] although they live, on average, seven years longer than men. Nor are the old themselves exempt from adopting these negative ageist attitudes as their own, at least until the actual experience of age turns out to differ from their expectations.

A 1991 study by Seccombe and Ishii-Kuntz analyzed negative attitudes toward aging in four age cohorts: middle-aged (55-64), young-old (65-74), old (75-84), and oldest-old (85+).[13] The results showed that the middle-aged (55-64) group, still on the brink of age, was most pessimistic, while the oldest-old, those living in its reality, were unexpectedly optimistic. The study supports the contention that younger people hold a more pessimistic attitude toward aging than do older people themselves.[14] Those just approaching old age were most negative, anticipating all its problems. The older participants who were actively experiencing its less dire consequences had found that they could cope. In this case, the prophecy is not necessarily self-fulfilling.

CULTURAL AGING

Different societies have different markers for defining old age. Becoming head of a tribe, being admitted to the council of elders, taking responsibility for religious ceremonies, becoming a grandparent, donning the apparel indicative of the respect that comes with age—these are positive signs of a culture's belief that age brings wisdom and honor. In gerontocracies such as China, where elders run the country, or in Japan, which still clings to the tradition (if not the substance) of reverence for elders, age is a status to be achieved, not a tragedy to be feared.

In the United States, the reigning culture of youth denigrates age. To achieve age is all too frequently to lose your career, regardless of your status or competence, or to fall prey to the perception that you must be losing your health, intellect, and sense of humor. Reduced fare passes on Amtrak and cheaper tickets for the movies are meager compensation for people who feel they have lost major roles in their career or family life.

The cultural stereotype of incompetence among the aging is competing with a new and equally dangerous stereotype: old people as pleasure-seeking hedonists, gleefully spending their children's inheritance in pursuit of material goods; or ignoring family ties and social responsibilities to careen mindlessly around the country in RVs. It's difficult to know which stereotype is more alarming.

IS THERE A USEFUL WAY TO VIEW AGE?

If the medical concept of age is too narrow and disease-focused, and chronological age too imprecise, how can we define age in a way that has meaning for life-course policy? We need a definition that is elastic and encourages the continuation of growth and change. One way to construct such a definition is to observe the individual's behavior and self-perceptions.

To a large extent, age is self-defining. The 58-year-old who feels his career has peaked and has nowhere to go but down, who says it's too late to learn to play tennis, who fears new political ideas and social mores, who obsesses about his bodily functions, and who spends his vacation at the same resort with the same people *is* old.

"Old" is more than an accretion of years. It is a state of mind, a message to one's self that the best is past and not much remains to be done. For people who believe it, that message is a prophecy. All one's minor aches and pains are magnified, and serious illnesses are catastrophic. A sunset or a beautiful autumn day is either ignored or seen as another symbol of the end of life. Life loses savor and meaning if one lives in constant expectation of decline and death. And if there is no future, why learn anything?

The people we observed and talked with during the writing of this book are not old. Elderlearners, whether they're studying chaos theory or the origins of jazz, the poetry of Anne Sexton or line dancing, Chinese cooking or psychoanalytic theory, are looking ahead. Their lives embrace change, and they implicitly or explicitly recognize that they are still growing and developing.

The 82-year-old woman who is confined by severe arthritis to her apartment, but who communicates with the world on SeniorNet, avidly follows the news on CNN and in the *Times*, invites her younger neighbors in for tea or Scrabble, and reads the latest mysteries is *not* old.

The people who take Museum of Natural History study trips down the Amazon, or journey with Smithsonian groups through the canyons of the Southwest are not old, even though their average age is usually in the late sixties to eighties. People who enroll in Elderhostels to study regional history or polyphonic music or the Civil War or oceanic biology are not old, even if they wear hearing aids and carry canes.

Age is almost incidental for active older people who are taking classes, volunteering in their communities, keeping in touch with friends and families, and reaching out to new experiences. They may have a momentary start when they face the mirror each morning and discover new bumps and wrinkles, but they're too busy to let it impinge on their sense of self. It's hard to indulge in self-pity when you've just spent a day learning to play the alto recorder, teaching the illiterate, reading to the blind, or cleaning litter off the local beach.

DISENGAGEMENT THEORY

Not long ago, the word "retirement" struck terror into the minds of grown men and women. When business was bad, my father would cry out in despair: "I've had it for sure. It's over the hill time. Here comes that damned gold watch." To him, in the 1940s and 1950s, retirement had exclusively negative connotations: uselessness, giving up meaningful work, diminution of income, and encroaching ill health and senescence.

The conventional wisdom of the time held that rapid physical disintegration was not only sequential to the cessation of paid work, but an all but inevitable consequence of it. Pop theory gave the retiree only a few years to live, even though census figures were beginning to contradict that pessimism.

As late as the 1960s, gerontologists and others who studied or worked with older people saw the latter phase of life as a progressive process of physical, social, and intellectual "disengagement," not only from paid work, but from previously sustaining relationships and interests. "Successful aging" meant graceful acceptance of this version of the end—acceptance of the gradual loss of friendships, social relationships, and previously enjoyed activities. In effect, although most were too polite to say so, retirement meant that death was the only remaining frontier.

Women in those years followed a somewhat different path. Since most were not engaged in paid work, they couldn't properly retire; and since the concept of shared responsibility for the home was still rare, life did not change much for older women. They still had homes to clean, meals to prepare, and laundry to wash; and since retired spouses tended to be underfoot, they had to cope with a new intrusion on their time. Arthritis might slow their working speed, but, short of total disability, they were expected to carry on. Moreover, women's substantial edge in longevity meant that they could not "retire" until widow-hood released them from their prolonged condition of voluntary servitude. And even then, ties of family and friendship, nurtured throughout the years, remained as tethers to life. Disengagement in women was rare and usually indicative of serious depression.

The "disengagement" theory of the mid-twentieth century was, like much research at that time, male-oriented. As elaborated by Cumming and Henry,[15] who viewed it as of great developmental significance, disengagement gave the mature individual time to prepare for the inevitability of death by providing a psychological and sociological process of withdrawing from society. This decreased social interaction was characterized as mutual and even beneficial. The individual not only withdrew into him or herself, but society also withdrew from the individual. Thus death, when it came, did not disrupt society's equilibrium. The process was seen as natural rather than imposed. Cumming and Henry compared it poetically to the "gradual and inevitable withering of a leaf or fruit long before frost totally kills it."[16]

In the 1960s, researchers who began questioning the disengagement theory found a "positive correlation between the extent of social interaction and psychological well being, a correlation that is even higher in persons aged seventy and over than persons aged fifty to seventy."[17] Older people who remained engaged with others, who stayed vitally connected to their environment, were generally healthier and happier than those who withdrew.

Neugarten, Havigurst, and Tobin measured psychological well-being as a sum of five ratings: "(a) takes pleasure from whatever the round of activities that constitutes his[18] everyday life; (b) regards his life as meaningful and accepts resolutely that which life has been; (c) feels he has succeeded in achieving his major goals; (d) holds a positive image of self; and (e) maintains happy and optimistic attitudes and moods."[19]

Their conclusion was that "people, as they grow old, are neither at the mercy of the social environment nor at the mercy of some set of intrinsic processes." Individuals continue "to exercise choice and to select from the environment in accordance with [their] own long established needs."[20]

Katherine S., age 74, greeted us at the door wearing a sweatshirt that proclaimed, "Things get better with age; I'm approaching magnificent." And she is.

Katherine says the real turning point in her life occurred at age 54 when she went back to Washington University to pursue a master of arts in teaching. Upon hearing this, one son sent her a story about an 84-year-old who had just earned a Ph.D. Her second son sent her an article on why women over 40 shouldn't be in school. She has remembered that double message through 20 years of continued learning. It has not stopped her from reading Plato, Rousseau, Shakespeare, and other classic authors, nor has it interfered with the searching, thinking, and wondering process that was unleased in her as a mature student when she felt the world was opening to her for the first time.

Since achieving her degree, Katherine has traveled and lived in Europe, learning French and attending the University of Paris. In their late sixties and early seventies, she and her husband joined the Peace Corps, training first at the University of Maryland, where they studied rural community development, and then in Fiji for six weeks before taking on their teaching assignments at the University of the South Pacific. More recently, Katherine has attended five Elderhostels as well as a number of sessions at the Fulbright Institute at the University of Arkansas where lectures are free to seniors.

Much of Katherine's learning is a result of her experience as a volunteer. She belongs to the Webster Grove Nature Study Society and the Audubon Society, works with foreign students, and uses what she's learned at the Botanical Garden in St. Louis to supply stunning flower arrangements for the library at Webster University.

Typically, Katherine underplays her own accomplishments and was eager to have us interview some of her friends, including a 92-year-old Ph.D. who continues to be actively involved in learning. Clearly, her second son's message acted as a challenge rather than a warning. Disengagement is not in her mental vocabulary.

Fortunately, disengagement is out of fashion with retirees in the mid-1990s, who are often vigorous and in good health, able to remain economically independent, and enjoy new possibilities for educational, voluntary, and recreational activities. Nevertheless, disengagement may still be the appropriate mode for those who want time for contemplation, reflection, or the solitary things they have always wanted to do. James Birren, using the day as a metaphor for lifespan, suggests that some forms of withdrawal may be life enhancing.

> These late hours offer us the opportunity to sort out the grain and chaff of the day, allowing us to discard the hulls of our experience to get at the kernel of deeper meaning. . . . Our afternoons and evenings should be spent in calm reflection, in the search for meaning.[21]

Personality, not theory, is the key factor in how much societal intercourse older people need and want, and both activity and disengagement can occur in those who are well adjusted to aging. The individual should never be subjugated to any theory. In the waning years of the twentieth century, our concepts of aging are in creative flux; we must discard old myths and shibboleths about aging to see clearly what the new aging looks like, what it means to society, and how we can best respond to its needs and potential benefits in nonprogrammed ways. As we suggest in the next chapter, looking at the continued potential for growth and development throughout the lifespan may give us the intellectual breathing space we need to create ways to nurture the potential of an older population.

NOTES

1. Quoted in William Evans and Irving M. Rosenberg, *Biomarkers: The Ten Keys to Prolonging Vitality* (New York: Simon and Schuster, 1991), p. 40.

2. Lauren Goldberg, "A Gerontology for the 21st Century" in *Who Is Responsible for My Old Age?*, edited by Robert Butler and Kenzo Kiikuni (New York: Springer Publishing Co., 1993), p. 110.

3. Edmund T. Lonergan, ed., *Extending Life: A National Research Agenda on Aging*. Institute of Medicine, Division of Health Promotion and Disease Prevention (Washington, DC: National Academy Press, 1991), p. 122.

4. Bortz, pp. 25–26, 34.

5. K. Patricia Cross, *Adults as Learners* (San Francisco: Jossey-Bass, 1981), p. 236.

6. Jonathan Swift, *Gulliver's Travels* in *The Portable Swift* (New York: Viking Press, 1948), pp. 432–35.

7. Bortz, p. 45.

8. Ibid., p. 122.

9. Ibid., p. 308.

10. Cited by Philibert, p. 251.

11. Butler and Kiikuni, pp. 58–59.

12. Bronte, p. 20.

13. K. Seccombe and M. Ishii-Kuntz, "Perception of Problems Associated with Aging: Comparisons Among Four Older Age Cohorts," *The Gerontologist*, 31, 527–33.

14. These results are similar to the Harris and Associates results discussed in Chapter 1. See the table on p. 5.

15. Elaine Cumming and William F. Henry, *Growing Old: The Process of Disengagement* (New York: Basic Books, 1961).

16. Quoted by Arnold M. Rose, "A Current Theoretical Issue in Social Gerontology," in *Middle Age and Aging*, edited by Bernice L. Neugarten (Chicago: University of Chicago Press, 1975), p. 185.

17. Bernice L. Neugarten, Robert J. Havighurst, and Sheldon S. Tobin, "Personality and Patterns of Aging" in *Middle Age and Aging*, edited by Bernice L. Neugarten (Chicago: University of Chicago Press, 1975), p. 173.

18. The exclusive use of the male pronoun was common in the literature of the 1960s. Researchers at that time were not as sensitive to the sexism of language as we have become in the 1990s.

19. Neugarten, Havighurst, and Tobin, p. 174.

20. Ibid., pp. 176–77.

21. James Birren, "Understanding Life Backwards: Reminiscing for a Better Old Age" in *Who Is Responsible for My Old Age?*, edited by Robert N. Butler and Kenzo Kiikuni (New York: Springer Publishing Co., 1993), p. 19.

CHAPTER 3

Life Stage and Development Theory

Implications for Learning

For today's older people there are neither models to copy, precedents to take note of, conventions to be guided by, nor experience to consult, either personal experience or social experience. Being your age in the last decades of the twentieth century is challenging indeed.

Peter Laslett, A Fresh Map of Life, p. 73

A daughter criticizes one of her mother's friends for wearing a bright red coat while driving a yellow convertible. "It's inappropriate; she looks silly." In other words, her mother's friend is not "acting her age." The daughter's intolerance is both dated and meaningless. If someone tells us to "act your age," we literally no longer know how to respond. The old theories of aging don't have much to say to those in the current generation who are compelled to invent new responses to new ways of aging. Older adults, children of older adults, helping professionals, legislators, and friends all need a new paradigm to understand appropriateness and help us see where older people fit on the cradle-to-grave continuum. Because today's conditions of aging have no precedents in human history, we must, as Laslett says, "create principles for ourselves and our successors."[1]

LIFE STAGE THEORY

Shakespeare's seven ages of man is a classical attempt to set out a life stage theory. Although glorious poetry, Shakespeare's model of aging makes deterioration an inexorable condition of the last stages of life. It begins after the fifth age, in which Shakespeare's middle-aged justice, "In fair round belly with good capon lin'd," is "Full of wise saws and modern instances" and still in the apogee of life. Deterioration comes rapidly in the sixth age, when the bespectacled and shrunken man's voice turns back "toward childish treble." The seventh stage of life is a senile return to childhood, to "mere oblivion,/Sans teeth, sans eyes, sans taste, sans everything."[2] There's not much room between stages five and six for piano lessons, tennis, and helping out at the church soup kitchen, which one might not enjoy anyway with age seven creeping up.

The adult life-stages literature of the 1960s and 1970s is only slightly more helpful because it typically lumped together and only cursorily treated ages beyond 65. However, both literature and experience indicate that a good retirement or old age does not equate to aimless leisure. Many developmental and practical tasks are still to be done; one still has miles to go before one sleeps. In her work on adult life cycle tasks and educational program responses, Vivian Rogers McCoy sets out the following tasks of the person over 65:

- disengaging from paid work
- reassessing finances
- being concerned with personal health care
- searching for new outlets for achievement
- managing leisure time
- adjusting to a more constant marriage companion [the home for lunch problem]
- searching for the meaning of life
- adjusting to a single life [after death or departure of a spouse]
- becoming reconciled to death
- problem solving
- managing the stress accompanying change[3]

All these tasks require formal and informal learning, and most of them can be addressed in structured ways in elderlearning programs.[4]

Gail Sheehy's best-selling *New Passages, Mapping Your Life Across Time* takes an inspiriting view of age as a potential passage from one high to another. Sheehy believes that through positive attitudinal, mental, physical, and sexual exercise, we can retain our vigor and journey to the "age of integrity." With a combination of luck and will, we can move through "The Serene Sixties" to the "Sage Seventies" to the "Uninhibited Eighties" and even to the "Nobility of the Nineties" and beyond without losing our zest for living.

The energy and spirit of Sheehy's pop language is a refreshing change from the more sententious exhortations of most gerontological literature, but the message is essentially the same. If we develop the right attitudes, if we eat sensibly and exercise regularly, if we keep the mind-body connection working through continued mental stimulation, we have a good chance to age without lassitude and depression. As Sheehy says, "Although death is inevitable, the way in which we age is not."[5]

GROWTH AND DEVELOPMENT IN AGING

Sheehy's "passages" seem at first glance closely akin to the stage theories of aging with their series of predictable events in chronological order. Stage theories graph as a flat series of plateaus separated by transitions. They are useful for looking at children's development, which is highly predictable. They are less useful for older adults who do not develop in a chronologically determined pattern.[6]

Sheehy's stages, however, are moving away from purely chronological or life phase markers. The stages are not fixed solely by time but are affected by the individual's evolving situation: retirement, grandparenthood, children leaving home, loss of spouse, changing health status. This recognition of the importance of the context of the individual's life moves Sheehy's work closer to the dynamic of developmental theory.

Developmental theory, as presented by Erik Erikson in the 1950s, or by Neugarten, Gould, and Levenson in the 1970s, shows a series of plateaus and *ascending* transitions. Development implies no theoretical or chronological limits to ego and cognitive growth, but posits an upward trajectory. We learn more, we understand more, we become broader, more empathetic. Margaret Mead used to chide Erikson because on the printed page his developmental stages were "upside down." Because of the conventions of print, the reader read "down" the page. She felt that typographically the sequence of life should read up.[7] Of course, increasing age does not guarantee this upward movement; some people never get past the middle stages of development, which Erikson called Identity versus Role Confusion or Intimacy versus Isolation.

What is critical here is that age itself presents no barrier to developmental growth; indeed, it can be an incentive as each age faces new societal expectations, challenges, and inner needs. To the extent that elderlearning activities support or encourage ego and cognitive development, they are growth activities. Erikson's seventh developmental stage—generativity—by which he meant "the responsibility of each generation of adults to bear, nurture, and guide those people who will succeed them as adults," and which he thought characteristic of middle age, serves today as an apt descriptor of the successfully aging who have a second chance at generativity in the grandparenting role. "Amid the threat of deteriorating physical vigor," said Erikson, "lies the opportunity for growth."[8]

Growth and generativity are outcomes for those who view retirement as an opportunity to rekindle their creativity through writing, music, art, dance, and crafts, and who are attempting, through their activities, to leave a record of their passage for their children and grandchildren. Educators have found that the study of genealogy is popular with older adults. Genealogy is a way not only to discover one's origins but to leave a record. Many older people embark on genealogy or family history on their own, ransacking libraries and public records, corresponding with distant relatives, consulting the Mormon Family History Centers, traveling to family homesteads and reunions, and interviewing survivors. Much computer software has been developed to help them structure and record their research. The process of learning involved in a thorough genealogical search is extraordinarily demanding, supplying years of challenge to fuel continued cognitive and ego growth.

The opposite of generativity is stagnation, which indicates lack of success in productive aging. Stagnating older people, those who have stopped growing or seeking new experiences, are neither interested in nor good candidates for further learning. Without deliberate intervention, they are unlikely ever to achieve Erikson's eighth and culminating stage, integrity.

Integrity (the positive opposite of despair) is best reached through reflection and consideration, as a person attempts to achieve an understanding of his or her life, a sense of wholeness through a search for meaning. When asked *why* they are learning, 37.7 percent of respondents to the Elderlearning Survey checked "as part of a search for meaning and wisdom."[9]

This quest for integrity also resonates with respondents' choices of what to learn. The urge to complete a life review is frequently expressed through journal keeping or the writing of an autobiography. The Survey confirms that renewed interest in literature, history, philosophy, religion, and journal keeping is an integral part of the search for meaning and wisdom.

What They Are Learning[10]	
literature, drama, humanities	46.5%
history, family history, genealogy	36.5%
philosophy, religion, self-actualization	33.1%
writing, journalism, journal keeping	24.0%

THE FOUR AGES THEORY

Our tour through the extensive adult life cycle/growth and development literature, has, of necessity, been brief. Another perhaps more relevant way of looking at how people change and grow is the "four ages" theory. The theory began in France, but has now also become an integral part of thinking on the subject in Germany, Great Britain, Australia, and New Zealand.

In *A Fresh Map of Life: The Emergence of the Third Age* (1989), Peter Laslett gives a useful definition of the four ages. What follows relies heavily on his work.

- **The First Age:** This age begins at birth and lasts approximately 20 to 25 years. It is characterized by an initial physical dependency and a continued financial dependency. Its major tasks are education, socialization, and preparation for work. The child ideally grows from total reliance on parents for protection, nurturing, and language to the ability to deal with the surrounding world in school and social life. A successful first age gives young people the educational tools and the sense of personal autonomy and identity that they need to strike out on their own.

- **The Second Age:** This is the longest of the ages and probably the most productive in the traditional sense because it spans the period of life between taking on the obligations of a job and marriage and retirement from paid work. It is characterized by familial and social responsibility. The major tasks are procreating, raising a family, supporting that family, and contributing to the economic health of the society. One of its main frustrations is lack of personal control of time so that many personally fulfilling activities must be deferred until the Third Age.

- **The Third Age:** Although not necessarily governed by calendar age, the Third Age is usually ushered in by retirement. It is, or should be, a time of fulfillment through activities that give men and women both pleasure and a sense of their own worth. These activities may include continued work, paid or unpaid; active pursuit of previously deferred interests; development of new interests; renewed commitment to society through involvement in politics and social programs; and renewed commitment to learning as a means of achieving creativity, self-fulfillment, a definition of values, and a deeper understanding of oneself and others.

   Given the revised longevity expectations of the late twentieth century, the Third Age may last as long as 25 to 30 or more years and may be a time of unprecedented growth and spiritual renewal. It is truly the Age Age, full of uncertainties and possibilities, fraught with potential problems. The Third Age is hard to define in a world in which 20 or 25 percent of the population is without a socially predetermined role but is healthy, energetic, and ripe with experience. It calls for the "invention of institutions and attitudes which we do not inherit and do not yet possess."[11]

- **The Fourth Age:** This stage, once called "old age" (and sometimes referred to as "the disability zone"), comes at various times, from age 60 to 110, or not at all. The lucky ones never reach it; the unlucky may spend many years in it. It is characterized by illness, frailty, dependence, and the imminence of death.

   The discredited "disengagement" theory may be an accurate description of this late stage of life when physical and perhaps even mental processes are in a state of rapid entropy. But even at this age, when mobility, activity, and participation are constrained, rehabilitative educational activities can be highly effective and can move some people back to a previous stage. Studies in nursing homes show that even the very old and feeble can regain some of their strength and enthusiasm for living by involvement in activities that demand physical and mental exercise.

The Fourth Age, however, lies mostly beyond the scope of this book. We do not wish to sweep it under the rug, but it is not directly relevant to our interest in elderlearning. Our primary concern is the Third Age, a time of enormous potential when the human being, though coping with wrinkles, sagging flesh, and reduced physical strength, is still growing and developing and can fashion a totally engaging life style. Third Agers can be a powerful resource for a society that needs all the help it can get. Their physical and intellectual energies, if positively directed, can contribute substantially to a more thoughtful, ordered, and compassionate society.

The Four Ages is a useful construct for evoking new ways of thinking about how we as individuals can manage our own lives as well as how society can make the necessary adjustments to the changing demographics of an aging population. The flexibility of the definitions of each stage, rooted in function rather than chronology, enables us to look at the singular human being rather than merely categorizing on the basis of a person's age.

A 70-year-old in fair health who is apathetic, has radically reduced her social contacts, and is becoming forgetful and slovenly about her person and home may be exhibiting the classic signs of "terminal drop." She is beginning her last journey. If we are locked into a life stage theory, we will say she is disengaging, comfort ourselves that this is normal, and gently let her go. On the other hand, she may be depressed by a low grade chronic illness or the loss of a spouse or friend, she may be eating a poor diet, or she may be terminally bored. In any case, rather than write her off, we can attempt to draw her back into the Third Age through stimulating intellectual activities and social intercourse. A family member can take her out to a concert or include her in a family trip, or ask her to make a casserole for a holiday get together. A friend can coax her to come along to a local fitness center or to take a painting class. In this case, behavior characteristic of extreme old age that does not have its source in serious physical illness may be reversed.

Thus, the Four Ages idea functions as a growth and development model, inviting medical, psychological, social, and educational interventions to help people function at levels appropriate to their situations and abilities rather than to their age.

UNIVERSITIES OF THE THIRD AGE

The possibilities of learning for older adults have been recognized in Europe for over 30 years by the creation of Universities of the Third Age.[12] In 1972, the French founded the Université du Troisième Age in Toulouse. They defined the Third Age as "'the period of life when one ceases all professional activity,' when men and women have absolute freedom to choose what to do with their time."[13] The idea spread quickly throughout Europe.

The first English-language University of the Third Age (or U3A) was established in Great Britain in 1981 by a group based at Cambridge University.[14] While the French model had relied on prepackaged university courses, the British moved toward more self- and mutual help groups. In Great Britain, U3A is run on an "experiential" model, bringing together a self-resourced coalition of learners and teachers with virtually no government subsidy. The Third Agers demonstrated at the early public meetings that they were "capable of organising their own activities and providing all the skills and expertise needed."[15]

Early organizing efforts for U3As in other locations were largely supported by foundations, and in 1986 the founders received a small government grant to help run a national office and develop further U3As. By 1994, there were nearly 250 U3As throughout the UK. They are largely self-reliant and supported by membership fees ranging from £15 to £50. As in the Institutes for Learning in Retirement found in the U.S., learners typically serve also as teachers. A wide variety of learning opportunities is made available in the arts, languages, science and technology, recreation, literature and the humanities, history, and such practical skills as first aid, lip reading, wine making and appreciation, advertising, dressmaking, and public speaking. U3A's active National Travel Club reflects the same passion for travel that the Elderlearning Survey reveals (see p. 76). The rapid proliferation of Universities of the Third Age testifies to their practical application to the developmental needs of an aging population.

It took only about four years for "Colleges of the Third Age" to spring up in Australia, where the sheltering institutions are not universities but TAFE colleges (which are similar to U.S. community colleges). A working group was established in Australia in 1985 to "examine the problems faced by older people in education, to assess what was there, but more importantly it was an exercise in revising stereotyped approaches to the needs of the elderly."[16] The working group wanted to "dispel views of older people in education as something of a mildly amusing anomaly" and to "redress the balance," giving them a return for the education taxes they have paid over the years.[17]

Certainly, the first four courses offered in Australia's colleges were anything but stereotyped. The choice was wide in sweep and appealed to a number of needs and interests: Motor Mechanics, Computer Studies, Modern Economics, and Recording Australian Folklife. One was practical and skills oriented, enabling students to deal with their own vehicles; the second was based on important new technology; the third is a classical field of study, highly quantitative and abstract; and the fourth gives older people a way to decipher and analyze the past, their nation's and their own.

From the beginning, demand has exceeded supply in Australia's Colleges of the Third Age. The problem has been handled on the refreshing principle of "first born, first in." The major complaint has been insufficient promotion (advertising)—students have a hard time learning about the availability of courses. (This lack of information about what is available was also cited as a barrier to learning by 19.3 percent of the respondents to the Elderlearning Survey.)

These variations in Universities of the Third Age are significant because they are direct responses to a perceived developmental need, "a social form without compulsion."[18] Early on, the founders of these universities realized that learning was an appropriate activity for those who were no longer tied to a life of full-time work and, combining institutional resources with the energy and knowledge of older people, put together new institutions to serve this population. Do not think the Europeans were ahead of the Americans. In 1962, 10 years before the first French Université, New York's New School for Social Research initiated the Institute for Retired Professionals, the model for today's 300+ Institutes for Learning in Retirement.

NOTES

1. Laslett, p. 138.

2. *As You Like It*, II, 7, 11, 154–66.

3. See Vivian Rogers McCoy's chart of Developmental Stages (1977) in "The Life Cycle," by Arthur W. Chickering and Robert Havighurst, *The Modern American College*, edited by Arthur W. Chickering and Associates (San Francisco: Jossey-Bass, 1981), p. 28.

4. As in much of the earlier adult development literature, this is a male-oriented series of tasks. What of the over 65 female who may have no work from which to disengage, who long ago figured out how to manage her leisure time (when she had any), and whose major new tasks as she ages may be caring for her own aging parents, nurturing relationships with her grown children, coping with the physical ravages that confront her in the mirror, or getting used to having a husband around the house 24 hours a day?

5. Gail Sheehy, *New Passages: Mapping Your Life Across Time* (New York: Random House, 1995), p. 422.

6. Robert C. Peck, "Psychological Developments in the Second Half of Life," *Middle Age and Aging*, pp. 88–92.

7. Mary Catherine Bateson, *With a Daughter's Eye* (New York: Washington Square Press, 1985), p. 261.

8. Quoted by Bortz, p. 260.

9. We did not find a positive correlation between advanced age and the search for wisdom and meaning. In fact, the opposite seems to be true: between ages 60 and 74, 39.6% checked wisdom and meaning as a reason for learning; between ages 75 and 95, only 32.7% did so.

10. This chart represents only 3 of the 20 choices on the questionnaire. See Chapter 6 for more complete information.

11. Laslett, p. 131.

12. In many ways, the emergence of the U3As parallels the rise of Institutes for Learning in Retirement (ILRs) in the U.S. ILRs are treated in detail in Chapter 8.

13. Dianne Norton, "A Brief History of U3A," *Third Age News*, 1994 Supplement, p. 1.

14. Rose Leaf, "University of the Third Age: Stretching the Boundaries—A Self-Resourced Coalition for Learning" in *Stretching the Boundaries: A Quarterly Experience*, Australian Consortium on Experiential Education, Inc., 32, 1994, p. 25.

15. Norton, p. 1.

16. "Colleges of the Third Age," *TAFE Newsletter*, 22 (September 1986), 7.

17. Ibid.

18. Laslett, p. 176.

CHAPTER 4

Confounding the Stereotype
The Cognitive Abilities of Older Learners

When I was young I was amazed at Plutarch's statement that the elder Cato began at the age of eighty to learn Greek. I am amazed no longer. Old age is ready to undertake tasks that youth shirks because they would take too long.

Somerset Maugham

INTRODUCTION

Negative stereotypes of aging have their most devastating impact on the public perception of the mental abilities of the old. To be old is commonly equated with "losing one's marbles," entering second childhood, or becoming disoriented, forgetful, and absent-minded. At best, the older person is mentally torpid, at worst, senile. The elderly suffer most from these stereotypes. Like other stereotypes, they can become self-fulfilling prophecies as their subjects accept and internalize the myths of aging and begin to act in accordance with them. In our research, we often heard healthy, competent older adults make statements like, "I'm too old to go back to school," "I'm too old to try a new way of mulching my garden," or "I'm too old to learn to use a computer."

Such statements illustrate what Ellen Langer, in her book *Mindfulness*, calls "entrapment by category," or "mindlessness."

> To be mindless is to be trapped in a rigid world in which certain creatures always belong to the Emperor, Christianity is always good, certain people are forever untouchable, and doors are only doors.[1]

It is "mindless" for older adults to allow the myths and falsehoods of the past to bar them from the joy of renewed learning. It is "mindless" to accept outworn assumptions about old age that suggest submission to life as a passive spectator is age-appropriate. It is "mindless" to accept that growth and development have age limits. In this book, we argue passionately against such "mindlessness" and for increased opportunities and resources for older learners; we embrace the belief that continued growth and development are not only possible but critical for the health and well-being of older men and women.

Fortunately, increasing numbers of older adults are ignoring outmoded ways of viewing themselves, living in a present reality in which they realize and celebrate their own vitality and continued intellectual ability. The rapidly increasing numbers of people over 65 who are working to improve their mental and physical skills are ignoring negative messages that say their mental abilities are irrelevant to their own experience as learners. Today's quintessential elderlearner resembles Supreme Court Justice Oliver Wendell Holmes, who, in his nineties, summoned his court-appointed male secretary to read to him: "Let's have a little self-improvement, Sonny." Shortly thereafter, President Franklin Delano Roosevelt came to call. He found Holmes in his library reading Plato. "Why do you read Plato, Mr. Justice?" he asked. Without missing a beat, the aging Holmes answered, "To improve my mind, Mr. President."[2]

Although Holmes' taste for Greek philosophy may not be the usual choice of people in their nineties, it is less rare than one would think. Mr. G. is 73 years old. After retiring unwillingly from a life of manual labor, he decided to pursue a college degree at Empire State College, New York State's nontraditional college for adults. He surprised the faculty mentor assigned to him by requesting that his first learning contract be devoted to a history of philosophy, beginning with the Greeks. At a meeting with Mr. G. a few weeks later, the mentor tried to evaluate his progress by asking how he was getting along with Aristotle's *Nichomachean Ethics*. "Oh, pretty well," said Mr. G. "It's sometimes hard to understand, and that makes me kind of tired, but I read for only 45 minutes at a stretch, and then I walk around like my doctor told me to. Back and forth in my room. While I'm walking around I tell myself everything I've learned in the past 45 minutes, and if I'm not sure of something, I look it up and keep on walking. That seems to make it stick in the brain, and then I go back to old Aristotle for another 45 minutes." Mr. G. then gave his mentor a clear, cogent summary of the *Ethics* couched in nonacademic vernacular but true to the spirit and meaning of the philosopher. He ended by saying, "Old A. thought we could find happiness by acquiring intellectual virtue. I guess that's what I'm after."

While neither Oliver Wendell Holmes nor Mr. G. represent typical older learners, they are not uncommon exceptions to the entrenched myth of inevitable decline, and their continued aspirations for intellectual growth are not unique. Acquiring intellectual virtue in the Aristotelian sense seems to be what a number of older learners are after, whether they articulate it in just that way or not. (See Chapter 6 for a discussion of why older people are pursuing learning.)

DECONSTRUCTING THE MYTHS

In the past 20 or 25 years, serious progress has been made in understanding cognition in the aged. Although greater knowledge has made the picture more complicated, it has also demolished the stereotype of life after 65 as a protracted slide into cognitive decline. Most important, it has been established that older people can and do continue to learn, many of them as well as they did when younger.

Some earlier studies of intelligence, which compared younger and older adults cross-sectionally and seemed to support the theory of significant decline, have been superseded by longitudinal studies that give a different picture. The old belief held that the intelligence curve plateaus in the thirties and, after holding steady for about 10 years, begins to go downhill. That notion has given way to the results of more sophisticated studies using more highly differentiated intelligence tests which show, among other things, that

> on measures of vocabulary and other skills reflecting educational experience, individuals seemed to maintain their adult level of functioning into the sixth, and even the seventh decade.[3]

Even skills that are likely to decline with age (memory, speed, visuo-motor flexibility) can be compensated for by the accretion of experience and education that is termed "crystallized intelligence." Moreover, barring organic brain disease, older people can actually improve their cognitive skills through training and exercises. The more one is involved in learning activities, the more one's ability to learn expands. Continuing learners are better learners.

Klaus and Ruth Riegel at the University of Michigan suggest that when significant intellectual decline does occur in older people, it comes shortly before death.

> In 1956 the Riegels gave intelligence tests to 380 German men and women between the ages of 55 and 75. Five years later they retested 202 of them. Some of the remainder had died, and others refused to be retested. When the Riegels looked back at the 1956 test scores of the subjects who had died, they discovered that on the average, the deceased subjects had scored lower than those who survived. Put another way, the low scores in 1956 predicted impending death.[4]

In the Riegels' follow-up study in 1966, they found that those who had died in the interim had lower test scores on the second than on the first test. They reasoned that there is a marked deterioration during the last five, or fewer, years prior to a natural death, what they called a "terminal drop."

This terminal drop is now a widely recognized, though not completely understood, phenomenon, and it leads to a statistical dilemma. Baltes and Schaie speculate that "if the researcher could foresee the future and remove from his study those subjects nearing death, he might observe little or no change in the intelligence of the remaining group."[5] Thus the 30 to 40 percent of 81-year-olds in the Werner Schaie study (discussed below) whose cognitive capabilities seemed to be affected by age might be significantly reduced if one were only able to read the future and know which of them were nearing death.

The salient point in the earlier examples of Justice Holmes and Mr. G. is that, despite aging, both still took for granted their ability to continue growing and developing intellectually. John Dewey was perhaps the first to remark upon the "paradox" of concurrent development and aging, the individual's ability to become increasingly wise and mature even while declining biologically in strength and health.

> That there should be a gradual wearing down of energies, physical and mental in the old age period, it seems reasonable to expect upon biological grounds . . . that maturing changes at some particular age into incapacity for continued growth in every direction is a very different proposition.[6]

Over the past 20 or 30 years, much research interest has focused on the maintenance or decline of cognitive function among the elderly. The field does not suffer from inattention. One researcher, seeking a comprehensive view of the narrowed-down topic of "learning and memory in the aging," found over 400 books and papers published in the five years prior to 1990, and interest has certainly not abated since then.

These studies deal with a number of rather different but important issues related to learning programs for older adults; these issues should be understood by those who legislate such programs into being, those who design them, those who pay for them, and, most importantly, those who will benefit from them.

PHYSIOLOGICAL AGING OF THE BRAIN

Does the brain age physiologically? Is it inevitable that we will suffer diminishing cognitive capacity over time? As the philosopher would say, yes and no. The brain is not just a piece of machinery that wears out and rusts with age, nor is it a hard disk that cannot expand beyond its huge but finite quota of bytes. The brain is more durable than any piece of machinery, more resilient than any hard disk, more miraculous than any other organ in the body, and more variable.

Our cognitive abilities may change with age in both positive and negative directions. It is true that the incredible ability of the baby's or young child's brain to absorb and use new information, to learn language, to take hold of every aspect of its culture, is never again duplicated in later life. Evolutionary necessity has given children an extraordinarily quick and efficient learning system which, if they were to continue to function at that level, would produce a race of geniuses. On the other hand, the skills and knowledge human beings accumulate as they grow older compensate for the loss of speed in acquiring that knowledge.

The extraordinary plasticity of the brain makes predictions regarding its physiological functioning difficult. Rat studies have repeatedly shown that early life enrichment results in brighter rats. Their brains are bigger and the connections (dendritic branches) are more numerous and longer. Animal experiments have demonstrated that environmental complexity can actually alter the thickness of the cortex and that trained animals have more folds in their brain (cognitive capacity) than untrained animals. Moreover, there are chemical differences between stimulated and unstimulated brains. When "grown artificially in a glass dish, brain cells react to the addition of noradrenaline by extending the nerve branches—just as with enrichment."[7] According to Jack Barchas of Stanford, "Behavioral events alter neurochemical function and altered neurochemical function can change behavior,"[8] creating a positive feedback loop. Some chemicals block the synthesis of protein in the brain; other chemicals stimulate dendritic branches. Since most of us do not wish to carve up the brains of living humans to compare the stimulated and nonstimulated, the trained and the untrained, the educated and the uneducated, we are left to infer the quantity of brain function through measurable physiological and intellectual functions.

Age does bring inevitable physiological decline of brain function if you measure levels of dopamine and noradrenaline, the chemicals responsible for brain stimulation. There is decline if you use a PET scanner to show that older people have lower metabolism of glucose in the brain. There is no decline if you consider specific areas of the brain, such as the visual cortex, which suffers not even minimal cellular deterioration, or if you consider blood flow, oxygen use, metabolism, and other physical measurements in normally aging brains.[9] There is no decline if you look at the variable results of physical brain tests on individuals; the range of effects varies from none to great. There is no decline if you measure the output of the brains of older people whose lives are intellectually rich against those whose lives are deprived of mental exercise and stimulation.

The decline in some functions, such as short-term memory, does seem age-related. Because we expect and even accept that older people may demonstrate some hearing and vision loss, some loss of muscle tone, and gradual deterioration of internal organs, we also take diminished cognitive capacity for granted. However, the brain is the most complex organ of all, the only one capable of continuing in a positive trajectory, of developing throughout life. There are no simple answers to questions about age and loss of brain function, or to questions about whether those losses are preventable or reversible.

If we exclude degenerative disease, we may conclude that older, active brains do not necessarily deteriorate in critical ways. The presumption that our brains wither as we age is unwarranted and may arise from the confusion between normal aging and the aging hastened by such organic brain diseases as Alzheimer's, multiple small strokes, and senile arteriosclerosis, the symptoms of which were once classified together as senility. Today we have, in most cases, the ability to distinguish these degenerative diseases from normal aging and to recognize that they are not the inevitable concomitants of growing older. Many famous men and women lived into their eighties and nineties without loss of mental acuity. But for every Michelangelo, Picasso, Frank Lloyd Wright, Bertrand Russell, or Georgia O'Keeffe, there are thousands of ordinary citizens who can also serve as daily examples of unimpaired intellectual functioning into great age. Certainly the presence among us of millions of fully functioning older people is eloquent proof that physiological deterioration of the brain is not inevitable.

NONPHYSIOLOGICAL FACTORS IN OLDER ADULTS' COGNITIVE ABILITIES

Despite the growing understanding of the influence of health, exercise, education, personality and social status on cognitive aging, there is a lack of theories relating the knowledge of such influences on cognitive aging to theories of biological aging.[10]

A dual aging process occurs in later life: the normal physiological changes wrought by time and the injuries (illness, environmental) that contribute to aging. These two processes can be called primary and secondary aging, but they do not occur at the same age or to the same degree in the population nor are they necessarily indicative of absolute decline. Although the aging processes may qualitatively change the way people deal with learning challenges, individuals can and do develop mechanisms to deal with these decrements. One factor in the maintenance or even increase of performance levels "is the increase in expertise gained through experience in various domains."[11] In a small city in mid-Ohio, an 84-year-old woman, who for the past 20 years has borne the responsibility of voter education for the League of Women Voters, is regularly consulted by political pundits, newspaper reporters, and candidates. Her political information, insights, and predictions are said to be infallible.

Warner Schaie has shown that the following social factors also affect decline in intellectual development:

- high levels of education, occupational status, and income
- high workplace complexity
- long marriage to an intelligent spouse
- exposure to stimulating environments
- utilization of cultural and educational resources throughout adulthood[12]

Social factors play a critical role in how we age cognitively. Those who are well educated, whether in schools or through self-initiated learning experiences; those who have worked at cognitively demanding jobs; and those who have been surrounded by family and friends who stress cultivation of the intellect have a clear advantage over those who lack such experiences. Studies have shown that "the degree to which substantively complex work increases intellectual flexibility remains the same across the life span."[13] Conversely, "both cultural and social structural factors may reduce the level of cognitive effectiveness of the elderly."[14] Routinized jobs, an undemanding social environment, mindless leisure time, and the powerlessness fostered by negative stereotypes can all hasten a precipitous decline of both mental and physical health.

At 101 years old, Ann G. spends summers with her son in Maine, where she continues her 70-year study of Chinese religion and culture, particularly her research on the Chinese "paper gods" (a form of home worship). She winters with her daughter in Florida where she swims laps, cooks secret recipe Chinese dumplings, and takes three-mile excursions to the market or post office on her tricycle.

Ann has lectured extensively on Chinese religion and culture; she has written four books about China, the last published when she was in her 80s. She and her late husband, who worked for the Rockefeller Foundation, spent much of their married life in the Far East, including Beijing, where she worked in the 1920s helping women to establish embroidery trades out of their homes.

Ann says she always wanted to retire to Beijing (or Peking as she knew it), but the Chinese government has made that impossible. So now, in late old age, she busies herself at her son's electric typewriter, transcribing her notes from earlier research on the Chinese gods so that they will be legible and available for other researchers.

For her hundredth birthday, Ann's son gave her a one-week boat trip up the Columbia River to trace the voyage of Lewis and Clark. She says that "the secret is to keep up and doing, keep up and doing, and to not stop, ever." Her ambition is to "live at least to the year 2000—then I will have lived in three centuries."[15]

The "Alumni Notes" of the *Harvard Medical School Bulletin* provide eloquent evidence of the continuing capacity of the aging intellect to carry on the cognitive activities of a lifetime. These notes are informal reports by older retired physicians on what they are currently doing. The notes reflect the sustained high level of intellectual accomplishment possible for those who have always been mentally active and testify to the persistence of intellect in those who have lived by that intellect.

John T. Edsall, who graduated from medical school in 1928 and is presumed to be in his nineties, reports as follows:

> I am taking part in a three-day "summer school" in July on the history of hemoglobin at the Wellcome Institute for the History of Medicine in London. I am still working on my monograph on that subject. Also I gave seminars in April and May at Washington University Medical School (St. Louis) and at the University of Delaware.[16]

Leo Blacklow, class of 1930, who practiced medicine for almost 60 years, retired in 1993 but still attends hospital grand rounds and keeps up with medical news. And his learning doesn't stop there. "Being a science major, I found myself very deficient in [literature]," he says. Now enrolled in a course at Boston College, he is reading the works of English humorist P.J. Wodehouse and the classic *Madame Bovary*.[17]

Other medical school alumni, now in their seventies and eighties, report learning German, studying health care delivery in China, earning a master's degree in humanities, doing karate for exercise and discipline, writing their autobiographies, going to divinity school, engaging in study-travel, teaching and learning in university-sponsored Learning in Retirement Institutes, working in third world countries for the World Health Organization and UNICEF, and volunteering in poor neighborhoods on public health issues. If there's cognitive decline among this group, they're hiding it well.

COGNITIVE COMPETENCE

What do psychological tests and studies measure? What working definition of "intelligence" is being explored? What does it mean to be cognitively whole or cognitively impaired? And what about Godel's theorem, which says you cannot use the system itself to objectively analyze the system? If this theorem is correct, one human brain is incapable of measuring another human brain.

Godel aside, let's start with a fairly simple definition of "intelligence." David Wechsler, creator of a widely used measure of I.Q., the Wechsler Scales, defined intelligence as "the overall capacity of an individual to understand and cope with the world around him."[18] Peterson agrees, but cautions that since we still cannot directly or precisely measure cognitive potential, the usual research strategy has been to infer the underlying traits of an individual by measuring performance in a number of settings.[19] However, this measure can only be an approximation because performance and ability are not necessarily synonymous. Performance may be altered by one's mood, state of health, or motivation.

The Wechsler Adult Intelligence Scale-Revised (WAIS-R) covers, but does not necessarily distinguish among, a broad range of cognitive skills and capabilities. The individual IQ (Intelligence Quotient), although reported as a single score, actually measures a number of different kinds of intelligence: information, verbal (comprehension, vocabulary), numerical, spatial, symbolic, etc. However, since, as Peterson cautions, cognitive capacity (or ability) and cognitive performance are not necessarily synonymous (over- and under-achievers are staple characters in life as well as in classrooms), we cannot directly or precisely measure cognitive potential.

An additional complication in looking at standard IQ scores is that the concept of IQ has an age factor built into it, so "cross-generational comparisons disadvantage older cohorts."[20] Until recently, each generation has scored slightly higher on IQ than the preceding one.[21] A person at age 25 whose score was 110 was supposed to have an approximate score of 100, whereas a person at age 75 who scored only 68 might also be thought to have the equivalent of a score of 100. IQ confusion aside, it is well to remember that although high IQ scores may be predictive of success in educational endeavors or in vocational competence, they cannot assure a person success unless other personality traits, such as perseverance and motivation, are also present.

Whatever its merits or demerits, standardized testing does not account for the discrepancy between the results of the tests and the observation of functioning in older adults. Timothy A. Salthouse, intrigued by the discrepancies between measured cognitive competence in psychometric tests and the individual's observed functioning in everyday situations, did a study of 90 professors recruited from the faculty of two distinguished universities.[22] Half the subjects were aged 21-42 years; half 60-79 years. All the subjects were currently active in their professions and comparable in socioeconomic status, fields of professional specialization, and recipiency of honors. On a battery of cognitive tests, the younger faculty performed significantly better than the older on six of the eight tests. A similar study of businesspeople showed similar results. Salthouse posits the following reasons for these results:

1. The types of intelligence measured by tests may be different from the types necessary for professional success.
2. Only the most successful individuals survive in the profession to late middle or old age.

3. Different standards of evaluation. The more rigorous demands of psychometric tests may lead to an uncovering of the greater abilities of the young vs. the old.
4. Differential amounts of experience may enable older persons to function as well as or even better than their younger colleagues despite the apparent loss of measured intelligence.

What Salthouse does not mention, and what may be the most critical factor here, is the difference in response to the testing process itself between young and old. Noncognitive factors such as visual and auditory acuity, health status, motivation to learn, level of anxiety, meaningfulness of the material, and the speed at which the test is paced play a strong role in the performance of older adults.[23] These factors enhance the uncertainty principle and can highlight, diminish, or distort age differences depending on what exactly is being measured, how it is being measured, and under what conditions. The usual research strategy has been to infer the underlying traits of an individual by measuring performance in a number of settings.[24]

If we suspend skepticism for a moment and agree that standard IQ comes as close as anything to a measure of intelligence, we still haven't achieved a perfect definition. Some individual components of intelligence may be more highly developed in older people, others may to some extent diminish with age. Moreover, as we shall see, we can't merely have a number of older adults take the IQ test and compare the results with a younger cohort and come up with valid data on decline in old age.

CROSS-SECTIONAL VERSUS LONGITUDINAL STUDIES OF COGNITIVE AGING

In looking at the question of whether the IQ declines with age, early researchers did cross-sectional studies, that is, they used groups of different ages, gave them the same test, and then compared the results. These studies seemed to lend support to the thesis that there *is* a measurable diminishing of intelligence as we age. Thirty-year-olds were smarter than 50-year-olds who in turn were smarter than 70-year-olds. There are many reasons why this might be so other than simple decline.

Different age cohorts were formed by different cultures and exposed to different educational philosophies. Different skills have been prized and taught and different educational values pursued. Over the past century, the emphasis on memorization has decreased, part of a gradual move away from data-based testing. Today's younger adults were taught in classrooms where knowing how to find information, to analyze it, and to construct logical arguments from it were stressed over remembering facts. Current tests reflect that change in emphasis. Moreover, younger adults have become, through long practice, more sophisticated test takers. After years of SATs, GREs, and all the other batteries of tests to which they've been subjected, they have a feel for the multiple choice format and know when and when not to guess. They are experienced with analogies, geometric puzzles, synonyms and antonyms, mathematical reasoning, and all the tricks of the tester's trade. Today's 75-year-old may do worse on tests, even on subjects he or she knows well, than the 35-year-old who knows less but is a more accomplished test taker.

Cultural differences between the generations may also come into play when it comes to recall of factual information. Each age cohort has encountered a unique sequence of social and environmental events. Designers of tests are learning to be sensitive to racial, ethnic, and gender differences; perhaps they must also learn to be aware of age cohort differences. Questions that rely on general information or language familiar to young or middle-aged adults may draw a blank from older cohorts for whom a rock is a geological artifact not a kind of music, and for whom RAM is a horned sheep with no connection to computer memory. Differences in schooling may be vast; the content of physics courses the current older generation took in college are probably taught in high school today.

Other factors may distort cross-sectional testing. Older adults tend to do poorly on timed tests. Their mental reflexes may be slower, their memories needing a bit of jogging before producing the desired information. As less experienced test-takers, their situational anxiety may also impede performance. Other factors that may impair their ability to test well include motivation (their scores are not, after all, critical to their passing a course or getting into law school), mood (depression, if present, has a dampening effect on the intellect), or state of health.

However, when some psychologists decided to challenge the results of cross-sectional tests by doing longitudinal studies, that is, by studying the same cohort of people over time, the results were different. Werner Schaie, one of the pioneers of the psychology of aging, reports a longitudinal study of patterns of intellectual decline in which individuals were tested over seven-year periods ending at ages 60, 67, 74, and 81. The study found that over the course of testing, 60 to 85 percent of all participants remained stable or improved on specific abilities. Measureable decline actually affected less than one-third of the study participants until age 74, and even by age 81 affected only 30 to 40 percent of the persons studied.[25] The question of how much of the decline among the 80+ population was due to normal aging patterns and how much indicated "terminal drop" remains unresolved.

Another such study in Puget Sound, Washington, tested the intelligence of a group of older people in their sixties and again after an interval of seven years. Surprisingly, the individuals in their seventies tested *better* than they had in their sixties. What factors could have caused this improvement?

Television has been suggested as a possible reason for this surprising outcome. The suggestion is equally surprising because television has gotten a bad rap for its influence on children and has even been blamed for the current decline in college entrance scores. Less active older people frequently turn to television, particularly public or cable television, which provides in-depth news, public affairs, history, and culture and nature programs for adults. If the soaps, game shows, and sitcoms are ignored, one can make a strong case for the educative capacity of television, even commercial television, which brings the whole world to a person's armchair and has made extreme old age bearable for thousands of older people whose minds are healthier than their bodies.

One can posit other possible explanations for improvement in mental capacity among some older adults. Relieved of a life of toil, they may use their leisure to pursue old or neglected interests or cultivate new interests that frequently blossom in hitherto unforeseen directions. There is ample anecdotal evidence that simply having the leisure to read, talk to friends and neighbors, volunteer for community service, go to concerts and plays, enjoy hobbies, or even just sit and think reinvigorates older people's lives. The most important reason for improvement in the mental capacity of older adults may be that the accretion of cognitive skills over a lifetime enables them to process new information. This accretion is commonly called "crystallized" intelligence.

FLUID VERSUS CRYSTALLIZED INTELLIGENCE

Another widely accepted way to conceptualize intelligence is the distinction between fluid and crystallized intelligence.

> Crystallized intelligence depends on sociocultural influences; it involves the ability to perceive relations, to engage in formal reasoning, and to understand one's intellectual and cultural heritage. . . . Thus, the amount a person learns, the diversity and complexity of the environment, the openness to new information, and the extent of formal learning opportunities are likely to be influential in the person's score. In general, crystallized intelligence continues to grow slowly throughout adulthood . . . . Continued acculturation through self-directed learning and education can encourage the growth of crystallized intelligence even after age 60.[26]

If crystallized intelligence represents the accumulation of knowledge over time, fluid intelligence depends upon such factors as "the ability to perceive complex relations, use short-term memory, create concepts, and undertake abstract reasoning."[27] In contrast to crystallized intelligence, fluid intelligence is less dependent upon instruction and acculturation. The concept of crystallized versus fluid intelligence is useful in thinking about growth versus decline of cognitive ability in older adults because it may account for some divergent IQ test results. For instance, while measures like short-term memory and visuo-motor abilities tend to drop with age, lending credence to the theory of cognitive entropy, "on measures of vocabulary and other skills reflecting educational experience, individuals seemed to maintain their adult level of functioning into the sixth, and even the seventh decade."[28] One researcher went back through studies from 1986-90 in which a group of younger people had been compared with older adults. Her research indicated that although variability *was* greater among older participants in measures of reaction time, memory, and fluid intelligence, the differences flattened out in crystallized intelligence.[29]

We have no desire to recapitulate all of the hoary arguments about the genetic versus the environmental components of intelligence. The nature versus nurture issue has recently been revived, turning it into a political as well as a scientific quagmire. This debate has no direct bearing on the subject of older adult learning except in the need to recognize that to speak of crystallized and fluid intelligence is also to speak of the difference between a person's specific cognitive strengths (fluid intelligence) and what he or she has learned through the culture, schooling, and general exposure to learning experiences (crystallized intelligence) of a lifetime.

This distinction between inborn (genetic/nature) and acquired (environment/nurture) capabilities may lie at the heart of the differences in learning abilities among healthy older adults. If the researchers are correct and fluid intelligence shows a greater rate of decline as one ages than does crystallized intelligence, then older adult learners may be at a disadvantage in some situations, at an advantage in others. The playing ground is not even.

Let us invent two women, Joan and Abby, whose inborn ability to learn is nearly identical at birth. Put Joan into a series of enriching life situations: parents who read to her from an early age; good schools with caring teachers; a job that involves continual learning for successful functioning; a social life with people who care about politics, art, and religion; and sufficient income to travel and pursue self-enriching interests. Put Abby, on the other hand, into a family that is indifferent to learning, into mediocre schools that she leaves after the eleventh grade, into a job that calls upon little beyond rote skills, and into a restricted social life with little opportunity to enlarge her horizons. At age 70, which person will have developed a rich, complex life that will lend substance to her crystallized intelligence? Which person is more likely to involve herself in further learning activities? Furthermore, if both women's fluid intelligence, which is dependent upon inborn abilities, has slightly declined, Joan will be able to compensate for this with the rich contextual background of her crystallized intelligence while Abby will have less learning to call upon. Joan's younger friends may speak admiringly of how "hip" she is for her age. Abby's friends may say "she's losing it."

THE BRAIN AS SUPER COMPUTER

A paradigm shift occurred in the 1960s with the emergence of the information processing approach, which has become a common conceptual framework for looking at how human beings think.[30] According to this approach, human beings are active seekers of information about the world, and they receive (or intake) this information from the senses. This information must then be recorded internally. Like computers, humans must *encode* and *store* information, first into short-term memory and then into long-term memory in such a way that it can be found and recognized at a later time. The processes by which one makes use of that information (accessing the memory) are, in computer terminology, *search* and *retrieval*; in traditional brain terminology, the processes are roughly analogous to learning and memory. Because cognitive changes that occur with age are typically specific, not global (we may forget names yet have perfect recall for events), the information processing approach, which looks at distinct functions and mechanisms, is "particularly well suited to study any changes in cognitive processing in later life."[31] If one were to attribute inability to recall a specific name or fact or event to disk "overload" rather than to loss of memory, the problem's emotional impact on the individual would be transformed.

Numerous research studies have looked at specific functions and mechanisms. Smith and Park studied "Adult Age Differences in Memory for Pictures and Images"[32] and found no strong evidence to suggest that older adults use visuo-spatial information any less than [do] younger adults." Burke and Laver looked at the common problem of increasing difficulty in remembering names and vocabulary that is self-reported by many older individuals (i.e, the TOT, tip-of-the tongue phenomenon). They found that such deficits are caused by a problem in language production and are totally distinct from language *comprehension*, which appears to be relatively unaffected by increasing age. To account for this problem, Smith and Park have developed a transmission deficit hypothesis,[33] which says that the ability to retrieve a specific word quickly does not involve semantic memory, which may be fully functioning, but does involve the retrieval mechanism, which has slowed. The person has not "lost" the word (he or she would readily recognize it on a multiple choice test), but simply needs more time to retrieve it. Dr. Barry Gordon, director of the Cognitive Neurology Division of the Johns Hopkins University School of Medicine says that "With age, the memory system is overloaded to begin with. You have more names to remember than before—and overload can take its toll on memory." However, "such name-blocking also may indicate that you have a rich, healthy network of connections."[34]

CONCLUSION

This chapter has been long but necessary. If we are to argue for the individual and societal benefits of including the oldest Americans in the learning society, we must demonstrate that they retain the ability to learn and to profit from what they learn. A definitive answer to the question of how far age affects one's cognitive capability is impossible. People vary as widely in their retention of intellectual ability as they do in their initial intellectual endowment. Moreover, the variations from study to study in content and methodology make absolute comparisons impossible. Nevertheless, some things can be said with reasonable certainty.

Barring physiological complications, people can and do have the ability to continue learning well into extreme old age. Moreover, certain compensatory factors, like the integrity of crystallized intelligence, the accumulation of knowledge and experience, the persistence of curiosity, and the ability to put new information into a broader, more meaningful context give elderlearners an equality and potential superiority over younger cohorts. The persistence and wisdom of the aging, and the strong desire to continue learning and to remain in touch with one's culture can compensate for minor declines in memory retrieval, spatial or motor intelligence, or other symptoms of aging that may occur. Millions of older people around the world are demonstrating every day not only their strong need and desire but their ability to continue learning throughout their lifespan.

NOTES

1. Ellen Langer, *Mindfulness* (Reading, MA: Addison-Wesley, 1989), p. 12.

2. Ibid.

3. Paul Baltes and K. Warner Schaie, "Aging and IQ: The Myth of the Twilight Years," *Psychology Today* (March 1974), 35.

4. Ibid., 36.

5. Ibid., 37.

6. John Dewey, quoted in James E. Birren and Betty A. Birren, "The Concept, Models, and History of the Psychology of Aging," *Handbook of the Psychology of Aging*, 3rd ed. (San Diego: Academic Press, 1990), p. 12.

7. Bortz, p. 198.

8. Ibid.

9. Ibid., p. 202.

10. Kaarin Anstey, Lazar Stankov, and Stephen Lord, "Primary Aging, Secondary Aging, and Intelligence," *Psychology and Aging*, 8,4 (December 1993), 562.

11. Carmi Schooler, "Psychosocial Factors and Effective Cognitive Functioning in Adulthood," *Handbook of the Psychology of Aging*, 3rd ed. (San Diego: Academic Press, 1990), p. 348.

12. K. Warner Schaie, "Age Changes and Age Differences," *Columbia Retirement Handbook* (New York: Columbia University Press, 1994) pp. 299-300.

13. Schooler, p. 349.

14. Ibid., p. 352.

15. "100-Year-Old Woman Pursues Study of Chinese 'Paper Gods,'" *Times Record*, July 13, 1995, 14.

16. "Alumni Notes," *Harvard Medical Alumni Bulletin*, 67,3 (Winter 1993-94), 51.

17. "Leo Blacklow '30," *Harvard Medical Alumni Bulletin*, 67, 3(Winter 1993-94), 37.

18. John Salvia and James E. Ysseldyke, *Assessment* (Boston: Houghton Mifflin, 1991), p. 179.

19. David A. Peterson, *Facilitating Education for Older Learners* (San Francisco: Jossey-Bass, 1983), p. 54.

20. Ibid, p. 62.

21. About four years ago, IQ scores began to drop. There is no general agreement among psychologists about why they once rose or why they are now dropping.

22. "Cognitive Competence and Expertise in Aging," *Columbia Retirement Handbook*, edited by Abraham Monk (New York: Columbia University Press, 1994), pp. 310-19.

23. Peterson, pp. 53-72.

24. Salvia and Ysseldyke, p. 54.

25. Schaie, "Age Changes and Age Differences," p. 296.

26. Quoted by Peterson, p. 59.

27. Ibid.

28. Baltes and Schaie, p. 35.

29. Claire K. Morse, "Does Variability Increase with Age? An Archival Study of Cognitive Measures," *Psychology and Aging*, 8,2 (June 1993), 156-64.

30. Eugene A. Lovelace, "Basic Concepts in Cognition and Aging," in *Aging and Cognition: Mental Processes, Self-Awareness and Interventions* (Amsterdam: North-Holland Press, 1990), p. 3.

31. Ibid.

32. Smith and Park, "Adult Age Differences in Memory for Pictures and Images," in Lovelace, *Aging and Cognition*, p. 92.

33. Ibid.

34. Quoted by Sherrye Henry, "Keep Your Brain Fit for Life," *Parade* (March 17, 1996), 8.

CHAPTER 5

Use It or Lose It

An unused engine rusts. A still stream stagnates. An untended garden tangles. It is a powerful and universal truth.

Walter M. Bortz

Old men should be explorers
Here and there does not matter
We must be still and still moving
Into another intensity.

T.S. Eliot, "East Coker"

Chapter 4 showed that cognitive functioning does not necessarily diminish with age, and that many of the world's towering intellects have aged like great wines, growing fuller and richer with time.[1] Given the absence of organic disease, the active brain that is "exercised" regularly and stretched to its limits will function longer and better than the inactive brain. Alfred Steiglitz, Albert Einstein, Jacques Barzun, Claude Monet, Arturo Toscaninni, Claude Pepper, Mildred Fenwick, Hume Cronyn, and Pablo Casals were all making major intellectual and artistic contributions well into their eighties and nineties. Miecyzslaw Horszowski, the great pianist, recorded Mozart, Chopin, and Schumann on his hundredth birthday. Strom Thurmond, the oldest U.S. senator in history, won another term in 1996 at age 93. Whether or not you admire his politics, you must admire his *chutzpah*.

Unfortunately, sustained healthy cognitive functioning as we age is not a given. It is affected by reciprocal relationships between continued cognitive activity, a healthy body, a positive state of mind, physical exercise, and a supportive social environment. Each of these components can transfer positive energy to the others; conversely, each can also transfer negativity to the others. This reciprocity is critical, but can be subverted or overcome where there is sufficient will. A longitudinal study by K. Warner Schaie gave powerful evidence of this reciprocity.

> Analyses from the Seattle study showed that people with cardiovascular disease tended to decline earlier in all mental abilities than those with no cardiovascular disease. Schaie then tried a fascinating intervention: he gave some of the cardiovascular disease victims training in inductive reasoning. Those who had received training had fewer episodes of illness and fewer clinic visits than those in the control group who had received no training.[2]

The implications of this research are mind-boggling but not out of line with other research (discussed below) that gives increasing support for the intimate connections between mental and physical health.

While entering the Elderlearning Survey data, we were impressed by the number of respondents who appended notes indicating an intuitive understanding of the importance of continued mental activity. Remarks such as "I need to keep the gray cells humming" or "exercise and learning are my lifeline" or "mental and physical activity keep me alive" are grace notes interspersed among the impersonal checks and numbers called for by the survey design. The respondents wanted us to know that they are doing their damndest to hold on to their intellectual abilities.

One of the respondents provides a moving example of how an active intellect can defuse the power of physical decline. This 79-year-old woman ascribed her recent low degree of participation in learning activities to a year of medical difficulties. She had undergone a knee replacement, two hip replacements, and numerous stubborn bone infections that had kept her hospitalized for weeks. Nevertheless, when asked to rate her health, she checked "good!" In a note appended to the survey, she said that she was looking forward to going back to her self-directed study of the Jewish origins of Christianity and also hoped to follow up on earlier studies of Native American art by taking an Elderhostel trip to the Southwest. "By the way," she concluded, "I'm also reading all Hillerman's and Erdrich's novels about contemporary Native American life. I started that project while I was bedridden."

This woman's outlook lends credence to Walter Bortz's contention that, excluding organic disease, the active brain resists deterioration. Abraham Maslow goes even further, saying that capacities clamor to be used, and cease their clamor only when they are well used. In contrast, the unused capacity or organ can atrophy or even become a disease center, thus diminishing the person. We know that "cerebral exercise" causes chemical as well as physical changes. Animal studies support the thesis that the active older brain develops in positive ways. The brains of rats whose lives are enriched show a higher content of noradrenaline than control groups.[3] Moreover, this enrichment enhances their cognitive capacity. Old rats, when placed in enriched environments, solve mazes faster than their deprived counterparts. "They are smarter."[4] There are also demonstrable connections between physiological changes in brain function and behavior. "Behavioral events alter neurochemical function and altered neurochemical function can change behavior."[5] Thinking (or mental action), like physical exercise, stimulates increased metabolic activity.

Brains certainly do age. But aging can be slowed (or made invisible) by active mental exercise in challenging learning situations. Blood supply, with its extra oxygen and nutrients, goes to the area being challenged—just as with a weightlifter's biceps.

George Bernard Shaw wrote in *Back to Methuselah*,

> If the weight lifter, under the trivial stimulus of an athletic competition can "put up a muscle," it seems reasonable to believe that an equally earnest and convinced philosopher could "put up a brain." Both are directive of vitality to a certain end.[6]

Although the muscle/brain simile may seem counter-intuitive—we don't visualize a brain as getting bigger with exercise or diminishing with disuse—this phenomenon is perfectly consistent with animal and human physiology in which stimulation of brain cells by an active energy source produces growth.

There are also strong relationships between physical measures of cerebral physiology and social function. The stimulation of social contacts and continued cognitive demands slows, if it cannot totally prevent, cerebral entropy. Over 30 years ago, Robert Butler, the noted gerontologist, recognized that cognitive function is sustained by active social involvement; he reported "unexpected" relationships between physical measures of cerebral physiology and social function. In 1968, Butler, wrote that maintenance of social contacts, social responsiveness, and goals in living were all associated with better brain function.[7]

However, social involvement can occur in many ways. The conventional wisdom, that even mentally healthy men and women deteriorate when removed from their home environment to a nursing home, is not always true, as the following anecdote recounted by a physician friend illustrates.

> Dmitra was an 86-year-old Greek woman living in Boston with her devoted son Dmitri and his wife Mary. Dmitri and Mary had vowed to each other that Dmitra would never have to leave their home. But for the past few years, it had not been easy for the couple to cope with Dmitra's increasing irritability and bad temper. Formerly a warm and loving grandmother who fit in well with the family's schedule and way of life, she now complained about Mary's cooking, about the noise the grandchildren made, and about the family's "neglect." She generally made everyone feel sad and guilty. Nothing they could do pleased her.

Because her mother-in-law was now unable to negotiate stairs, Mary had rigged up a pulley system with a basket that could be lowered down with written requests and returned with mail, snacks, newspapers, or loving notes. But the basket became a dreaded vehicle for constant demands, complaints, and near paranoid charges. Dmitra's room was either too hot or too cold. She was either hungry and demanding a meal an hour after lunch or sending back an uneaten midday treat. She demanded that someone change the TV channel, and then, five minutes later, change it back. She had stopped reading and was no longer interested in politics or what was going on at the Greek Social Center. She would ask Mary or Dmitri to come up to keep her company, but when they did she told them to go away. Even her favorite granddaughter was afraid to go into Dmitra's room because she would be accused of switching her grandma's medicines or sneaking out with boys or taking drugs.

Like many recent immigrant families, this was a close one, and there were constant visits by aunts, uncles, and cousins, all of whom wanted to spend time with Dmitra, but she sent them away, saying that they were just there to steal her jewelry. Her son was the only one she would talk to, and even he suffered her tirades.

Finally, their previously happy family life threatened by the omnipresence of this miserable old woman, Mary spoke the unspeakable: she suggested that Dmitra be put in a nursing home. Her husband reluctantly agreed. They searched for the best place they could find and a month later drove Dmitra to its door. The nursing home director suggested that the family not call or visit for a few days but give Dmitra time to grow accustomed to her new surroundings.

The next two days were difficult for Mary, who felt a double guilt for having institutionalized her mother-in-law and for not visiting her. Then, on the morning of the third day, the phone rang. It was Dmitra. Her voice had lost its querulous whine and sounded brisk and upbeat. "If you're coming to visit me today," she said, "I have a few errands for you to do. I want you to stop at the library and get out some books on modern Greek history, and I'd like you to find grandpa's old Greek records."

"Sure," said Mary, "but why, mother?" "Oh," answered Dmitra, "I've been asked by some of my friends here to give a course on modern Greek history, and I thought I'd also like to play them some real Greek music. My roommate gave a course on Jewish rituals a few weeks before I came, and everybody said it was good, but mine is going to be much better. I'll wow these old ladies."

In an ironic twist on the usual story of the accelerated decline of the institutionalized, Dmitra, given the opportunity to play a constructive role among her peers, had recovered her sense of self. Nor was this a momentary upward blip on a downward trajectory. Dmitra followed the course on modern Greek history with one on Greek cooking, which she was allowed to demonstrate in the institution's kitchen, and then coaxed her new friends into forming a reading group. She was apparently re-energized by the active learning and teaching that now engaged her time. She ate and slept better, negotiated her way around the nursing home without a wheelchair, and was a graceful hostess to her family when they visited.

This real story vividly illustrates the power of the mind-body connection. Renewed cognitive activity in a setting where learning would have an immediate payoff in peer recognition enabled Dmitra to regain much of the psychological and physical ground she had lost over the past few years. Her learning enhanced not only the quality of her life but of her family's life as well. She may or may not live any longer, but certainly she is living better and will leave behind a legacy of positive memories.

On the other hand, anyone who has ever visited a poorly run nursing home can attest to the reality of brain atrophy in a nonstimulating environment. This reality is now recognized in first-rate retirement centers and domiciliary institutions where efforts are made to provide regular opportunities for social intercourse and mental exercise, e.g., birthday parties, line dancing, bridge, current events discussions, and crafts instruction.

A rapidly increasing body of evidence supports the idea that mental exercise increases brain function, but an important study by Dr. David Snowdon, currently being conducted at the University of Kentucky's Chandler Medical Center, may come up with more definitive data. In what is called the "nun study," teams of renowned scientists are working with the School Sisters of Notre Dame on a longitudinal study of aging and Alzheimer's disease, comparing disease and death rates of the more educated with those of the less educated.[8] So far, 550 sisters have agreed to participate in all aspects of the study, including brain donation after death, which will give the researchers the first opportunity to do a large-scale study of the aging human brain, comparing the brains of the cognitively active with those of the less active. Early papers coming out of the study were so suggestive of the positive effects of continued learning that many of the nuns reported they were signing up for courses and increasing the amount of their informal learning activities.[9] There was also significant evidence of the connection between longevity and the level of education. Sisters with a bachelor's degree or higher were more likely to survive to old age while maintaining their ability to perform self-care activities.

"Education is one of the most powerful and mysterious variables," says Dr. Richard Suzman of the National Institute of Aging. A high level of education seems to be associated with longevity, and there has been a dramatic increase in the education levels and the longevity of today's older adults.[10] Numerous studies have shown that better educated people are healthier as they age, but the reasons for this have not been definitively pinpointed. It may be that through their education they have learned how to take better care of them-

selves, or that the links between education and higher income have contributed to a healthier life style, or that some genetic characteristics are at work. It
has been suggested that "by stimulating the brain, education may establish
more neuronal pathways early in life as well as prompt people to remain
cognitively active throughout life."[11] However, this effect is not limited to
formal education. K. Warner Schaie, director of the Penn State gerontology
center, says that even the self-educated, "those who led very active lives—
traveling, reading books, taking courses—maintained intellectual function
much longer than those who became couch potatoes."[12]

In the meantime, while waiting for still more definitive studies, "use it or
lose it" remains a practical prescription for continued mental competence as
we age.

PHYSICAL EXERCISE AND INTELLIGENCE

The evidence that using the brain strengthens it, that we can indeed "exercise" the brain to keep it functioning at a high level, is undeniable. Millions of
older learners have already chosen to use it rather than lose it as they engage
in a variety of demanding learning activities, from chess to international affairs
to chaos theory.

But what about physical exercise—walking, swimming, bicycling—activities seemingly unrelated to brain function? A growing body of evidence
supports Bortz's contention that the increased metabolic activity induced by
physical exercise results in a higher level of metabolic activity in the brain with
beneficial results for memory.

> A review of biological changes commonly attributed to the process of
> aging demonstrates the close similarity of most of the changes subsequent
> to a period of enforced physical inactivity . . . at least a portion of the
> changes commonly attributed to aging is in reality caused by disuse and, as
> such, is subject to correction. There is no drug in current or prospective
> use that holds as much promise for sustained health as a lifetime program
> of physical exercise.[13]

Goggin and Stelmach maintain that physical exercise "can minimize and/or
slow the rate of decline in some cognitive and physiological functions."[14] In
1985, Salthouse found that older adults who were physically trained had faster
response times (RT) than age-matched adults who were untrained; he concluded that although the differences in RT between younger and older adults
cannot be completely eliminated, those who exercise clearly have an advantage over those who do not.

A study by Robert Dustman divided 43 sedentary subjects, aged 55 to 70,
into three sections.

. . . one did aerobic exercises; one did flexibility exercises; and one group remained inactive. The aerobic exercise group improved in all the expected physical measurements over the other two groups . . . [but] their cognitive abilities [also] improved! Exercise, three hours a week for four months, led to "clear improvement" in intelligence.[15]

At a study done at McMaster University in Canada in 1988, 15 subjects (10 men and 5 women; mean age 66 years; age range 60 to 85) were tested before and immediately after 45 minutes of exercise and then compared with a control group on memory, mood, and cognitive function. Results showed greater improvement in six of the eight scores of cognitive function in those who exercised as compared to the control subjects. The difference was particularly marked in the logical memory test score. This finding represents an improvement in short-term memory, and corresponds to earlier research findings.[16]

In a somewhat similar study done on a larger population in 1989 at Scripps College, a series of cognitive tasks was given to 62 older men and women who reported that they regularly exercised vigorously and to 62 relatively sedentary men and women. All the participants were screened for neuromuscular and central nervous system disorders. The first test session covered vocabulary and measures of working memory reaction time. The second session consisted of three written tests of reasoning and two subjective well-being questionnaires. The performance of the exercisers was significantly better on measures of reasoning, working memory, vocabulary, and reaction time. Subsequent analyses showed that neither self-rated health, medical conditions, nor medications contributed to the differences between the exercise and nonexercise groups.[17]

These results seem valid even for the old-old. Ambulatory volunteers from a nursing home in Canada, with a mean age of 84.5 and 9.3 years of education, all shown to be normal on a mental status test, were divided into an exercise and a control group. The first group underwent a single 15-minute standardized session of nonstrenuous exercise while the control participants watched a video of similar exercises for 15 minutes. Tests of meaningfully cued memory were given pre-exercise, immediately post-exercise, and 30 minutes post-exercise. The results were statistically higher memory retrieval in the immediate post-test period for the exercised group.[18] In a study of nursing home residents in the Netherlands, the recall capacities of 40 patients (average age 83) improved markedly after an exercise program.[19]

Clearly, physical exercise, which is routinely prescribed as medicine for the heart and lungs, is also good medicine for the brain. Most programs for older adults, whether at senior centers, local agencies, or OASIS centers, regularly combine intellectual and physical activities. The 73-year-old student mentioned in Chapter 4 who alternated between reading Aristotle and walking around the room was on to something.

DIET AND COGNITION

Although there is little argument about the positive effects of a balanced diet on the prolongation of life and health among the elderly, not much is known about how specific dietary components relate to cognition. While Eleanor Roosevelt took garlic pills to keep her mind in good condition and our mothers told us that fish was brain food, few scientific claims have been made on behalf of specific foods or substances. Some recent work at Tufts University's Human Nutrition Research Center on Aging suggests some "limited evidence that insufficient folate and vitamin B-12 might be involved in the age-related increase in cognitive impairments."[20] Vitamin deficits were particularly marked in those who scored at the lower 5 or 10 percent of standard neuropsychological tests.

> Low vitamin B-12 status was associated with poor performance on tests of both memory and abstract thinking, low folate status was related to poor performance on the test of abstract thinking, and low folate intake was related to poor performance on both tests. These results remained significant after controlling for age, gender, education, and income level.[21]

A recent mouse study, reported in the *Proceedings of the National Academy of Sciences*,[22] suggests that vitamin E in doses about 13 times the recommended level might play a role in protecting brain tissue protein from damage as we age, but as yet no definitive human studies of the effects of vitamin E have been carried out. In any case, further research on cognition and diet will likely indicate the importance of sound nutritional practice. We are what we eat.

EFFECTS OF COGNITIVE TRAINING ON OLDER ADULTS

Intellectual decline with age is not inevitable; it may even be reversible. Although a relatively new area of research for psycho-gerontologists, cognitive training is generating a lot of interest. A 1986 Penn State study reporting on 229 subjects, ranging from ages 64 to 90 with an average age of 73, showed that the effect of positive intervention on mental functioning is critical. Half the subjects showed *no decline* between 1970 and 1984. The researchers then provided five one-hour training sessions to 71 subjects and re-tested them. "Those individuals who showed declined intellectual ability . . . responded more favorably to the training than did those who had shown no change over the fourteen years."[23]

A number of studies have demonstrated that it is possible to improve performance in such cognitive tasks as face-name memory, problem-solving tasks, and fluid intelligence abilities.[24] The ability of mnemonic training to substantially improve memory in the aged is almost universally acknowledged though rarely practiced. On a more prosaic level, crossword or jigsaw puzzles are handy do-it-yourself brain conditioning exercises.

Sherry Willis posits a number of interesting questions deriving from this research.[25]

> 1. Does training involve the remediation of pre-existing performance levels or is it moving older adults to a new level of performance beyond their earlier capacities? In other words, is it reversing decline or simply yielding gains beyond the prior skill level?

> 2. Is training aimed at improving a specific skill (e.g., memory) as effective as strategy training in improving broader factors like speed, motivation, or attitude which have an effect on a broader spectrum of cognitive skills?

> 3. Is self-instruction or practice as effective as training?

> 4. What are the long-term effects of cognitive training? Are the newly learned skills retained?

In one study of older adults who received initial training in 1979, with booster training sessions in 1981 and 1986, it was found that

> Significant training effects . . . indicated that subjects were able to continue to profit from cognitive interventions as they advanced from young-old to old-old age. Moreover, training subjects even into their late seventies and early eighties continue to perform at a level significantly above their baseline level (prior to training . . . 64% of the training group's performance was consistently above baseline, compared to 33% of the control group).[26]

Clearly "there is no longer any question about the ability of older adults to learn and to benefit from education, but there is an astonishing lag between what is now known about development over the life span and what our major social institutions prescribe for the different stages of life."[27] The linear life plan, in which education is clustered in the first two decades of life, no longer makes sense; education is needed throughout the lifespan to help us accommodate changes in the nature of our work, navigate passages from one stage of development to another, accommodate new personal and professional situations, and respond to the challenge of successful aging.

To a greater extent than we have heretofore realized, we have significant power over the shape of our own old age. According to Dr. John W. Rowe, director of the MacArthur Foundation Consortium on Successful Aging, "Only about 30 percent of the characteristics of aging are genetically based: the rest—70 percent—is not."[28] This idea is carried even further by Dr. Gerald E. McClearn, a gerontological geneticist: "By age 80, for many characteristics there is hardly any genetic influence left."[29] This liberating concept means that individuals *can* choose to engage in the kinds of physical, social, and intellectual activities that will help keep them bodily and psychologically healthy, even though they cannot change their heredity or past experience.

CREATIVITY AND WISDOM IN AGING ADULTS

Two stereotypes rub up against each other when we look at creativity and wisdom among older adults—one favoring youth, the other favoring age. Creativity is an attribute commonly associated with the young: poets, artists, mathematicians, theoretical physicists, the unbearded youths whose startling discoveries and innovations changed the world. Creativity is often perceived as the exclusive product of the high energy, mental acuity, and dexterity of youth. Keats and Mozart, reaching the heights in their youth, serve as the archetypes of youthful vigor and artistic drive.[30] Verdi, Picasso, and Monet, who peaked much later in age, are regarded with some condescension as exceptions to the rule.

Wisdom, on the other hand, is traditionally associated with age: "With the ancient is wisdom; and in length of days understanding" (Book of Job); "Knowledge comes but wisdom lingers" (Alfred, Lord Tennyson). Wisdom is also connected with creativity as art's highest culmination: "Raphael paints wisdom, Handel sings it, Phidias carves it, Shakespeare writes it, Wren builds it" (Ralph Waldo Emerson).

People are presumed to get wiser with years and experience, to gain a seasoned understanding of the world and its follies. In ancient times, and in most Eastern civilizations today, age is directly associated with the accretion of wisdom. Confucius is depicted as a bearded sage. Homer made Nestor the oldest and the wisest of the Greeks who fought the Trojans.

Our preoccupation with wisdom and creativity may be rooted in the belief that these two capacities represent our highest aspirations and are what distinguish human beings as a species from the animals. The Elderlearning Survey respondents rated these qualities high indeed. When asked "why" they are learning, 47.2 percent checked "to engage in creative activity," and 37.7 percent checked "as part of a search for meaning and wisdom."

Dean Simonton, in "Creativity and Wisdom in Aging," defines creativity as

> the ability to innovate, to change the environment rather than merely adjust to it in a more passive sense. So, we create scientific theories, compose artistic masterpieces, and construct imaginative utopias.[31]

Simonton defines wisdom as

> a broad perspective on life, discerning a larger view of life's meaning than permitted by hand-to-mouth subsistence. Presumably such wisdom allows individuals to reach an equilibrium with themselves, others, and the world that smooths over the vicissitudes of mundane existence.[32]

The scientist setting out to study creativity and wisdom obviously has difficulty in setting up quantitative or qualitative parameters for these sticky terms. For creativity, one solution is simply to measure output: the number of papers and books published, works of art produced and shown, and at what age. Using these quantitative measures, a number of studies support the common understanding that poets, mathematicians, and theoretical physicists do peak in their twenties or thirties, although exceptions can be cited, such as Frost and Einstein who kept rising to new peaks of creativity as they aged. In such domains as history, philosophy, literature, and general scholarship, most researchers feel that the age curve for creativity probably shows maximum output around age 40, with only a modest decline after that.

However, if one makes a distinction between quantity and quality, the proportion of major products (masterpieces or works of truly seminal meaning) tends to fluctuate randomly over the course of most careers, neither increasing nor decreasing with age. "Those individual creators who are the most productive will also, on the average, tend to be the most creative" across their lifespan.[33] The single factor that seems to inhibit creativity markedly is illness.

May Sarton, a poet, novelist, and essayist who, though suffering cancer and stroke, wrote well into her late eighties.

> I have always looked forward to old age, and the reason, as the poems make clear, is that I have known so many great old people. Well, I looked forward to old age wrongly because I imagined it would be serene and uncluttered, and rightly because it would make it possible for me to grow and to create poems and books that have growth in them. I am convinced that we are on earth to make our souls. And to that extent old age, of course, is the most thrilling time of all. Because we are coming close to an end, this conviction that the making of a soul is of paramount importance is very much with us.[34]

Sarton's "wrong" anticipation that old age would be serene and uncluttered is echoed by the 45 percent of Elderlearning Survey respondents who named lack of time as a barrier to their learning. Our lives do not get less complicated and the maintenance of homes, health, social obligations, and family relationships do not become less demanding when we age.

Sarton's "right" anticipation, that old age would be a time of growth, a time to "make our souls," has resonance for the vision of the Third Age as a time of continued development. The chambered nautilus, Oliver Wendell Holmes's "ship of pearl," is an apt metaphor for the ideal life—its shape an expanding spiral in which the inhabitant lives in the largest and newest chamber, "shaping his growing shell," leaving the "past year's dwelling for the new." This is a dynamic vision of life, each age, each stage, going beyond what has been to what can be.

In February 1996, the *New York Times* best seller list included *Tiger in the Grass* by Harriet Doerr (age 85) and *Having Our Say* by Sara and Elizabeth Delaney, African-American sisters (ages 99 and 100, respectively). Three years after her husband's death, 65-year-old Harriet Doerr had returned to school to complete a B.A. in European history; in 1984, at age of 73, Doerr's first novel, *Stones for Ibarra*, won the American Book Award. The Delaneys have no previous book; they were busy working as a school teacher and a dentist. Presumably, no one ever told Doerr or the Delaneys that they were too old to be creative. They, and thousands of other older adults who have joyfully entered into the creative process, have what Humphrey Trevelyan called, "this divine discontent, this disequilibrium, this state of inner tension [that is] the source of artistic energy."[35]

The inner drive towards creativity, frequently truncated or denied by the demands of "getting on" in life—earning a living, raising a family, attending to the multiple chores of existence—can have a joyous resurgence in later life. As outer demands lessen, inner needs emerge. The resultant flowering of creativity is eloquently expressed by hundreds of the Elderlearning Survey respondents who seized the last question, "Describe an informal learning project that you have undertaken on your own," as an opportunity to write about what they are doing. A North Dakota woman is quilting—inventing new patterns and trying out variations on old ones. A retired salesman in Georgia has "gone back to black and white photography," setting up his own dark room and working on "soft focus" landscapes and "portraits of the folks who still live in the old cabins." Other respondents reported writing poetry, children's books, and short stories; making fanciful jewelry; trying out new pottery techniques; writing and producing plays for local drama societies; and acting, singing, sculpting, painting, or composing choral music.

For some Third Agers, creative pursuits are an extension of what they have been doing all along; for others, they are a return to what they did when younger until interrupted by the imperatives of making a living and nurturing a family. For them, growing older has meant a release and a return. Still others, older adults who had neither opportunity nor conscious desire to engage in creative activity when younger, have also seized the leisure of retirement to explore new facets of their interests and abilities. No one who has witnessed the intensity of concentration among older adults in writing, painting, and music classes will ever again maintain that creativity is the exclusive province of youth. These people are indeed "making their souls."

Wisdom is obviously more difficult to measure than creativity. Wisdom is developmental, an accretion of knowledge and understanding over time, and its "products" may be tangible (books, works of art, brilliant speeches) or intangible (deep understanding, inner peace, influence on the young, or the ability to teach, mediate, reconcile). To make value judgments about another's degree of "wisdom" is presumptuous and impossible. Nevertheless, new studies have shown that "even though the acquisition of wisdom is by no means guaranteed among elderly citizens, the individuals who are most wise will be disproportionately found among. . . older subjects."[36] Some studies suggest ways in which early creativity and late wisdom may converge "in the content of creative products that evince the acquisition of wisdom."[37]

In any case, the time-honored myth of the wisdom of age is not only comforting, it seems to be compatible with reality.

NOTES

1. As a friend remarked upon reading this, eventually even great wines turn to vinegar. Certainly the brain shares the ultimate mortality of the body it inhabits, but we are making the case for prolonging its vigor for as long as possible.

2. Bronte, *The Longevity Factor*, p. 56.

3. Bortz, p. 198.

4. Ibid., p. 201.

5. Ibid., quoting Jack Barchas of Stanford University, p. 198.

6. Ibid., p. 199.

7. "The Facade of Chronological Age" in *Middle Age and Aging*, edited by Bernice L. Neugarten (Chicago: University of Chicago Press, 1968), p. 241.

8. David A. Snowdon, Sharon K. Ostwald, and Robert L. Kane, "Education, Survival and Independence in Elderly Catholic Sisters, 1936-88," *American Journal of Epidemiology* (1989) 130, 999-1012. http://www.coa.uky.edu/nunnet.

9. Sharon M. Reynolds, "Aging with Grace: The School Sisters of Notre Dame Study," *Odyssey* (Winter/Spring 1993), 2-7. A 1996 report on an interim study within the framework of the "nun study" carries startling implications, which, if they prove valid, could totally change our understanding of organic brain deterioration. A comparison of autopsied nuns' brains with autobiographical material written by those nuns at an early age indicates that poorly developed writing skills may be predictive of late life Alzheimer's. Exactly what this means is not yet completely understood. http://www.coa.uky.edu/nunnet.

10. Kolata, C3.

11. Jane E. Brody, "Good Habits Outweigh Genes as Key to a Healthy Old Age," *New York Times*, February 28, 1996, C9.

12. Ibid.

13. Bortz, p. 142.

14. Noreen L. Goggin and George E. Stelmach, "Age-Related Deficits in Cognitive-Motor Skills in *Aging and Cognition: Mental Processes, Self-Awareness and Interventions,* edited by Eugene A. Lovelace (Amsterdam: North Holland Press, 1990), p. 152.

15. Bortz, p. 206.

16. D.W. Molloy, D.A. Beerschoten, M.J. Borrie, R.G. Crilly, and R.D.T. Cape, "Acute Effects of Exercise on Neuropsychological Function in Elderly Subjects," *Journal of the American Geriatric Society*, 36,1 (January 1988), 29-33.

17. Louise Clarkson-Smith and Alan A. Hartley, "Relationships Between Physical Exercise and Cognitive Abilities in Older Adults," *Psychology and Aging*, 4,2 (June 1989), 183-89.

18. M.J. Stones and D. Dawe, "Acute Exercise Facilitates Semantically-Cued Memory in Nursing Home Residents," *Journal of the American Geriatric Society*, 41 (1993), 531-34.

19. Bortz, p. 207.

20. Paul J. Jacques and Karen M. Riggs, "B Vitamins as Risk Factors for Age-Related Diseases," *Nutritional Assessment of Elderly Populations: Measure and Function*, edited by Irwin H. Rosenberg (New York: Raven Press, 1995), p. 234.

21. Ibid, p. 246.

22. "Where's the Vitamin E?" *U.S. News and World Report*, June 10, 1996, 102.

23. Stones and Dawe, pp. 531–34.

24. Sherry L. Willis, "Current Issues in Cognitive Training Research" in *Aging and Cognition: Mental Processes, Self-Awareness and Interventions*, edited by Eugene A. Lovelace (Amsterdam: North-Holland Press, 1990). pp. 263-280.

25. Ibid.

26. Ibid., p. 276.

27. Harry R. Moody, "Education in an Aging Society," *Daedalus*, 115, 1 (Winter 1986), 208.

28. Brody, C9.

29. Ibid.

30. Keats died at 26 and Mozart at 35. We can only speculate to what extent their art might have been enriched and deepened with age.

31. Dean Keith Simonton, "Creativity and Wisdom in Aging" in *Columbia Retirement Handbook*, edited by Abraham Monk (New York: Columbia University Press, 1994), p. 320.

32. Ibid.

33. Ibid., p. 323.

34. May Sarton, "A Literary Perspective," *Perspectives on Aging: Exploding the Myths*, edited by Priscilla W. Johnston (Ballinger Publishing Co., 1981), pp. 122-23.

35. Ibid., pp. 117–18.

36. Simonton, p. 325.

37. Ibid., p. 326.

CHAPTER 6

A Profile of Elderlearners

You don't grow old; when you cease to learn you are old.

Reuel L. Howe

The Elderlearning Survey (ES), designed as part of the research for this book, consists of four densely packed pages focusing on the who, what, where, how, and why of learning in the older population, a total of 151 variables. (See the appendix to this book for a reproduction of the survey form.) In late 1995 and early 1996, a total of 3,600 surveys were mailed to people who ranged in age from 55 to over 96. Of the 912 surveys received (a 25.3 percent return), 860[1] were suitable for entry into the ES database, which has subsequently been analyzed with the help of a professional statistician.

The 860 respondents provide a "snapshot" of elderlearners. 78.8 percent were from mailing lists supplied by organizations directly involved in elderlearning: Elderhostel, Institutes for Learning in Retirement, OASIS Centers, and a travel/study group sponsored by the Smithsonian. These respondents, by virtue of their inclusion on these lists, had already been identified as elderlearners or potential elderlearners. The other 21.2 percent were from the AARP mailing list and from a miscellaneous private list. If this were a more scientific study, the AARP and miscellaneous respondents might be considered as a control group, but we make no such claims.

To aid in understanding the data, which at some points in the text are broken out by group, we have used the following designations:

Group Designations		
Code	Respondents	# of Useable Responses
107	AARP	117
207-A	Elderhostel	147
207-B	Elderhostel	87
307	Institutes for Learning in Retirement	237
407	OASIS	181
807	Study/Travel Group	27
907	Miscellaneous	64
	Total	860

Overall, the high response rate was gratifying. A four-page questionnaire is a rather daunting prospect for most people, especially when they must supply their own stamps to return it. Those who responded offer an invaluable cross-section of geography (all 50 states are represented), income levels, and educational backgrounds.

Although the ES asked for little beyond check-off answers to the questions, it called forth an unexpected outpouring of written responses, some long and detailed. Respondents seized the apparently rare opportunity to talk about what they were doing and what it meant to them. Ignoring the usual anonymity of questionnaires, more than half of the respondents signed their names or put their addresses on the return envelope.

Given below are the raw numbers in each category along with percentages of the whole; more complicated correlations and relationships, such as those between income, educational background, and learning styles will be considered later in the chapter. Deviations from the total number of 860 reflect missing data (not all people answered all questions).

WHO ARE THE LEARNERS?

Gender		
Males	282	32.8%
Females	577	67.2%

The lopsidedness of these figures will surprise no one with experience in adult continuing education. It is true today of most forms of continuing education that more women than men participate, and this is especially true of adult learning. Elderlearners turned out to be no exception to the rule. Women outlive men by an average of seven years; "for every 100 men 65 years

of age and older, there are about 150 women."[2] However, the age disparity
here is only partially explained by women's higher survival rate. Figures from
the National Center for Education Statistics for participation in learning
activities of persons 55+ over the past 25 years have consistently shown the
percentage of participation by women exceeding that of men. For instance, in
1975, 20 percent more women than men reported taking classes.[3] As you
move down the socio-economic scale, the disproportion between men and
women grows wider. The ES figures on men's participation would have been
lower if it were not for groups 307 and 907, which had an atypical number of
male respondents. In group 407, a lower socio-economic group, females
predominated. Something in the socialization of working class men must
block their participation in continuing education activities.

Marital Status		
Single	76	9.0%
Married	451	52.9%
Divorced	83	9.7%
Widowed	_243_	_28.4%_
	853	100.0%
Age		
55-59	16	1.9%
60-64	82	9.6%
65-69	258	30.2%
70-74	248	29.0%
75-79	167	19.5%
80-84	62	7.3%
85-89	18	2.1%
90-95	4	.4%
96+	_-0-_	_0.0%_
	855	100.0%

The clustering between ages 65 and 79 is typical of courses, travel groups,
and other formal learning activities we have observed. We speculate that the
fall-off after 79 is only partially explained by increasing disability or mortality
rates. Supplementary explanations might be that as people grow older and
increasingly unable or unwilling to participate in learning activities outside the
home, they are dropped from mailing lists; and that older people simply might
not wish to bother filling out such an intrusive survey instrument. However, as
we shall see, advanced old age does not necessarily mean cessation of learning
activity.

Living Arrangements		
Alone	329	38.3%
With spouse/partner	450	52.4%
With friend(s)	17	2.0%
With children or relatives	33	3.8%
In retirement community	29	3.4%
	858	99.9%

Today's older adults are independent, as the small number of those living with children or relatives would indicate. Moreover, many of those who report living alone are well into their eighties and even nineties.

Income Category		
0 to $19,999	121	16.1%
$20,000 to $39,999	269	35.9%
$40,000 to $59,999	165	22.0%
$60,000+	195	26.0%
	750	100.0%

The income distribution is more spread out than we had expected, even though the sample was skewed toward the high end by 27 respondents from a study/travel group (807) on a rather expensive natural history cruise as well as by some of those on the private list (907), which was composed largely of professionals and academics. 110 respondents (12.8%) chose not to answer this question; money *is* the last taboo, even in the anonymity of a survey.

Work and Retirement			
Working for Pay		148	17.6%
Salaried full-time	(20 2.4%)		
Salaried part-time	(83 9.9%)		
Self-employed	(45 5.3%)		
Retired		693	82.4%
		841	100.0%

The 19 people who didn't answer this question were mostly women. We assume that most of them had never worked outside the home, so did not consider themselves retired. A further breakdown of these figures and a discussion of their implications can be found in Chapter 11.

Volunteering			
Do volunteer work		626	72.9%
Full-time	(22 2.6%)		
Part-time	(348 40.5%)		
Occasionally	(256 29.8%)		
Do not volunteer		233	27.1%
		859	100.0%

Clearly, these statistics give the lie to those who would say older citizens are takers, not givers. They also reveal a vast reservoir of talent and experience that can be deployed toward making this a more caring society. (See Chapters 11 and 12 for further discussion of volunteerism.)

However, volunteering is more a woman's than a man's game: 74 percent of women reported volunteer activities as compared to 67 percent of men. Furthermore, in the part-time category (1 to 3 days per week), the percentages are 43 for women and 35 for men. Given the history of gender roles, this is no surprise. Until recently, men worked and most women stayed home to care for the family, help neighbors, and volunteer at schools, hospitals, and social agencies. Volunteerism as a role is still ingrained in most of the women who now comprise our older generations. The real surprise is that older men are also using their retirement to give generously of their time.

Levels of Education		
Grade school	10	1.2%
High school	153	17.8%
2-year college	150	17.5%
4-year college	231	26.9%
Graduate or		
professional school	<u>314</u>	<u>36.6%</u>
	858	100.0%

At the highest range, these figures are possibly skewed by the respondents' misunderstanding of the meaning of graduate or professional school. We suspect that this item was confusing; a significant number interpreted it to mean any professional school (dental hygiene, business studies, nursing, hair dressing) as well as the master's and doctoral degrees that were intended. Nevertheless, there were a significant number of highly educated respondents, particularly in groups 307, 807, and 907.

Race or Ethnic Background		
African American	17	2.0%
Asian American	7	.8%
Caucasian	802	94.1%
Hispanic	4	.4%
Native American	12	1.4%
Other	10	1.2%

The ethnic background figures present a graphic picture of the frustration and shame of American education. Although educators are trying valiantly to increase access and diversity at all levels, most are failing to provide for or attract minorities in any significant numbers. The ES confirms this fact. The number of non-Caucasian elderlearners in the ES would have been even smaller had not group 407 included 12 African Americans from one OASIS group in California. That single, racially integrated group accounted for 70.6 percent of the African Americans who responded.

There are many possible explanations for minorities' low participation in formal elderlearning activities, but the most important is probably their typical level of completed education. The amount of formal education is generally accepted to be the most important predictor of participation in adult education; those who have spent the most years in school are most likely to participate in adult and continuing education activities.[4] The current older generation has had less education (as measured by years of formal schooling) than younger people, and the disparity is widest among minorities whose youthful access to education was much more restricted. The following figures on comparative years of formal education are from a 1978 study by the Federal Council on Aging.[5]

Years of Formal Education		
Age	Whites	Blacks
60-64	12.2	8.5
65-69	11.6	7.9
70-74	10.1	6.6
75+	8.8	5.9

Because this study was done almost 20 years ago, the numbers today would undoubtedly look somewhat different. The 60- to 64-year-olds are now closer to 80 to 84, and the current levels of education for present-day 60- to 64-year-olds are somewhat higher than they were in 1978, but the number of years of formal schooling still goes down as ages go up. No evidence indicates any lessening in the relative disparity between whites and blacks in the amount of completed education.

In *Aging in Black America,* James Jackson et al. advance another reason for low participation of blacks in educational activities.

> Poor jobs and low income during post-adolescence and young adulthood will be reflected in poor job histories across the life span, which is again reflected in lower retirement opportunities and resources in old age.[6]

Deliberate and well-meaning efforts to increase access for blacks and other minorities to Third Age learning can have only limited success as long as the underlying structural causes of *de facto* segregation from the mainstream are unchanged and until the differences in health, income, and educational opportunity are addressed. Moreover, anyone black or white, whose earliest memories of school are negative, is unlikely to be an eager candidate for further education in later years. We must also remind ourselves that to explain is not to excuse our as yet unsuccessful efforts to remedy the situation.

Health (as self-rated)		
Excellent	248	30.6%
Good	462	57.0%
Fair	93	11.5%
Poor	7	.9%
	810	100.0%

Some may question the validity of a health status that is self-rated and self-reported, but most medical researchers accept such measures as important because they reflect the way people feel about themselves and govern how they function in their lives.

> In the matter of health status, . . . subjective ratings have often proved more predictive of a sense of well-being than have relatively objective measurements. An individual's positive perception of health status affects the behaviors taken in response.[7]

The information relating to self-rated health status may be among the most important to come out of the ES. The categories were deliberately selected so as to mandate a break between excellent/good and fair/poor. No one could take cover in the middle. That being so, it is significant that 87.6 percent of this sample of elderlearners, 55 to 95 years of age, declared their health to be excellent or good. Whether they are healthy because they are learners or learners because they are healthy is an interesting question, but clearly the two are related.

The correlation between age and health emphasizes the rather surprising perception of good health that characterizes this group.

Self-Rated Health by Age						
Age Group	Excellent	Good	Fair	Poor	Total	% Total
55-59						
number	5	5	4		14	1.7
percent	35.7	35.7	28.6			
60-64						
number	38	34	4		76	9.4
percent	50.0	44.7	5.3			
65-69						
number	79	142	25	1	247	30.7
percent	32.0	57.5	10.1	.4		
70-74						
number	66	133	26	2	227	28.2
percent	29.1	58.6	11.5	.9		
75-79						
number	41	97	19	2	159	19.8
percent	25.8	61.0	11.9	1.3		

Self-Rated Health by Age (continued)						
Age Group	Excellent	Good	Fair	Poor	Total	% Total
80-84						
number	15	34	11	1	61	7.6
percent	24.6	55.7	18.0	1.6		
85-89						
number	2	11	3	1	17	2.1
percent	11.8	64.7	17.6	5.9		
90-94						
number		3	1		4	.5
percent		<u>75.0</u>	<u>25.0</u>			
Col. Totals	246	459	93	7	805	100.0%
% by Category	30.6%	57.0%	11.6%	.9%	N.A.	N.A.

Again, the perception of excellent/good health predominates across the age spectrum. The major exception occurs in the *youngest* group, where 28.6 percent of 55- to 59-year-olds reported themselves in only fair health, a larger percentage than in any other age group even when fair and poor are added together. This result could be aberrant because the number of respondents in this age group is limited, but it may also be based on younger people's greater awareness of any deviation from the health norm to which they are accustomed or which they expect. If an 85-year-old man awakes with an arthritic pain in his hip, he may simply dismiss it as unimportant. After all, he is still in generally good health and surviving. If a 55-year-old woman awakes with a similar pain, she may be concerned.

Those in the excellent/good category outnumbered by large percentages those in the fair/poor category, even in the 75 to 95 groupings. These statistics destroy a whole set of stereotypes, but are synchronous with recent research showing older adults as a group to be more healthy and less in need of health and custodial care than has been predicted. A simplified chart with the perception of health reduced to two categories—excellent/good and fair/poor—clearly illustrates these results.

Self-Rated Health by Age, Two Categories Only				
	excellent/good		fair/poor	
age	number - percent		number - percent	
55-59	10	71.4	4	28.6
60-64	72	94.7	4	5.3
65-69	221	89.5	25	10.5
70-74	199	87.7	28	12.4
75-79	138	86.8	21	13.2
80-84	49	80.3	12	19.6
85-89	13	76.5	4	23.5
90-95	3	75.0	1	25.0

Again, the number of persons age 55 to 59 and those past 84 are too few to be statistically significant, but the important findings are how positively elderlearners feel about their health, and how slow the decline in health is as they age.

We can only speculate as to which comes first, a continuing involvement in learning that generates the perception (or reality) of health, or good health that generates involvement in learning. However, the former gains credence when we recall the 79-year-old woman (see Chapter 5) who, despite multiple orthopedic operations and subsequent infections, rated her health as "good."

WHAT ARE THEY LEARNING?

The following areas of learning are listed in the order of the frequency with which they were checked. The instructions asked respondents to check "ALL of the areas that describe your significant learning projects, both formal and informal, during the past two years." A significant learning project was defined as "one that takes 10 or more hours." Some respondents checked just one or two; others checked a great many.

What They Choose to Learn		
music, art, dance, arts-related crafts	505	58.7%
travel or travel-related	444	51.6%
literature, drama, humanities	400	46.5%
politics, foreign affairs, current events	316	36.7%
history, family history, genealogy	314	36.5%
health and nutrition	307	35.7%
philosophy, religion, self-actualization	285	33.1%
computers, computer programs, new technologies	277	32.2%
finances, financial planning, investing	250	29.1%
sports, leisure, or recreation	211	24.5%
nature, biological sciences	210	24.4%
writing, journalism, journal keeping	206	24.0%
gardening or agriculture	191	22.2%
languages or multicultural learning	162	18.8%
environment or environment-related studies	133	15.5%
field of current or previous career	127	14.8%
physical sciences (astronomy, geology, etc.)	123	14.3%
community development or community building	95	11.0%
building, construction, home repair	94	10.9%
learning for a new career	25	2.9%

We cannot be sure whether these areas of study should be viewed simply as winners and losers in a popularity contest or whether the numbers actually represent significant learning projects undertaken. In any case, the areas certainly tell us the subjects in which the respondents are most interested,[8] and the data should, therefore, be useful to program planners.

At the end of the survey, respondents were asked to describe their informal or self-planned learning. The strong interest in the first 9 or 10 areas above is consistent with what they reported they were learning on their own.

WHY ARE THEY LEARNING?

A young friend recently asked, "These people you're writing about don't need to learn new stuff to get a job or keep the one they've got, they don't need credits and degrees, and you can't take learning with you. Why are they doing it?" I could answer with pleasure and statistically valid conviction "They're doing it because they enjoy it."

Why They Are Learning		
for the joy of learning	685	79.7%
to pursue a long-standing interest or hobby	498	57.9%
to meet people, socialize	461	53.6%
to engage in creative activity	406	47.2%
to pursue new interest or hobby	373	43.4%
to fill time productively	343	40.0%
as part of search for meaning and wisdom	324	37.7%
to fill blanks in previous education	214	24.9%
to fulfill community service purpose	182	21.2%
to help in my present job	40	4.7%
to prepare for new job/career	21	2.4%

"Joy of learning" is clearly the hands-down winner. People starred it or circled it, put multiple exclamation points after it, wrote "This is number one," rank ordered it first (although the instructions said nothing about rank ordering), or simply checked nothing else. If a survey result can be eloquent, this one is. "Joy" held its high ranking even when correlated with age (which lowered the other percentages but barely fazed this one).

The "meet people" answers gave out two messages. For some few respondents this seemed to be the only reason for learning, and their responses to other parts of the survey, particularly "what you choose to learn" were minimal. The impression was that they did little learning for its own sake, but undertook learning activities as a means of accessing social activities. Many of those who answered the question in this way were living alone, whether single, divorced, or widowed. "Meet people" as a reason for learning declines with age (62 percent at age 55 to 25 percent at age 95) and also declines in tandem with self-reported health. It is one of two "whys" that clearly correlate with gender—45 percent of males checked this reason, 58 percent of females.

The other variable that is influenced by gender is "search for meaning and wisdom"—32 percent of males and 41 percent of females checked it. When correlated with age, "search for meaning" moves counter-intuitively down— from 50 percent at ages 55 to 59 to 17 percent at ages 85 to 89. Perhaps older people have already found meaning in their lives.

The relatively high ranking of creative activity is not surprising but con- firms the highest ranking given to the arts in "What They Choose to Learn." The desire "to engage in a creative activity" as a motivator for learning apparently rises along with income levels from 45 percent to 68 percent and shows a similar rise, 20 percent to 53 percent, with increasing levels of education from grade school to four-year college, and then drops slightly to 48 percent among those who have gone to graduate school. The apparent dulling of creativity by postgraduate work will come as no surprise to many educators.

"To fill time productively" seems the product of the work ethic and runs fairly consistently across age, gender, income, and education. Both "longstanding interests" and "new interests" decline with age, although the former not as much as the latter.

Write-ins in the "Why" section were frequent and thematically consistent, most of them variations on the following: "to stretch my mind," "to exercise the gray cells," "to keep my brain working," "to stay young by staying in touch with the world," and "learning keeps me alive." These elderlearners have anticipated the message of this book.

HOW DO THEY LEARN: LEARNING STYLES AND PREFERENCES

By asking respondents to check "the learning resources with which you are personally most comfortable," the ES gave us the opportunity to match learning styles with the learning choices people actually make. We were especially interested in finding out whether reading, learning alone, and self- generated learning were predictors for significant involvement in self-directed learning activities. The results are not conclusive, but suggest that this is true.

Learning Styles and Preferences		
reading	642	74.7%
classes, workshops, seminars	588	68.4%
travel	479	55.7%
group meetings	444	51.6%
discussion	437	50.8%
hands-on activities	356	41.4%
television	295	34.3%
learning alone	196	22.8%
self-generated learning	190	22.1%
with friend or colleague	178	20.7%

Learning Styles and Preferences (continued)		
computer programs	117	13.6%
field work	85	9.9%
experimenting	82	9.5%
Internet	45	5.2%

At first glance, these figures say two things: 1) the older generation is still a print-based generation; and 2) the older generation is highly social, preferring to learn in the company of others, in group meetings, classes, workshops, and discussions.

The preference for classrooms may stem at least in part from expectations raised by previous educational experience which, for older generations, was predominantly formal. When 75-year-olds were in high school and college, chairs were arranged in rows, not circles; the syllabus was prescribed; and the teacher was far more authoritarian than today. Although older adults are delighted to be relieved of papers, tests, and grades, many are still uneasy when the teacher or professor, eschewing lectures, relies on class discussion to raise issues and cover the material. However, over a fifth of the respondents checked a preference for self-generated learning and learning alone, a preference that was predictive for "high" independent learners, those in the upper 25 percent of amount of hours per month spent in independent learning.

The extraordinary preference for learning through travel is the unexpectedly dominant theme emerging from the ES results, carrying through the What, How, and Where sections of the survey. (See discussion in Chapter 10.) On the other hand, the relatively low ratings for computers and Internet are belied by the respondents' narrative accounts of their learning.

WHERE ARE THEY LEARNING?

Where a person learns has strong correlations with age, income, level of education, and learning styles. The high numbers in the first section, "on your own," held fairly steady across the different groups and other variables. Despite the stated preferences for learning in groups, most learning is done on one's own.

Learning on Your Own		
at home	655	76.2%
through travel	473	55.0%
in libraries	406	47.2%
in museums, galleries	365	42.4%
at work or volunteer activity	338	39.3%
outdoors	214	24.9%
in nature centers	88	10.2%
total # responses	2,539	

There are few surprises here, although one wonders about the 23.8 percent who say they are *not* learning at home. Don't they ever read at home or watch an educational television show or learn a new household skill? Or is it that they don't call any of those activities learning? The biggest revelation is the large number who say they learn in libraries, but this holds up in the next section as well, where libraries are cited as the most commonly used community resource.

Using Community-Based Resources		
libraries	353	41.0%
churches, synagogues	245	28.5%
social clubs	151	17.6%
hospitals, health facilities	105	12.2%
community centers	92	10.7%
senior centers	88	10.2%
parks	84	9.8%
local or city agencies	76	8.8%
YMCA/YWCA	36	4.2%
total # responses	1,230	

The number of total responses as well as the percentages drop when one moves from where older adults learn on their own to where they learn in the community, although the use of libraries and churches remains fairly consistent. The surprises are that churches and synagogues do not rate higher and that local or city agencies rate so low. Churches might be the most appropriate institutions to increase the numbers of black elderlearners. According to a 1993 study, 47 percent of aged blacks attend church at least once a week and 29 percent reported that they participated in church activities other than services one to three times per week.[9]

The relatively strong showing for hospitals and health facilities is indicative of a new role that the health community has chosen to play. Hospitals and clinics are no longer just places you go when you are ill. Many are becoming true health centers, practicing preventive medicine for the whole family, and responding especially to seniors' needs. They have exercise and diet programs; post-heart attack programs; classes in nutrition, disease prevention, and relaxation techniques; and videos that provide information on a broad spectrum of diseases and injuries. They are becoming a one-stop shopping emporium for health, especially for older adults.

However, use of community resources is uneven. The poorer and less educated are heavier users than those at the other end of both scales. This result is not only expected but may be intentional on the part of resource-poor, local government-sponsored centers and agencies, but it is equally true for YMCAs, health facilities, and churches.

Use of Senior Centers by Group		
Group	# Persons Responding	% of Group Total
107	19	16.2%
207	64	27.4%
307	67	28.3%
407	106	58.6%
807	1	3.8%
907	1	1.6%

Groups 807 and 907, at the high end for income and education, score highest in their preference for learning alone and for self-generated learning. Their low use of other community-based resources is consistent, including use of libraries, for which their combined total is 36 percent, slightly below average for the group. Presumably they buy rather than borrow books.

Group 107, which frequently proved the exception to whatever general statements could be drawn from the ES results, was consistently at the bottom of the scale in the use of all learning resources, aligning itself alternately with the low end of the socio-economic scale in its use of resources that one accesses on one's own, and with the high end of the socio-economic scale on its non-use of community-based and education institutions.

Learning Programs for Seniors		
Elderhostel	318	37.0%
Learning in Retirement Insts.	306	35.6%
church study groups	184	21.4%
OASIS	169	19.7%
local or city agencies	108	12.6%
55 Plus	82	9.5%
alumni organizations	65	7.6%
Shepherd's Centers	<u>10</u>	1.2%
total # responses	1,242	

Because three of the programs, Elderhostel, Learning in Retirement Institutes, and OASIS, were among those from which the ES mailing list was gathered, we would expect those programs to rate high. However, there was significant cross-over, particularly between the Elderhostelers and the members of Learning in Retirement Institutes, but also between OASIS members and the other two.[10] The number saying they learn in church study groups was slightly lower but fairly consistent with those who cited churches and synagogues as a community-based learning resource.

Professional continuing education meetings and workshops were not included in the ES, but a number of respondents wrote them in under "other."

This mode of continuing to learn in one's own career area seemed to occur irrespective of age and gender, but was closely tied to education and income, which probably means that if you had an interesting job or career, you are more likely to wish to continue meeting your old colleagues and learning in that field.

Educational Institutions		
local public schools	98	11.4%
community colleges	211	24.5%
four-year colleges	127	14.8%
universities	208	24.2%
total responses	644	

Here again, no big surprises, though perhaps some confusion. The number of respondents citing schools as a source of their learning is higher than one might have expected given the National Center for Educational Statistics (NCES) census data (see Chapter 1). The numbers are compromised by the fact that Elderhostelers and Institute members were split as to whether they should count courses taken on campuses but not directly given by the college or university. Some did, some did not.

Formal Courses for Credit	
Number taking formal courses for credit	49
Percent of total respondents	5.7%
Range of courses taken:	1-15

# of Courses taken	# of Respondents
1 course	27[11]
2 courses	6
3 courses	4
4 courses	4
5-8 courses	4
10 courses	1
12 courses	1
15 courses	2

Mean   2.959   Median   1.000

Formal Courses: Noncredit or Audited		
Number taking informal courses	398	
Percent of total respondents	46.3%	
Range of courses taken	1-70	
Of those 398 who reported taking noncredit courses:		
1 course	100	25.1%
2 courses	89	22.4%
3 courses	45	11.3%
4 courses	54	13.6%
5 courses	20	5.0%
6 courses	29	7.3%
7 courses	4	1.0%
8 courses	15	3.8%
9 courses	3	.8%
10 courses	12	3.0%
11+ courses	27	6.7%
	398	100.0%
Mean 4.209 Median 3.000		

Of the 49 older adults who said they had taken courses for credit, 41 were under 75 years old (4.8 percent of the total number), and only 8 were over 75 (1 percent). The number of courses taken ranged from 1 to 15, with a median of 2.959 and a mean of 1.000. The assumption is that if the courses were for credit, they were given in a college or university.

However, 419 people (48.7 percent) answered the question about how many noncredit courses they had taken or audited; 293 of these respondents (74.2 percent) were under 75 years old, and 25.8 percent over 75. The number of courses taken ranged from 1 to 70, with a mean of 4.209 and a median of 3. We do not know by what institutions or organizations these noncredit courses were offered, but the list could certainly include hospitals, museums, community centers, and churches.

BARRIERS TO LEARNING

The most striking result here is that 200 learners, 23.3 percent, reported *no barriers at all!* Some wrote in the margins indignant or even boastful notes saying things like "I see *no* barriers to my learning!!!" or "Nothing could stop me from learning." For the rest, time, despite retirement, is apparently the big barrier. With lives filled with travel and volunteer, family, and social activities, seniors must give learning high priority if it is to be a major component of their lives, as it clearly is.

Barriers to Learning		
time	384	44.7%
distance	227	26.4%
money	183	21.3%
lack of information about		
what is available	166	19.3%
lack of motivation	109	12.7%
insufficient offerings	108	12.6%
fear of new technologies	58	6.7%
physical handicap	54	6.3%
lack of confidence in	43	5.0%
learning ability		

K. Patricia Cross says that understanding the barriers to learning is important because "it is usually the people who 'need' education most—the poorly educated—who fail to participate." (This is borne out by the ES which showed that barriers to learning decline as the level of education rises.) Cross categorizes these barriers as situational, dispositional, and institutional.[12] The "dispositional" barriers included in the ES (lack of motivation, lack of confidence, and fear of new technologies) were checked by only 5 percent to 12.7 percent of respondents. Given that roughly 20 percent of those who answered the survey were from low income and low education backgrounds, and might be presumed to be diffident about their learning prowess, the results say something positive about the psychology of older adults. On the other hand, the relatively high ranking of "lack of information" and "insufficient offerings" suggests that institutions are failing to reach older adults or to get their messages across. The situational barriers (time, distance, money, and physical handicaps) are a different story. Time issues must be addressed by the learners themselves, although some reasons for the shortage of time, as detailed below, defy time management techniques. Educators can, if they are serious about reaching an older adult population, address the issues raised by distance through new systems of delivery of educational services (see Chapter 10). In this society, no human being should be deterred from taking full advantage of the system's learning resources by lack of money, but that is an old battle that will not easily be won. However, if the surprisingly high self-rated health figures are related to high participation in learning activities, the argument can be made for a trade off: dollars spent on learning resources can save dollars spent on health care.

The numerous write-ins in the "other" category of the barriers section, which got more write-ins than any other, are revealing. The most frequently cited barriers were

problems about night classes, night driving	15
caring for disabled spouse or family member	12
transportation	10
poor health	8
lack of time because of volunteer activity	6
family obligations, eyesight, still working	4 each

Other barriers cited include laziness (2), hearing (3), recent move (3), language, lack of energy, burn out, dyslexia, disinterested spouse, slowing down, disinterest, lack of traveling companion, procrastination, and recently changed churches (apparently a major upheaval in the respondent's life). Since people are, in general, reluctant to use the "other" category, each write-in must be assumed to be occurring elsewhere throughout this population.

In Chapters 10 and 12, we discuss ways in which all barriers, but particularly the situational and institutional ones, might be eliminated, or at least moderated.

FORMAL AND INFORMAL LEARNING

In developing the ES, we were particularly interested in finding out how much formal (credit and noncredit) and informal learning was actually taking place, and what factors predispose toward learning. We were particularly interested in the differences, if any, between those who were predominantly formal learners and those who were informal (self-directed or independent) learners. To this end, we have looked at the data from a number of perspectives: correlating learning with gender, age, health, income, education, and learning styles; looking at the correlation between the number of learning choices respondents listed and the hours they reported as spent in learning; and seeking information that will help institutions understand and find ways to encourage elderlearning.

Time Spent in Formal Learning		
Number answering question	553	64.3%
Hours per month— range	1-160	
Mean	17.47 hours	
Median	12.00 hours	
Time Spent in Informal Learning		
Number answering question	674	78.3%
Hours per month—range	1-300	
Mean	27.86 hours	
Median	20.00 hours	

Summary: Formal and Informal Learning

The ES results as they relate directly to the amounts of formal and informal (or independently generated and designed) learning taking place among older adults need further discussion. To understand the results, it is important to know what definitions of formal and informal learning the respondents were using. The following excerpts are from the letter that accompanied the Survey:

> **Formal learning** is learning that takes place in any formal or organized setting: a school, university, Elderhostel course, or other learning program that has a predetermined structure.

> **Informal learning** is either self-initiated and planned or takes place within an informal group that structures its own learning projects (e.g., local library reading groups, Great Decisions discussion groups, gourmet cooking or investment clubs, etc.). Examples of informal learning abound among older adults. Some people are pursuing complex family history projects that involve many hours of learning the skills of genealogy; others are involved in volunteer activities that demand vital new learning; still others may be pursuing old or new interests in history, politics, philosophy, literature, computers, and the sciences; many are driving themselves to become proficient at surfing the Internet; and some are rereading Austen or Trollope or honing a skill like photography, playing a musical instrument, doing water colors, or learning Italian in preparation for a trip.

We cannot vouch for how well or poorly respondents understood this distinction between formal and informal learning or whether their answers concur with our definitions. In some cases, misunderstanding was apparent, e.g., when a computer class was described as informal learning, perhaps because the students wore jeans or the class took place in the back room of a store. In general, most of the respondents seem to have understood these distinctions.

However, if we had been able to conduct in-depth interviews with the respondents about their learning (as Allen Tough did in his seminal study of self-generated learning), the hours reported for informal learning would likely have doubled or tripled.[13] The concept of informal learning is so new to most people that they have a difficult time assigning the "learning label" to much of what they do. In the few one-on-one interviews we did conduct, we had to encourage even professionals to report the reading and research they did in their fields, whether at home or at work, as time spent learning. (The old equation between "learning" and "schooling" persists.) Had their revised responses been substituted for their original ES responses, the mean for "informal" learning would have been significantly higher. Similarly, when initiating conversations about learning with casual friends and acquaintances, we were able, through persistent probing, to discover a wealth of learning experiences they hadn't even thought to mention: learning to bake bread, to use a spreadsheet, to construct and maintain a compost heap, or to lead a reading group discussion. Tough and Hiemstra,[14] who did lengthy structured interviews with adults across a broad socio-economic spectrum, revealed the extraordinary degree to which adult learning is informal. Older adults are no exception.

Our own research revealed that older people are learning in numbers and amounts of time expended at a rate far exceeding even our original expectations. The average (mean) amount of time spent per month in *formal learning* (classrooms or other situations where the content, duration, methods, and goals are set by a teacher, group leader, or institution) is 17.75 hours. The lowest scoring group (907) reported 12.10 hours; the highest scoring group (307) reported 23.57 hours. The range was from 1 to 160 hours per month.

The average (mean) number of hours per month spent in *informal* (non-classroom-based or self-directed) learning was 27.86. The lowest scoring group (407) reported a mean of 25.41 hours; the highest scoring group (907) (which was, paradoxically, the lowest scoring group in formal learning) reported an average of 42.91 hours. The range was from 1 to 300 hours per month.

What Do the Numbers Mean?

The questions we asked were difficult. Most of us never think about our learning in terms of the number of hours we spend, and we certainly don't sit around counting the hours we spend in informal learning. For most respondents, this was probably the first time they had even thought seriously about the learning they do on their own.

Nevertheless, 78.5 percent of the respondents took time to thoughtfully answer this strange new question. Among the 21.5 percent who did not answer the question, many circled the blank with question marks or wrote things like "varies," "many," "impossible to figure out," or "lots and lots," tantalizing hints that the numbers could have been even higher. These hints became especially frustrating when the same people who refused to be pinned down to numbers wrote narratives about learning projects of significant breadth and depth that sounded as though they would have consumed enormous amounts of time.

To understand what distinguishes those who do a lot of learning from those who do not, we looked at the upper 25 percent and the lower 25 percent of both formal and informal learners (high learners and low learners) to see what variables could predict their level of learning. The most consistent thing we found was the number of items they had checked for "What You Choose to Learn." Those who checked the greatest number of items turned out to be high learners, formal and informal; those who checked the fewest were among the low learners. Learning level in turn correlated with the amount of education completed. Those with a high level of education had more varied interests than those with a lower level. More interests meant more subjects. More subjects meant more learning. The desire to learn arises from the habit of learning. The more learning you have, the more you want.

The percentage of high learners varies little from age to age: 60- to 64-year-olds have a slight edge, and then the numbers are evenly divided from 65 to 79. Because our sample contained a few very old, very high learners, the curve seems to ascend again after age 85. We would like to think that is because elderlearners are healthier.

Only marginal correlations appeared between the incomes of high and low informal learners, although the highest and lowest income brackets have more high learners than the middle income brackets. High informal learners are self-employed in greater numbers, and report somewhat less volunteer work, although they score highest of all the groups in citing community development as a reason why they learn. They also tend to be high formal learners.

An unexpected finding about high informal learners was that they are *low users of community or institutional learning resources* (see above, "Where Are They Learning?"). Although we had never thought about it, this finding makes sense as a significant marker for informal learning. The high informal learners choose *not* to go to senior centers, local or city agencies, or colleges or Institutes to satisfy their learning needs. They prefer to do it on their own.

Group 307, members of Institutes for Learning in Retirement, were the highest formal learners, averaging 23.6 hours per month in classes, significantly above the median of 17.8 for all groups.

Group 907, the miscellaneous group consisting largely of professionals and academics, took the honors as informal learners, averaging 42.9 hours per month, whereas the median for all groups was 27.9.

Is this disparity among how groups choose to learn mainly dispositional or mainly circumstantial? In any case, the question is fertile ground for further research.

NOTES

1. The remaining 52 either arrived too late to be used or contained insufficient information to be useful.

2. "On Behalf of Older Women: Another Reason to Protect Medicare and Medicaid." *New England Journal of Medicine,* 334,12 (March 21, 1996), 794.

3. Peterson, p. 44.

4. Ibid., p. 42.

5. Cox, p. 154.

6. James S. Jackson, Linda M. Chatters, and Robert Joseph Taylor, "Roles and Resources of the Black Elderly" in *Aging in Black America* (Sage Publications, 1992), p. 5.

7. Beth B. Hess, "Postword: Where We Are and Where We Might Go," *Aging in Society: Selected Reviews of Recent Research*, edited by Matilda W. Riley, Beth B. Hess, and Kathleen Bond (Lawrence Elbaum Associates, 1983), p. 256.

8. Psychology was a serious omission from this list, but many of the respondents included it in the "philosophy, religion, self-actualization" category or wrote it in.

9. Jacqueline M. Smith, "Functions and Supportive Roles of Church and Religion" in *Aging in Black America*, (Sage Publications, 1992), pp. 124-47.

10. We have no explanation for one anomaly. The number of people who said they used OASIS was *less* than the number of OASIS respondents. Apparently, the sense of identity is cloudy in some OASIS groups.

11. Some of the respondents to this question entered a "1" in the blank space; others simply checked it. We had to enter checks as a "1," even though we suspected that some of the checks may have represented more than one course.

12. K. Patricia Cross, *Adults as Learners* (San Francisco: Jossey-Bass, 1981) pp. 97-99.

13. Tough's research in the 1970s marked the first time anyone had paid serious attention to self-directed learning. See Chapter 9 for further discussion.

14. Allen Tough, *Adults' Learning Projects* (Toronto: Ontario Institute for Studies in Education, 1971); R.P. Hiemstra, *The Older Adult and Learning* (Lincoln: University of Nebraska Press, 1975).

CHAPTER 7

Older Adult Learning in Colleges and Universities

In age the passions cool and leave a man at rest, and then forthwith his mind takes a contemplative tone; the intellect is set free and attains the upper hand.

Arthur Schopenhauer

THE GRAYING OF THE CAMPUS

During the 1970s and early 1980s, an unprecedented number of adults started appearing on college campuses. They came for a variety of reasons: to fill in perceived blanks in their earlier education; to earn degrees deferred by early marriage, children, or the need to work; to advance old careers or enter new ones; or to enrich their lives through further learning. This first wave of students, largely female and middle class, was soon followed by tens of thousands of working class men and women. Spurred by the decline of industrial jobs and the rise of "knowledge" jobs, and supported in part by their companies or unions, these working class students sought new skills to secure their economic futures.

As the "graying of the campus" began, institutions were slow to recognize that their academic and administrative structures presented adults with a series of hurdles. One hurdle was class hours. Faculty were reluctant to teach evening classes, but working people could not make 10 a.m. labs or mid-afternoon office hours. Because some basic courses were never taught at night, adult students were effectively shut out of critical degree programs. Even when evening classes were offered, administrators often neglected to extend the hours of vital campus offices and services, such as admissions, registration, counseling, libraries, and cafeterias. Parking arrangements had to be made and academic adjustments worked out to remove the physical education requirement from some degree programs. New forms had to be printed which did not require parents' signatures indicating responsibility or permission. Even those administrators who recognized the need to respond to a burgeoning adult market were sometimes helpless in the face of institutional inertia.

Eventually, the scheduling was somewhat painfully sorted out. Adult students could not only earn degrees at night, they could deal with the registrar, visit the library, see an advisor, and stop in at the resource center or snack bar. They even began to feel welcome.

As the flood of adult students increased, classroom dynamics changed. These students carried with them an imposing weight of real world experience. For some faculty, they were a delight: challenging, commenting, enriching the theoretical bent of academic teaching with their practical knowledge. For less secure faculty, they were an alien species: too old, too blue collar, too unaccustomed to the politesse of academia. They were frequently outspoken, disruptive, and a threat to professorial authority.

There were other bumps along the road. Accomplished but non-degreed social workers were required to take beginning social work courses and even spend semesters in field work. Skilled hackers who had taught themselves the ins and outs of computer programming and knew far more than many of their professors had to enroll in Computer Science 101. The technical manager of a factory producing TVs and VCRs was expected to take basic electronics courses. People with professional expertise of all kinds found themselves sitting in classes they could easily have taught.

By the mid-1970s, a few institutions began to realize that teaching people what they already knew wasted everyone's time. With impetus from organizations like the American Council on Education (ACE), the Council for Adult and Experiential Learning (CAEL), and the Educational Testing Service (ETS), the practice of prior learning assessment (PLA) began to expand.

Prior learning assessment is a means of evaluating the learning students bring with them, its breadth, depth, and equivalency with what is taught in the classroom, and a means of assigning appropriate credit to that learning if warranted. Assessment is carried out through a variety of mechanisms, including proficiency examinations; credit for military, corporate, and union experience; performance observation; extended oral testing; or development of a self-compiled portfolio that includes identification of learning, documentation, and narrative explanation. As of the last survey, over 1,400 colleges and universities offered some prior learning assessment options.[1]

As time went on, more and more faculty (and traditional-age students) acknowledged that adults brought new life to the classroom. They were not simply going to college because it was the next step after high school, or because their parents wanted them to be there. They were there because they *wanted, needed* to be. These new students, many of them paying for their own learning, were committed to it. They had strong goals—career, professional, and personal—that impelled them to endure the disruptions and make the sacrifices in money, time, and quality of life that going back to school entailed. They were also consumers, determined to get their time and money's worth.

To the extent that it has succeeded, continuing education for adults of working age has been driven by market imperatives rather than by a long-range concern for assisting human development over the lifespan. The demographics were compelling. In the 1980s, the baby boomers were passing beyond college age, and adult students could fill their places in the classrooms. Resource opportunities were also seductive: tuition assistance plans from employers and unions; partnerships with major corporations; and government subsidies for job-related training. Market imperatives extended the dominance of credentialism, which was a valid response to competitive job markets, and promoted middle class lifelong learning for those wishing to "get ahead."

The comparatively new field of adult learning, though flying the banner of "learning never ends," was implicitly thinking in terms of middle-aged adults whose career goals were uppermost and who were therefore dependent upon credits and degrees. Much of the faculty opposition to these "new" students was based on the fear that their institutions would emphasize practical learning over theoretical, and promote vocationalism rather than scholarship.

ADULT AND OLDER ADULT ENROLLMENT IN COLLEGES AND UNIVERSITIES

The limited shift in thinking that took place on campuses in the 1970s and 1980s, as colleges began to accept that adults were on campus to stay and that accommodations must be made to serve their needs, has not yet been extended to Third Agers. There is a notable absence of interest in older adults, even among those in continuing education who should be supporters. The programs of two recent national education conferences are a case in point. The 1994 and 1995 CAEL International Conferences had over 90 sessions on each of their programs, but not a single lecture, workshop, or even poster session that pertained to elderlearners. At the 1995 National Research Institute's Annual Conference on Lifelong Learning, out of 5 major speakers and 54 papers presented, *not one* addressed issues of older adult education or even mentioned the explosion of learning in the over 55 adult population.

In 1972, 8.6 percent of all college students were 25 or older. By 1988, that percent had grown to 39.1, reflecting an enormous demographic shift. John Brademas, arguing for greater attention to adult students, estimated that their enrollment was growing three times as fast as the U.S. population.[2] Each year since the 1970s, the average age of college students has gone up, stabilizing in the mid-1990s at around 37 to 39. The figure is somewhat higher in community colleges, and somewhat lower in universities.

Of the vast numbers of adults registered for college courses, few are elderlearners. According to 1992 figures from the National Center for Education Statistics,[3] the number of students 65 years and older enrolled for credit in U.S. colleges and universities is as follows:

All institutions	63,588
Four-year colleges	19,394
Two-year colleges	44,172

These sparse numbers represent just .04 percent of all registered students. Not surprisingly, most of these are part-time (58,066); only 6,500 are full-time. Moreover, 61 percent of all registrants are women, although that percentage drops to 51 for full-time students. Older women also make up 55 percent of registrations for graduate school.[4]

These dismal numbers are compromised by poor reporting. Many colleges and universities do not track ages beyond 49, choosing to lump all other students in the 50+ classification. One large eastern public university that has a sterling reputation for successfully serving adult students still uses the 50 and over formula. Even using the additional 15 years between 50 and 65, only 4.8 percent of its undergraduate and 5.3 percent of its graduate population show up in the 50+ category.

A Census Bureau study of adult learning that broadened the inquiry to find out if respondents had participated in *any* formal adult education in the past year[5] got a much different response. For purposes of the study, adult education was defined to include all non-full-time education activities, including college attendance, work-based classes, adult literacy classes, or classes taken for recreation and enjoyment. Of those over 65 years old, 3,750,000 said "yes," they were taking or had recently taken a course, a figure equivalent to 13 percent of the over 65 population. While 13 percent is low compared to our survey data, it is dramatically higher than the .04 percent said to be enrolled in credit classes and suggests the existence of a large untapped population of elderlearners that the colleges are not reaching.

The Elderlearning Survey (ES) reveals some interesting figures on adult choices for formal education. The following chart records where Survey respondents are taking courses.

Institutional Choices for Formal Education	
Institution	**Percent Reporting**
public schools	11.4%
2-year colleges	24.5%
4-year colleges	14.6%
universities	24.1%

Clearly, the public schools are only minimally involved. Although the public school system is widespread and has the potential to be a major provider of older adult learning, a 1980 survey found 60 percent of school districts were serving fewer than 50 older adults annually. Peterson attributes this result to a mind set that says schools are for children, and to a lack of financial resources and interest.[6]

All the ES figures related to courses taken must be looked at with caution. Some respondents, who reported taking classes, workshops, or seminars in the past two years at an institution, did not enter any checks or numbers in the following question which asked for the number of formal courses taken and whether they were credit, noncredit, or audited.[7] Some people who attended Elderhostels or who are members of Institutes for Learning in Retirement counted their participation as taking courses, although most did not. Moreover, many students checked two or more kinds of institutions, so that a total of the percentages would be statistically meaningless. The low percentage for the four-year colleges is at least partially accounted for by the large number of private, high-tuition institutions that can offer older students no state-approved funding subsidies, but even these colleges should ponder the implications of the relative numbers.

WHY OLDER ADULTS AREN'T IN COLLEGE

There are a number of reasons why more people over 65 are not enrolled in colleges and universities. First, the unique attribute of colleges and universities is their ability to grant credits and degrees. They are our society's verifiers and certifiers of learning achievement. The transcript evidence which they, and only they, are empowered to issue as "proof" of learning is of immediate practical use to working adults. Such adult students need a degree or certificate to keep their present job or move up to a better one, to change careers, to acquire the cachet of a postsecondary degree, or simply to validate their learning.

None of these categories routinely applies to those older adults, who are already retired and have no further need to advance in their careers. Most older adults are also beyond the need for degrees to bolster their egos, and validation of their learning is, or should be, an internal process. This doesn't mean they don't need or want further learning; it just means that they may seek other less expensive and less formal means of acquiring it.

Second, the prevailing style of traditional academia is neither attractive to nor appropriate for the majority of older learners who want to learn at their own pace and without the need to perform in prescribed ways. Third Agers are impatient with the rigmarole of papers, tests, grades, and enforced attendance over a protracted period of time. Retirement means an end not only of work-driven "thou shalts" but, for many, of any outside pressures to achieve. Older adults engage in learning because they want to, not because they have to. And their rewards are internal, not letters on a grade report. Many of them would echo the words of one survey respondent in his mid-seventies who wrote, "I already know what I know, and more important, I know what I don't know. I don't need a professor to reward me for the former or to remind me of the latter."

Third, per-class tuition fees are far beyond most retirement incomes, and there are currently no grants or loans to help a septuagenarian study anthropology or French poetry. The sharply reduced fees for those over 65 in some state colleges as well as free auditing privileges at the professor's discretion tend not to be sufficiently publicized, and the "space available" restrictions applied to auditing courses make older adults de facto second class citizens.

Fourth, because seniors are not viewed as a promising "market," they are not typically included on mailing lists or in marketing plans. They can't take courses that they don't know about. According to the Survey, "Lack of information about what is available" is the *fourth* most important reason older people give for not taking more classes.

Fifth, no real effort is made on most campuses to offer (and publicize) courses that might be attractive to older persons, such as courses in oral history, cross-cultural studies, or journal writing, to name just a few that recur in people's self-directed learning, and that might merit a legitimate place in an intellectually rigorous institution.

Sixth, and possibly of primary importance, the level of older adults' previous formal education is low compared with the average of the total adult population. Among older age cohorts, the number of years of completed schooling drops. Today's young-old, those 65 to 69, have completed a median 12.4 years of education; those 85 to 89 have completed a median of only 10.3 years of education.[8] One of the few things we know for sure about adult education is that the more one has the more one wants. It stands to reason that older people who have had less experience of education will not opt for formal learning at as high a rate. Those older adult learners in the Survey who say they lack confidence in their ability to learn are more likely to test the waters in some shallower cove.

BARRIERS TO COLLEGE AND UNIVERSITY PARTICIPATION IN OLDER ADULT LEARNING

All these reasons aside, more older adults would attend colleges and universities if the institutions wanted them to. Participants in Institutes for Learning in Retirement and Elderhostelers (see Chapter 8) take pride in their affiliation with the host college or university, buying its logo T-shirts, postcards, and notebooks; supporting its teams; and contributing to its fund drives. Those who register for or audit courses tend to be enthusiastic about their professors, their fellow students, and their own prowess. However, most colleges are still caught up in the process of learning to accommodate working-age adults. Their administrators are still remembering a gentler, kinder nine-to-five day. Their faculties are still arguing about whether their educational mission is compromised by allowing practical, job-related learning to mingle with the dispensation of purely abstract knowledge. There is little interest in and less enthusiasm for accommodating Third Agers.

American colleges and universities, which pride themselves on being open forums dedicated to new ideas and social reform, have so far adamantly resisted change in their own structures and policies. The most leftist faculty are the most conservative when it comes to modifying what they teach, how they teach it, and to whom. Current political correctness is confined to gender, class, and race; it does not extend to age. Because the struggle to accommodate an adult working age population is so recent, and the changes engendered by it still so tenuous and so strongly resisted by faculty, further accommodations to seniors might be difficult to achieve. In conversation with our teaching colleagues, many of them well over 65 themselves, the authors' preoccupation with elderlearning has either been viewed as a mild eccentricity or ignored as beneath notice. Outside the psychology and gerontology departments, interest in any aspect of elderlearning is nonexistent.

To administrators, who are currently under enormous pressures to lower costs and become more efficient, an older clientele with limited means, no moneyed sponsors, and a new set of problems is not attractive. Nostalgia for the old status quo of "one main customer: the undergraduate student who seeks a first-time college education, usually full-time, on campus, where classes are scheduled between 8:00 a.m. and 5:00 p.m."[9] accounts for administration's meager response to new opportunities and new social needs. Many of the same institutions that stretched themselves to meet the imperatives of returning middle-aged adults, haven't yet begun to consider that an even older constituency, one that is growing more numerous and politically powerful, might benefit from their services. And these students prefer *daytime* classes!

The real question, as framed by the authors of the 1995 survey, *What the Public Wants from Higher Education*, is whether colleges and universities want to continue to pursue as their major business the provision of first-time, on-campus education or whether they want to go into the newer business of providing true lifelong learning.[10] There are compelling reasons why the latter course might be both intellectually and socially desirable.

NON-CLASSROOM STRATEGIES FOR FOSTERING ELDERLEARNING

Some institutions *are* beginning to acknowledge their role in satisfying the learning needs of older adults without forcing systemic change. A few are now not only permitting seniors to audit their classes free, they are *publicizing* the fact. Over 300 colleges and universities are sponsoring Institutes for Learning in Retirement on their campuses, and 1,500 are extending their services by sponsoring Elderhostels. Some, broadening their vision of the institution as a community learning resource, have opened their doors to the public for free lectures, exhibitions, performances, and discussions, widely publicizing these in the appropriate media. The benefits of institutional hospitality go both ways: the colleges and universities, by opening their doors, contribute to the possibility of intergenerational learning and understanding. Younger students can better understand the potential for lifelong learning in their own lives when sitting next to an older person whose comments arise from a rich experience of life. Conversely, older students' learning is stimulated by the fresh perceptions of their younger classmates as well as by their healthy skepticism and dislike of cant. Elderlearners enjoy their dual or triple roles as co-learners with younger students, as mentors, and, on occasion, as mentees.

Look closely at the audience at a typical college public lecture or performance. Except for rock concerts and extremes of performance art, students are frequently in the minority; the rows of gray, white, and bald heads you will see are *not* all faculty. Welcoming older adults to the campus guarantees an audience for events that might otherwise be sparsely attended, thus avoiding embarrassment for both host institution and visiting scholars or artists. The "generosity" of the college is appropriately recognized as contributing to the community's quality of life, and may help defuse town/gown tensions. Such good publicity is also a handy argument against city council complaints of too much tax-exempt property on city rolls.

On the other side of the equation, older adults are able to benefit from lectures and performances that they might otherwise be unable to afford. Some colleges have a specific policy to encourage elderlearners on their campuses. Dartmouth has made arrangements with Kendal at Hanover, a nearby retirement community, to support a variety of learning opportunities, both on campus and in the retirement community itself. A regularly scheduled bus runs between the college and the retirement community, allowing Kendal at Hanover residents to audit classes, get to the library, and attend special lectures and other events without the perils of driving, weather, or parking. In a survey of resident satisfaction, 95 percent of the respondents felt that proximity to Dartmouth was one of Kendal's greatest assets.

> A college town provides many opportunities—would I have ever believed I would again be auditing classes in the same classroom in which I sat so many years ago and taking advantage of the countless opportunities that a college atmosphere offers? To me, this is retirement living at its best.
>
> *John Adams, Kendal at Hanover resident*

... the move to Kendal at Hanover was a fine decision, giving me access
to Dartmouth sports and numerous activities related to keeping my mind
alive with study courses, often led by College faculty, plus access to
entertainment. ...

Dick Gruen,[11] Kendal at Hanover resident

The attractiveness of college communities as retirement destinations has
long been recognized by realtors, tax collectors, and local chambers of commerce. Those retirees whose financial resources are sufficient to enable them
to relocate at will are important resources for towns and cities. They pay high
taxes but make minimal use of tax-supported services (such as public school
systems), and they pump money into the local economy for goods and services.
They are a primary source of volunteer labor for many community organizations and charities, and they show up to vote in higher numbers than any other
sector of the population. They are truly ideal citizens.

The triangle area of North Carolina has become a retirement mecca thanks
not only to its temperate climate but in great part to the presence of the
University of North Carolina, North Carolina State University, Duke University, and Research Triangle Park, all of which offer multiple opportunities for
Third Age learning.

Further west in North Carolina, the city of Asheville has benefitted from
being a college town. The University of North Carolina at Asheville is host to
the Center for Creative Retirement (CCR), one of the most interesting
attempts in the country to both serve an older population and convert it to a
community asset. The Center for Creative Retirement, under the direction of
Ronald Manheimer, draws upon the structure of other Institutes for Learning
in Retirement for its College for Seniors, but goes beyond them in a number of
important ways. CCR ties itself to the host university not only through shared
courses but through its Senior Academy for Intergenerational Learning (SAIL),
which matches retired professionals with University undergraduates as tutors
and mentors, thus cementing intergenerational ties. It connects to its community through Leadership Asheville Seniors (LAS) which, with civic leaders,
political activists, and others, explores ways to match seniors' talents and
expertise with community needs. Through Seniors in the School, CCR also
links the community to a sizeable number of CCR members who tutor, mentor,
and present enrichment programs in the public schools.

Princeton, New Jersey, is another example of the drawing power of a
distinguished university; the city has an extraordinary population of retired
professors, writers, artists, statesmen, scientists, bookish financiers, and lesser
mortals who share a love of learning. They are attracted by Princeton University, although Princeton is not notable for its hospitality to the community, as
well as by the other colleges, universities, music schools, and theological

seminaries that cluster in the area and offer a mind boggling array of intellectual possibilities.

On a notably smaller scale, Brunswick, Maine, with a population of 21,000+ and snow bound most of the winter, is hardly a stereotypical retirement destination, but it has a rapidly increasing number of born-in-Mainers choosing to return for their retirement, as well as older people "from away," many of them attracted by Brunswick's small town ambiance and the presence of Bowdoin College. For $25 per year, townspeople can become official "Friends of Bowdoin," which entitles them to receive a weekly newsletter in which they can learn about events on campus that are open to the public. They also receive invitations to special association-sponsored events (e.g., dinners, trips to Boston museums, lectures, and concerts). Although membership is open to everyone, the "friends" are predominantly retired older adults. When Yevtushenko reads his poetry or Barney Frank talks about "Jews and Blacks" or a string quartet plays Bartok, the friends are there, frequently outnumbering students and faculty. The "friends" also tend to be generous to their academic benefactor at fund-raising time, another potent reason for all colleges to cultivate their good will.

Examples of academic hospitality to older people can be cited across the country. A few institutions, including Eckert College in Florida, have built on the natural synergy between older people and higher education by using excess campus space to build retirement housing. Similar projects are in the planning stages at many other institutions.

Nevertheless, despite all this good news, the gap between what is happening on campuses and what could be happening is enormous. On most campuses, education and education resources remain age-segregated; the elderlearner is always the "other," and classes lack the stimulation of intergenerational discussion and points of view. Segregated programs for older adults, because they are noncredit and outside the regular course offerings, are not held accountable in the same way for quality of content and delivery. They send a message that older students are "different" in fundamental ways from other students. These ghettoized programs also tend to have small budgets, are frequently dependent upon grants or gifts, and are vulnerable to space shortages and staff cuts.

As on so many societal issues, community colleges have been in the forefront of responding to the practical learning needs of elderlearners. Less wary of losing their status as arbiters of intellectualism, they have reached out to older adults with a number of innovative programs that address hot-button subjects: planning for retirement, health, finances, computers, exercise, and the arts. Some public institutions have developed funding strategies that enable them to offer these courses tuition-free for adults over 60 or 65, and others have worked out self-funding mechanisms whereby the students pay a nominal amount per course that goes directly to the teacher without further administrative costs. Although community colleges show up as a strong resource for learning in the ES, a 1993 survey of 1,224 community colleges found that despite population trends, fewer than 25 percent of the responding institutions offered programming for older students,[12] a number far too low to meet the needs of a rapidly aging population. Because of poor reporting strategies, this result might mean that community colleges have only limited offerings of interest to or designated for older adults, or it might mean that they are not offering courses on an age-segregated basis. The latter possibility has much to recommend it.

Higher education is too central to this country's lifelong learning system to turn its back on emerging needs. Its responsibilities, as delineated in Fischer, Blazey, and Lipman's *Students of the Third Age*, should include

- helping older generations to understand today's values, culture, and technology
- acting as a catalyst for mobilizing older adults to maintain productive post-retirement roles
- fostering diversity in intellectual, cultural, and social life by educating students of all ages about aging and ageism
- fostering the effective use of society's limited resources by reducing older adults' need for health and social services by increasing their mental vigor through education[13]

If the agenda outlined in these four points is followed, colleges and universities would become an integral part of the lifelong learning system.

IMPORTANT ROLES COLLEGES AND UNIVERSITIES MIGHT PLAY

Despite the structural changes that have occurred as adults flocked to the classrooms in the past 25 years, all too many educators still feel and act as though "virtually all the knowledge necessary for the life course can and is to be acquired in the First Age."[14] In a chapter on "The Obsolescence of the Educational System," which is as applicable to the U.S. as it is to the U.K., Laslett contrasts the conventional education systems with their hierarchies, coerced learning, exams, credits, attention to maintenance of "standards," and other paraphernalia of formal education with the ideals of the University of the Third Age. If we believe in intellectual development over the lifespan, then colleges and universities, as well as public schools and other educational institutions, must become supply side parties; they must recognize the need to prepare people for the Third Age and to facilitate their access to the classrooms, libraries, art collections, grounds, and sporting facilities that the educational system maintains. Education should be a lifetime partnership in which all components of the learning system have a role to play.

Colleges and universities can take a number of specific steps that demand relatively minor adjustments in their current structures and priorities.

- They could initiate collaborative intergenerational learning projects of which positive models abound in the literature.
- They could provide professional development seminars for faculty to discuss how to adjust teaching methodologies for students who are not "empty vessels" and whose learning styles may be different.
- They could provide more interdisciplinary courses and practices. These should not be viewed as peripheral parts of the curriculum but as mainstream ways of thinking about the domains of knowledge outside the regimen of departmental structures.
- They could provide classes in learning skills for self-directed learners; these could include use of libraries and online resources, how to plan a self-directed learning project, the identification of resources, analytic and critical thinking, and self-evaluation of projects.
- They could appoint some faculty or advisors to serve as mentors and resource people for self-directed learning projects.
- They could schedule daytime seminars in current issues in politics, economics, the environment, constitutional concerns, the arts, justice, crime, violence, pornography, etc. to be led by specialists or panels of experts who can illuminate different sides of topics of current concern. Older people are among the most avid followers of current events but they may rely too heavily on a narrow spectrum of partisan commentators.

These steps would go a long way toward serving the older adult population without altering the institution's mission, curriculum, academic standards, methodologies, or even schedules. The argument that colleges and universities cannot divert their scarce resources can be countered by reminding them that "there is no shortage of [older persons] capable of keeping our cultural capital in working use."[15] Third Agers can see to it that galleries and libraries stay open, that researchers have assistants, that exams are graded, and that younger at-risk students have tutors and mentors. Older adults thrive on being needed. They would grow in self-esteem if their discretionary time could be spent in contributing volunteer labor to the institutions they most respect.

NOTES

1. Lois Lamdin, *Earn College Credit for What You Know*, 2nd ed. (Chicago: CAEL, 1992), Appendix J, "Colleges & Universities with Comprehensive Prior Learning Assessment Programs," pp. 195-241; for further information on prior learning assessment see, besides Lamdin, Urban Whitaker, *Assessing Learning: Standards, Principles, & Procedures* (Chicago: CAEL, 1989).

2. "Universities Must Treat Adult Education as a Fundamental Part of Their Mission," *CHE*, 6, 33 (May 12, 1990), B1, B2.

3. "Higher Education Enrollment," Table 172, NCES, U.S. Department of Education, 1991.

4. Ibid., Table 171.

5. *Participants in Adult Education 17 Years and Older, by Selected Characteristics of Participants*, Table 344, NCES, U.S. Department of Education, 1991.

6. Peterson, pp. 253-54.

7. For statistical purposes, noncredit and audit were treated as the same because many respondents were unclear as to the difference. If a respondent checked 1 noncredit and 3 audits, it was recorded as 4 noncredits.

8. These figures are from the 1980 Bureau of the Census, adjusted for 1994.

9. Don A. Dillman, James A. Christenson, Priscilla Salant, and Paul D. Warner, *What the Public Wants from Higher Education: Work Force Implications from a 1995 National Survey*. SERC Technical Report Number 95-52 (Pullman, WA: Washington State University, 1995).

10. Ibid., p. 31.

11. The quotes from residents and the preceding data are from *Keynotes*, Newsletter of Kendal at Hanover, September 1994, p. 2.

12. Brenda Marshall Beckman and Catherine Ventura-Merkel, *Community College Programs for Older Adults: A Resource Directory of Guidelines, Comprehensive Programming Models, and Selected Programs*, League for Innovation in the Community College, 1993, p. iii.

13. Richard Fischer, Mark Blazey, and Henry Lipman, *Students of the Third Age* (New York: MacMillan, 1992), p. 17.

14. Laslett, p. 163.

15. Ibid., p. 170.

CHAPTER 8

Other Sources of Formal Learning

In the past few years I have made a thrilling discovery . . . that until one is
sixty one can never really learn the secret of living.

Ellen Glasgow

Formal, classroom-based continuing education is commonly associated
with colleges and universities, but the involvement of these institutions
with elderlearning is, as we have seen, limited. The bulk of older adult
formal learning is less likely to occur on a campus than in a church or
department store or community agency. Nevertheless, the two most highly
visible institutions serving elderlearners, Elderhostel and the Institutes for
Learning in Retirement, maintain close organizational ties with traditional
higher education, although their course structures, methodology, and content
are deliberately different from standard postsecondary fare. The other formal
programs to be discussed in this chapter are almost totally divorced from
academia.

ELDERHOSTEL

Elderhostel was begun in 1975 in part as a counter-response to the idea that
the proper role of old people is disengagement. The unique combination of
study, travel, and social interchange that Elderhostel embodies was specifically
designed to challenge older adults, to excite them to new experiences and
opportunities, and to offer them stimulating intellectual activity. As Dr. Harry
R. Moody, an Elderhostel board member, has written, "In retrospect, Elderhostel
seems obvious. Elderhostel was not an idea whose time had come but rather an
idea that was long overdue."[1]

The concept of Elderhostel (or Elderhosteling in its frequently used verb form) is perhaps the most well known of all American Third-Age learning activities. The numbers alone are impressive: beginning in 1975 with an initial enrollment of 220, Elderhostel has grown to over 300,000 registrants per year, a 1,400-fold increase in 20 years. Of these participants, 235,000 are enrolled in domestic programs and 65,000 in overseas programs.[2] Most of these are "repeaters." One woman told us that over the past nine years she had attended 34 Elderhostels.

Currently, about 1,500 colleges, universities, and other learning institutions in the U.S. participate in Elderhostel, as do 60 learning organizations in 55 countries overseas.

The Elderhostel formula is simple. Participants travel to the site of learning for one- to three-week programs with groups of 15 to 40 people 55 years or over. Accommodations are on college campuses, in conference centers, or in local inns or hotels, and instruction is given by college professors or accredited experts. Noncredit courses are accompanied by field trips and extra curricular activities, and ample provision is made for social interaction. There are no grades, tests, or homework; immersion in the subject matter is for the pure joy of learning.

By policy, all courses are centered about liberal and humane studies. The superficial and frivolous are avoided (new strategies for playing Scrabble or instruction in making Christmas wreaths out of wine corks are not part of the curriculum). Only one topic is expressly forbidden—aging. Elderhostel offers "age-segregated programming but with an explicitly 'age-irrelevant' curriculum,"[3] a paradox that keeps the focus on "new powers that can be unleashed in the later years, rather than those which are lost with age."[4] This policy has led to some criticism; David A. Peterson says that "Reluctance to admit that the later years involve any uniqueness or interest contributes to the stereotypes that old age is to be avoided, ignored, or denied and leads to an attempt to be middle-aged forever."[5]

One may argue with the philosophy of Elderhostel, but the formula clearly works. The heft of today's catalogs gives some indication of the scope of the program. Elderhostel's 1995 Spring-Summer U.S. and Canada catalog is 140 tabloid-size pages in dense format; it describes roughly 20 courses per page for a total of about 2,800 courses that encompass the arts (haute and pop); literature; history; the social, physical, and biological sciences; nature and the environment; and imaginative combinations of all of the above. The International Fall 1995 catalog is only slightly less awe inspiring: 120 pages with learning opportunities in 57 countries, including Antarctica, Fiji, the Galapagos, and Tonga. The offerings include not only courses that draw on the natural and historic resources of the local venues, but walking tours, bicycle programs, cruises, barge journeys, and home stays.

A hostel, in the traditional sense, is a place of temporary shelter for travelers, a sparse lodging for people on the move. The word has also been used to denote a residence for students. The name Elderhostel was originally conceived of in those terms, connoting adequate but certainly not luxurious lodgings. In our first conversation with Elderhostel President Bill Berkeley in 1994, anticipating a discussion of lofty theoretical issues, we asked him to talk about the major challenges confronting Elderhostel. Berkeley's answer was prompt and succinct: "Bathrooms." Although older adults delight in most aspects of campus living and are good sports about cafeteria style food and minor inconveniences, they are not prepared at age 70 or 80 to share bathrooms with strangers. The bathroom issue has led to a considerable softening of the meaning of "hostel," a sort of comfort creep. Some universities now house hostelers in nearby motels, and the program descriptions always include an indication of the level of plumbing accommodation to be expected.

The Elderhostel organization has done some basic demographic studies to find out in what ways the population they're serving has changed between 1983, 1989, and 1994. Although the changes are not dramatic, the percent of males in the U.S. and Canada programs has gone up slightly but is still below one-third of the total number of participants (the figure is somewhat higher in the international programs). The number of participants 70 years or older (U.S. and Canada) has risen from 43 percent in 1983 to 58.3 percent in 1994, and the education and income levels are also going up.

According to ES data, 40 percent of Elderhostelers had an income over $40,000, and 66.2 percent had a college or graduate education. Eight individuals, or just over 3 percent, were other than Caucasian.

Berkeley and his staff are not comfortable with these demographics. To broaden the population they serve, they have instituted "hostelships," an effort to ensure that people of limited income can participate. Hostelships are funded by setting aside a small portion of each hosteler's tuition and making the money available to interested but less solvent elderlearners. Berkeley has also tried a number of recruiting strategies to broaden the racial mix, including persuading some black colleges to join the network, but to date he has met with little more success than have other adult education programs.

The appeal of Elderhostel for Third Agers is easily understood. Programs are intellectually challenging without being threatening and hostelers are not burdened with an imposed need to "perform." They combine the romance of travel to interesting places with the opportunity to learn and socialize with interesting peers. Elderhostel's association with colleges and universities gives it a certain cachet. Participants are energized by the mental and social stimulation and feel that they have gained something of permanence that will enhance their lives. Indeed, the term "Elderhostel" has become so engrained in our language that when we speak to colleagues or older adults about elderlearning, the immediate reaction of many is to assume we're talking about Elderhostel. The two terms have become virtually interchangeable in the public mind.

The pervasiveness of Elderhostel in older adult culture is also manifested in other ways. When we were younger, we used to joke that at cocktail parties a useful conversational gambit might be to talk about Club Med or ask for advice about time-share resorts. Now at gatherings of older people, a conversation can usually be initiated by saying something like "Sorry if I start nodding off tonight, but I just got back from an Elderhostel in New Zealand," or "If you were signing up for an Elderhostel in Arizona would you rather study Hopi pottery and kachinas or Navajo weaving?"

But if the enthusiasm of Elderhostelers is easily understood, the reasons for the colleges' participation are somewhat less clear. Hosting an Elderhostel is a major logistical undertaking. The campus coordinator, working with the state program director, has to choose faculty and course descriptions, prepare the dorms or secure outside accommodations, work out a food system, handle the logistics of field trips and special events, arrange for security, and attend to the hundreds of niggling details that make the difference between success and disaster. All this is typically done for a financial return that is barely positive.

So why do they do it? In the beginning, some institutions were just grateful to be able to use their facilities and staff during spring and summer breaks and to enable instructors to augment their salaries by teaching an Elderhostel course. Now, however, with an increasing demand for courses at different times of year, many colleges are using rented motel or hotel space and feeding students off-campus, which ups the cost and cuts the profit margin. Berkeley says the sponsoring institution usually breaks even or a little better. It "depends on the way they keep their books."

Teaching an Elderhostel frequently serves as professional development of a kind different from that which most faculty have experienced. Faculty are freer to conceive courses that reflect their own interests, that break out of the semester strait jacket, that may be unashamedly interdisciplinary, and that break down barriers between orthodox and unconventional subject matter and teaching strategies. For many faculty, it's a heady experience to teach a population that is only there for the sake of learning. Interviews with teachers who have worked with elderlearners sound a repeated note of wonderment at the power of the experience their students bring to class and the "joy" in learning that they convey.

Administrators are also invigorated by the experience of managing an Elderhostel. In an interview, Anne Robichaud, the engaging site director and part-time lecturer in the Assisi program in Italy, said that she had given up a better paying position to work for Elderhostel because "I get so much back from the Elderhostelers; they're so interesting and so well informed, and so generous to me and to each other." Anne's father had recently died, and she had just returned to Italy after a hasty trip home for the funeral. With tears in her eyes, she described what it was like to find four "graduates" of the Assisi program awaiting her arrival in Massachusetts. They had traveled from their New England homes to bring food, to help the family with funeral preparations, and to show their love and support.

Elderhostels are also good public relations vehicles, carrying the message that the host institution "cares" and has a broad vision of education. Within the college community, younger students begin to understand that "learning never ends" is more than just a poster slogan. Such casual contacts as brushing past older adults in the halls between class breaks, eating next to them in snack bars, and showing them how to use the library's online services erode intergenerational barriers and help move the institution toward the ideal of a true learning community.

We suggest a note of altruism in the participation of 1,500 institutions in the Elderhostel program. There are other returns than financial and public relations. Host colleges and universities are helping to usher in an era in which there is wider public acceptance of the idea that lifelong learning for older adults is a valid social goal with predictably positive outcomes.

ELDERHOSTEL SERVICE PROGRAMS

Many Third Agers are willing to pay substantial sums to study Florida's Coral Reef while residing in an air-conditioned motel in Key West, or Big Band Jazz in an oceanfront hotel in San Francisco, or Basic French in a Quebec country inn, but recently Elderhostel has persuaded hundreds of upper middle class seniors to pay for the privilege of performing manual labor in conditions of serious discomfort.

For $2,984 (including airfare),[6] a person can go to Indonesia for three weeks to teach English and help with maintenance projects. Or, if that sounds too physically demanding, for $3,776, he or she can fly to Russia from Los Angeles to provide consulting help to businesspeople, health care professionals, or government administrators. A low budget trip, eight days in Arkansas for only $500 (not including airfare), earns the privilege of repairing furniture for the elderly poor, teaching literacy, and participating in community quilting; for $556, one can do recreational therapy in the Adirondacks at a camp for children with life threatening diseases.

Elderhostelers interested in these programs are warned that food and accommodations may be more "basic" than they are used to, that the work will be demanding and sometimes frustrating, and that there is no guarantee things will run smoothly in developing countries. They will work frequently at menial tasks, while living in crowded quarters where they may share a bathroom with several strangers and have to put up with potentially inept or even hostile local officials. Despite all these disincentives, they still register.

As of 1994, Elderhostel's partners in this Service Program have included Habitat for Humanity International, Global Volunteers (providing citizen-to-citizen contact in the service of world peace), Oceanic Society Expeditions (ecology-related field research expeditions), the San Bernardino National Forest Association, and Double "H" Hole in the Woods Ranch for seriously ill children. These joint ventures, tapping the altruism of the older generation for the betterment of humanity, are run on the premise that volunteering to help other people is part of a commitment to learning and can add meaning to life at any age. Their popularity testifies to the truth of Erikson's description of "generativity" as a positive component of old age.

The Service Programs brochure is quite specific in making the linkage between each volunteer activity and learning. In the traditional language of advocates of experiential learning, it points out that when people are engaged in "significant, genuine service that meets real community needs," learning will occur both as they share their skills and knowledge and as they increase their understanding of the community and of broader social issues.

Learning outcomes are deliberately structured into the Service Programs in three ways. First, it is assumed that informal learning will occur as participants tap into their old skills, learn new ones, work in teams, and face personal challenges. However, this experiential learning is augmented by field trips and discussion of what has been learned. Second, some learning is formally taught: practical skills; the philosophy of the partner organization; knowledge of the history, culture, and environment of the local area; and sensitivity to the social fabric of the community. Third, beyond the formal and informal learning components of the program, participants are given structured time for integrating what they have learned into their lives. "Time for people to think, talk, reflect or write about what they did and saw helps them to incorporate the service experience into their broader life experience in a more meaningful way."

The success of Elderhostel's Service Program is a dramatic illustration of how we might harness older Americans' willingness to give of themselves through volunteer activity, as well as their energy, zeal, and commitment to helping others, to the cause of bettering the lives of the less fortunate around the world. One woman said, "After retiring you're inclined to feel totally selfish. This is a way to give back to the world. It's nice to feel useful."[7]

INSTITUTES FOR LEARNING IN RETIREMENT

Prior to the emergence of Elderhostel, the Institute Movement was already tapping into educated older Americans' passion for learning. Predating the

Universities of the Third Age in the United Kingdom and elsewhere, the first Institute for Retired Professionals (IRP)[8] was started at The New School for Social Research in New York in 1962 by a group of retired teachers. Another Institute followed at Syracuse University in 1975 and at Harvard and Duke universities in 1977. By 1995, over 200 Institutes were in existence and another 40 were in the start-up phase. About 240 colleges and universities from coast to coast have either sponsored or are considering sponsoring this self-governing form of elderlearning. The number of members in each Institute ranges from 40 to 800, but the average is about 220, which means that over 50,000 Third Agers are currently affiliated with postsecondary education through this vehicle. This sizable figure does not appear in the usual data on adult participation in higher education because Institute courses are simply not counted.

It is difficult to talk about the Institutes in ways that their members would recognize because they have evolved in such different directions, taking on some of the coloration of the sponsoring college or university. The PLATO Society at UCLA is the purest peer-run organization. Founded by a group of retired professors, it has proudly retained its original intellectual orientation. Like its academic host, PLATO retains the 15-week semester. Class size is limited to 18, and everybody in a class has responsibility for delivering at least one paper. Harvard's Institute has highly selective admissions criteria and doesn't allow any "how to" courses. The Brooklyn Institute for Retired Professionals and Executives is more eclectic. Its Fall 1994 catalog featured such courses as The History of Microbiology, Jewish Mysticism, and American Playwrights, as well as such "how to" courses as Bridge, Folk Dancing, and Managing Your Money. Institutes hosted by small or community colleges are, like their host institutions, responding to a different set of learning goals and values than those typically found in large universities and Ivy League colleges. They may focus more on the pragmatic, and are more prone to ask outsiders to "teach" some courses rather than relying solely on members' expertise.

Despite great diversity in demographics, and even philosophy, the Institutes' similarities are sufficient to link them in a common cause. The majority of them have been administratively linked since 1987 to Elderhostel's Institute Network, which serves as a coordinating mechanism, publishes a newsletter, and holds leadership workshops across the country.

The major issues agitating the Institutes we visited include parking (a thornier issue in some locations than Elderhostel's bathrooms), shortages of classroom and office space, the number of members to be admitted and the criteria for admission, the degree of oversight and control to be exercised by the host institution, the number of courses an individual can take simultaneously, how to improve the quality of course leadership, the academic level of what is taught, and the amount of overhead the Institute has to pay to the institution.

Most of these issues are discussed and resolved without undue acrimony, but occasionally the level of controversy escalates and positions harden. The Institute for Retired Professionals at the New School for Social Research in New York had its quarrel with the host institution hit the *New York Times*. The New School felt that some Institute courses did not meet its standards for academic quality;[9] that some students were taking too many courses; that the classes were taking up too much space; that the group was insufficiently diverse; and that the older students who tended to "hang out" at the school were negatively impacting its efforts to recruit younger students (this last was implied if never stated). Boiled down to essentials, the major issue was control. An image-conscious dean, who was quoted as saying, "This is a university. We're not a social-service center,"[10] came up against a group proud of its self-governing autonomy. Because of the caliber of its members and the reputation of its host institution, which was renowned for its progressive stance and strong social concerns, the resulting public clash brought irate mail from older students and adult education professionals around the country.

An embarrassed administration handled this dispute in a time-honored way: a commission was convened to take a fresh look at the needs, issues, and opportunities in education for older adults. The commission's final report gracefully declined to take sides, but broke interesting new ground, recommending not a cutback but an expansion of the New School's programs for older learners outside the IRP. It further recommended that the Institute ease space and other frictions by redrawing its course schedule to bring it closer to the School's calendar. The Institute could create greater diversity by establishing a new community service program to provide services to the school itself and a way to earn scholarships for participants. The IRP was also advised to place new emphasis on small seminar-type study groups where serious peer learning can take place, and IRP members were urged to accept *greater* responsibility for administration, thus freeing the director for other conceptual and operational duties. The commission report, while suggesting structural changes that might ease the tensions, was in favor of expanding and strengthening the IRP program and granting it more autonomy rather than cutting it back.

New Institutes may originate through action by the sponsoring college, university, or other learning institution (Carnegie-Mellon University empowered its dean of continuing education to "do something" to increase alumni involvement), or within a group of elderlearners who work together to persuade a college to serve as sponsor. During the developmental phase (anywhere from a few months to two or more years), the Elderhostel Institute Network can assist with workshops and professional consultations until the new Institute is up and running and eligible for full membership status.

Typically, the host college or university provides space and a varying degree of administrative guidance. The Institutes are usually self-governing, making their own decisions about program guidelines, courses, dues and fees, and other by-law issues. Some are financially independent; membership dues and course fees allow them to forego any direct financial support from the college. They may have access to an office, a phone system, a mail permit, or a special rate for printing and copying materials, with or without reimbursement. Others are more dependent, at least in the early years, on actual dollar outlays by the host institution.

Institute governance can be an easy or a thorny issue. Typically, the dean of continuing education or someone in an analogous position is nominally in charge. He or she attends the Institute's leadership group meetings in an advisory capacity, allocates space and resources, serves as boundary spanner between the Institute and the college administration and faculty, and, in general, acts as a facilitator. The Institute members elect their own officers— usually the heads of the membership, admissions, hospitality, and program committees.

Unlike "traditional" adult education programs, Institute courses are given in daylight hours and run for 6 to 15 weeks. They tend to be heavy in surveys in the arts and humanities, interdisciplinary studies, local history, community and intercultural issues, foreign affairs, and current events. The mix of practical and theoretical studies varies, and there are almost always special lecture series, social events, and sponsored expeditions to nearby museums, galleries, historical sites, and theatrical and musical performances.

Institute courses are largely peer-designed and peer-led. The Third Age is about developing wisdom, putting it all together, and integrating the learning of a lifetime. What more natural way to do this than by sharing knowledge and understanding with peers. Institute members tend to be highly educated (52.5 percent hold graduate or professional degrees) and many of them have previously taught. Within the Institute, they may volunteer to coordinate courses, either in their previous field of specialty or in some new field of interest they have pursued in depth. On occasion, college faculty are invited to give a lecture or course, and in some Institutes graduate students have been invited to talk about their research projects or run a seminar on a topic growing out of their research, but these are not the norm.

The level of teaching is often uneven. Successful businesspeople, newspaper executives, physicians, and accountants do not necessarily possess sterling pedagogical skills. We sat in on courses that would have passed muster at an elite university and on others that bravely limped along with minimal content and even more minimal student participation. Quality control is largely by registration: if a group leader's previous course was interesting, his or her next course will attract a sufficient number of students. If it was ill-conceived or boring, word will have spread to avoid it.

The quality of teaching, or group leadership as it is more often called, is an issue of concern at most of the Institutes. With the help of the Elderhostel Network, the Institutes are devising classes, workshops, and tutoring mechanisms to help members learn the rudiments of course design, presentation, group dynamics, and facilitation of discussion that are the hallmarks of successful teaching.

While researching this section of the book, we visited four different Institutes, observing volunteer and intergenerational activities as well as sitting in on classes. In one case, we even attended a meeting of the leadership. In all cases, the level of discourse was high, as was the energy level and the sense of group esteem. Everyone we met wanted to make certain that we understood how important it was that they were teaching and learning together in an academic setting. Members take pride in their participation in the Institutes. They identify strongly with the host campus, are missionary in their zeal to convince outsiders of the worth of what they are doing, want each course to succeed, and expend themselves to that end.

We sat in with a group in Ohio who were studying local history with an elderly gentleman who had lived most of that history. Now frail and partially paralyzed on his right side, he had been driven to school by one of the class members and helped into the classroom by another while the first parked his car. He was greeted and eased into his chair by a woman, apparently an old friend, who took his notes out of his briefcase and arranged them on the table in front of him. His hand-outs were distributed by two others who had positioned themselves in the front row for that purpose. The ensuing brief lecture was given rapt attention, and the following discussion was spirited if not particularly focused. The group was enchanted by pictures of the town's old wharf, market, and city hall, places they had known in their childhood, and they were eager to add their reminiscences to the formal history. There was in that classroom a sense of community, of support for each other, and of excitement at the evocation of the past. We, as outsiders, caught a glimpse in that classroom of the richness of elderlearning, its emotional as well as its intellectual value.

Once again we must ask, what's in it for the sponsoring colleges and universities? If Elderhostels offer potential financial rewards, Institutes are simply an expense. They cost administrative time; they devour, at least at start-up, office expenses (phones, postage, materials, copying services); and they take up scarce classroom space during the middle of the day, the academic prime time. We won't even bring up parking; it's too tender a subject.

In addition to these real costs, Institutes also bring diversity to the campus, and diversity, although desirable, often means conflict. An institution geared to 18- to 24-year-olds must make adjustments for people who may walk a bit slower, dress differently, and complain that the music in the cafeteria is too loud. The abrasion potential is great, but rarely materializes. Instead, most students seem at least bemused to be rubbing shoulders with their grandparents' peers and respond positively to the occasional overtures toward intergenerational learning.

But if the Institutes are worthwhile as models of lifelong learning for younger students, they are also a potential resource for their host campuses. As we noted, participants' pride in being identified with higher education is often generously expressed at fund-raising time, and they are frequently willing to volunteer for jobs that stretch the college's ability to staff offices and keep libraries and museums open longer hours. On some campuses, professors have even found qualified elderlearners willing to read student papers, grade exams, and lend a hand with research projects.

NON-COLLEGE-BASED FORMAL LEARNING

Elderhostel and Institutes for Learning in Retirement are among the best known resources for Third-Age learning, but their identification with colleges limits their primary appeal to largely white, economically comfortable, and highly educated populations.

Other, less well-known, formal learning structures, variously organized and funded, tend to serve a more diverse population. Many of these organizations are community-based and vary widely from location to location. Community senior centers or local and state agencies may focus on services to seniors: Meals on Wheels, transportation to health facilities, financial advising, provision of home health services, and regular social get-togethers. But they may also offer exercise classes, folk dancing, and bridge lessons, which may be as life enhancing as a course in the Russian Revolution. The content of elderlearning is less relevant than the level of interest and cognitive exercise that it elicits from its participants.

Because we cannot cover all the rich variations on the theme of elderlearning, we have chosen to identify a few that offer a vision of what is currently being done and could be done to extend not only life but the quality of life for all older citizens.

OASIS

OASIS began in 1982 when Marylen Mann, a teacher, wrote a grant proposal for a project to serve older adults. Subsequently funded by the May Foundation, OASIS now has 25 OASIS centers, each housed in a May-affiliated department store. Department stores, which by their nature must be located either in the heart of cities or in malls with access to public transportation, are a magnet for a diverse population for whom shopping and recreation are intertwined. As OASIS sites, stores provide free space and utilities, as well as access to a broad spectrum of clients, many of whom would hesitate to venture onto a college campus but are perfectly comfortable in classrooms on the tenth floor behind bedding.

Thanks to its mercantile locations, its explicit mission of inclusiveness, and its flexible programming, OASIS attracts a different and more varied population of Third Agers than we have seen in any other setting. Our visit to the OASIS center located in Kaufman's department store in Pittsburgh was an eye opener in what imaginative administration and programming can do for an older population. Kaufman's provides space and utilities, sends in cakes on members' birthdays, holds special OASIS discount days, invites members to participate in promotional events, and provides a generally welcoming atmosphere.

The Pittsburgh OASIS began in 1989 under its present director, Anita Lopatin, a retired social worker who knows her city, its history, its needs, and all its major players. Starting with three members—herself, her husband, and her mother—she began her campaign to establish the Pittsburgh OASIS by sending out announcements to every social service agency, civic group, church, and local official in the city and the adjoining suburbs. By the end of the first year, this OASIS had 1,000 members, and by 1995, the number of people on the mailing list had grown to 35,000.

May Foundation funding must be matched by local funds. Lopatin has secured her match from the most stable and prestigious of community leaders: the local gas and electric companies, the County Department of Aging, hospitals, health systems, local foundations, and arts organizations. Similarly, she has involved as learning resources a wide network of schools, colleges and universities, churches, social service agencies, and individuals. City hospitals put on a day-long health and wellness seminar each month. A retired CPA teaches the popular course on taxes. Professors from Carnegie-Mellon University were involved in a recent grant-funded course on Re-Emerging Russia. Arts organizations offer discounts to music, dance, and theater events that are well attended. The facilities of a community college were used for a computer course, and the OASIS theater group puts on a play a year under the auspices of a local theater company.

The Pittsburgh Oasis group is widely representative of varying neighborhoods, and of diverse ethnic, religious, and racial groups. It celebrates Martin Luther King day with music and speeches and with the same fervor it gives to Christmas and Chanukah. One way in which Lopatin has attracted diversity is through "Preserve Your Heritage" programs that focus on the culture and language of the many ethnic groups that were attracted to jobs in what used to be called "Steel City." Currently, Polish, Italian, and German groups are meeting regularly, learning or re-learning the languages, cooking, and customs that constitute their culture.

Lopatin waved aside our questions about the economic status of her membership. "Everyone wears their best clothes to come to the center," she says, "so it's difficult to know how rich or poor they are." This lack of stress on people's backgrounds was obviously appreciated by one woman who said, "Nobody here knows the 65 years of shit that I come with, and nobody cares."

Although she has never tried to find out what their incomes are, Lopatin says that when a trip or activity that entails some cost is announced, she has come to know which members will probably not be able to participate unless she asks them to take on a planning or "escorting" role, the reward for which is a reduced fare. She has also managed to set aside special funds for occasional "scholarships."

This OASIS group holds a special place in the community. The chorus, led by two former music teachers, is a staple feature of many Pittsburgh events, meetings, and festivals, and OASIS members are frequently asked to participate in such events as fashion shows and focus groups for local colleges, businesses, and candidates. OASIS is also known as a good source of volunteers. When people are needed to go door-to-door for contributions; do phoning, mailing, and office backup; help out at hospitals or children's homes; or any of the hundreds of nonpaid chores that keep a community healthy, organizations have learned that a single call to the OASIS center produces as many willing and able older adults as they need.

Throughout the country, OASIS centers vary in their makeup, focus, and direction, but the ES allows us to make a few generalizations about them. First, they are the most ethnically and racially diverse of the formal elderlearning programs on which we have data. Twenty respondents (11.2 percent of the sample) were non-Caucasian, accounting for 40 percent of the total minority representation in *all* the groups, although OASIS respondents as a whole were only 21 percent of the total survey population.

They also have a larger proportion of women than any of the other groups, only 38.9 percent of whom are married and living with a spouse. The other 61 percent of women are single, divorced, or widowed, so it comes as no surprise that 68.5 percent include "to meet people" as a reason for their participation. This largely female population tends to have low to moderate incomes, modest educational backgrounds (45 percent have a high school diploma or less), and a higher volunteer rate (84 percent) than any other group. Their reported hours of formal and informal learning are considerably lower than the mean for all groups. However, their enthusiasm for learning, as measured by comments in the margins of the Survey, is intense. Clearly, OASIS is successfully serving a population for which there are few other appropriate learning resources.

LaFarge Lifelong Learning Institute

The LaFarge Lifelong Learning Institute (LLLI) in Milwaukee is unique in that it had its origin in a religious institution. It was organized in 1967 to meet the physical, social, psychological, and spiritual needs of the retired School Sisters of St. Francis. Named after John LaFarge, a Jesuit priest whose *Reflections on Growing Old* is still a classic reference on aging, the Institute quickly grew beyond its specific religious identification to become a nonprofit, nondenominational educational institute separate from the religious congregation.

Today LLLI, committed to the educational well-being of older adults, annually enrolls about 2,500 students over 50 in a menu of more than 120 courses that ranges from Acts of the Apostles to Shakespeare, Forest Resources, American Indian Music, Balloonology, and the wonderfully named Caves, Crypts, Cathedrals.

Although preserving the traditional school structure of teachers, courses, and semesters, LLLI has no tests, grades, or homework, and students learn at their own pace. They may take a given course until they feel they have the knowledge or skill they set out to acquire. For example, they may take anywhere from one to three semesters of Spanish I before choosing to advance to Spanish II.

All the teachers are volunteers, some from academic backgrounds, others skilled in a particular subject or craft. An Educational Exchange Program offers opportunities for intergenerational learning, such as a class on the Magic of Electricity shared with a group of sixth graders, or a country western dance class in which rappers and waltzers high-step together. LLLI seems to be successfully fulfilling its goal as an "anti-aging center," providing "opportunities for growth in wisdom and enhancement of personal dignity."

Other Formal Learning Resources

Formal learning programs for older adults occur in thousands of local, county, and state agencies across the country, as well as in senior centers; 55 Plus Centers; churches and synagogues; local foundations, hospitals and health organizations; city, county, and national parks; YMCAs/YWCAs\YMWHAs; and courses by mail, radio, and television. All these venues differ according to their target population, their resources, and their agendas, but certainly, if their various programs were well publicized, fewer senior citizens would complain of insufficient resources or lack of knowledge of learning resources.

According to ES data, community resources for groups are less used than those community resources (libraries, museums, parks) that can be accessed on an individual basis. The population that turns to community centers or senior centers for formal learning experiences tends to be poorer and less educated. The educational programs available are usually confined to crafts, games, health and exercise, and finances, and emphasize the practical over the theoretical.

The surprise in the survey was that church and synagogue study groups (cited by 21.4 percent of respondents) did not receive a higher ranking as program providers; they are probably the most accessible providers of educational services to older adults through Sunday school classes, Bible study, discussion groups, social concerns, and general values instruction. According to Peterson, three-quarters of all adult education programs in 1979 were offered by churches, and over 5 million people participated in church programs annually.[11] He cites a Harris study (1975) that reported that "Seventy-seven percent of the older respondents . . . had been to a church or synagogue in the past year, substantially more than the number who had been to a library (22 percent)."[12] Either society has been radically secularized in the past 20 years or the ES respondents are uniquely nonchurch oriented, but ES figures do not support Peterson's claims for the dominance of churches in adult education. However, in 1983, in a partial reversal, Peterson said that "the potential of the church has not been fully developed," although he saw signs then that "religious bodies [were] becoming more aware of the needs of older people and that the future may include more educational programs for the elderly by churches."[13] Unfortunately for our purposes, such programs, if they occur, will probably not be tracked or documented.

One can argue whether travel/study programs, such as those sponsored by museums, or alumni, professional, or other affinity groups and by profit and nonprofit organizations, provide formal or informal learning experiences, but they are undeniably the most popular of all learning resources. Chapters 9 and 10 offer further discussion on travel as a means of learning.

A number of other organizations provide formal learning, but time and space forbid our going into detail about their programs. However, a real contribution is being made by 55 Plus, the Shepherd's Centers, YMWCAs, YMWHAs, health care centers, local public access cable television, and other creative local programs that serve older adults. Elderlearning opportunities, despite funding difficulties, are growing rapidly. What is most needed is to devise better connections between individuals' needs and interests and program availability, as well as to find ways to get the institutions' messages out to the community of older adults.

NOTES

1. Eugene S. Mills, *The Story of Elderhostel* (Hanover, NH: University Press of New England, 1993), p. 6.

2. These and the following statistics are from a phone interview with Bill Berkeley, executive director of Elderhostel, January 25, 1996.

3. Mills, p. 155. Quoted from H.R. Moody, "What Can We Learn from Elderhostel?," private paper (January 1990), p. 2.

4. Ibid., p. 156.

5. *Facilitating Education for Older Learners*, pp. 292-93.

6. This and the following prices and destinations are from a 1994 Elderhostel brochure.

7. Enid Nemy, "World of Opportunities for Tirelessly Retired," *New York Times*, August 11, 1994, p. C8.

8. The Institutes go by many different names: e.g., Institute for Learning in Retirement, Institute for Retired Professionals, Academy for Lifelong Learning, Center for Creative Retirement, Worcester Institute for Senior Education, Institute for Lifelong Learning, Third Age Center, Explorer's Institute, PLATO, The Living and Learning Institute, and The Renaissance Society. We shall refer to them generically as "Institutes."

9. The argument for academic quality is difficult to make in a context where students are receiving neither grades nor credit. If the level of the courses is considered sufficiently challenging by the students (who in this case happen to be high intellectual achievers and stringent critics of their own academic fare), one must ask, "Where's the beef?"

10. Maria Newman, "Elderly Angered by Changes for Courses at New School," *New York Times*, February 7, 1994, B7.

11. Peterson, p. 258.

12. Ibid.

13. Ibid., p. 259.

CHAPTER 9

Older Adults' Self-Directed Learning

Now shall I make my soul,
Compelling it to study
In a learned school
Till the wreck of body
. . . Or what worse evil come.

William Butler Yeats, "The Tower"

The still sparse literature on older adult learning places emphasis mainly on the kinds of *formal* learning experiences in which those past 55 or 60 are engaged. There are some data on the numbers of participants in college credit and noncredit courses, community programs, Elderhostels, Learning in Retirement Institutes, and the like, but little data (or seeming interest) exist for the kinds of learning Third Agers are accomplishing on their own.

Independent learning projects, self-initiated and self-designed, constitute a direct response to the learner's own interests, needs, and life style choices. The individual learner sets the goals of the project, decides what resources will be used (usually in accordance with an intuitive or deliberate understanding of his or her own learning style), gauges the learning tasks at comfortable levels, and decides when the task is complete.

The self-directed learning project typically begins with a question, a problem, a need to know, or a curiosity. It is frequently triggered by some event or change in the person's environment. A spouse's heart attack may make imperative an understanding of cardiac diets or of the basics of low fat cooking. Election to the chair of the local arts council may be the impetus for a study of Robert's Rules and sustained research and consultation on how to be an effective leader. Hearing that a favorite author has won the Nobel Prize may spur one to go back and read all of that writer's fiction as well as some critical work. Such projects may be complicated and stretch out over years; some may be circumscribed and doable within hours or weeks. The important thing is that these projects are "owned" by the learner who is in control of what is learned, when the learning starts, where it goes, and when it is complete. There are no outside strictures or time limits, no imposition of subject matter, no questions of credit. Such a project is especially appealing to older adults, who might echo the sentiments one woman wrote at the bottom of her Elderlearning Survey: "As you can surmise from my answers, I love to learn but no longer want to be taught. Lecture sessions now seem to inspire me to write limericks or odes to buzzards."

SELF-DIRECTED LEARNERS

Self-directed learners have many different faces. The myth is that only extraordinarily self-directed individuals engage in self-directed learning. The fact is that almost all of us will choose to learn something on our own at some time in our lives. A census of self-directed learners might look not at all like the usual census of adult learners: white, middle class, and well educated. Such characteristics may be more true of learners in formal settings than of self-directed learners, who showed up in our survey as a much broader population, spanning gender, race, income, and education differences.

In 1971, Canadian researcher Allen Tough was among the first to turn his attention to self-directed learning and learners. In a series of in-depth interviews covering blue collar factory workers, men and women at the lower end of the white collar job scale, teachers, politicians, and housewives, he found that most of us are self-directed learners and that this informal learning goes on throughout the lifespan. Tough's research has led him to believe that what occurs in the classroom is merely the tip of the iceberg. He estimates that 70 percent of all adult learning is self-planned, a figure that holds true for the elderlearners in our survey.

Tough, who conducted his seminal research in Canada in 1970, used the minimum number of seven hours (the equivalent of a working day) of deliberate learning sessions within a period of six months as his criteria for a learning project.[1] However, he found the typical learning project to be far more ambitious, involving 100 hours in which the person's primary intention was to learn. Some educators were skeptical, but subsequent studies in Canada, the U.S., Europe, Africa, and New Zealand confirmed Tough's startling findings on the prevalence of self-generated learning.

About 90 percent of all adults conduct at least one major learning effort each year. The average person conducts five distinct learning projects in one year—that is, in five distinct areas of knowledge, skill, or personal change. The person spends an average of 100 hours per learning effort in a year, which adds up to a total investment of 500 hours in all of his or her efforts in the year. That is almost 10 hours a week, on the average—a lot of time![2]

Tough also notes the existence of "high learners,"[3] who spend about 2,000 hours a year on 15 to 20 projects. A few credible "high learners" surfaced in the Elderlearning Survey, those who said they spent anywhere from 150 to 250 hours per month (2,400 to 3,000 per year) in learning activities for self-directed projects. For example, one ambitious respondent said he was studying philosophy, anthropology, religion, and history to "find man's place and purpose in the universe." Other respondents with similar diligence, though less scope, were studying the history and practice of painting, designing computer applications for a son's business, doing research on the ecosystem of southern California, and keeping up with professional engineering literature.

Although the typical independent learner may seek help or subject matter expertise from a variety of acquaintances, experts, or pre-programmed resources (e.g., textbooks, study guides, computers, television "courses"), the impetus, the subject, and the point at which the learning is deemed complete are at the sole discretion of the individual.

THE STRUCTURE OF SELF-GENERATED LEARNING

A self-generated learning project usually goes through the following stages:

- the idea (or impetus)
- the plan
- the search for resources
- the learning
- the evaluation of the learning as complete

These stages may or may not be systematically approached. The learning may expand beyond or contract within the original intent. Outcomes may or may not be satisfactory. Despite frequent changes of direction, glitches in the learning process, or interruptions caused by environmental changes in one's life, surprisingly successful learning continues.

Unless the learner is of an unusually orderly turn of mind, self-directed learning projects are rarely outlined or planned in detail. Like Topsy, they just grow as newly discovered resources attract and interests expand until, at some point, the desired information or skill is deemed acquired or complete. The criteria for completion are internal—when the individual has learned enough to solve the problem, to improve skills, to perform satisfactorily, or to satisfy curiosity. Some projects are narrowly focused and can be accomplished within hours or weeks, e.g., learning how to prune roses. Others are never-ending, e.g., the quest for the perfect rose. One woman, after eight years' work on her family genealogy, could go no farther and had to declare herself finished; she complained that she was bereft, likening her state to a post-partum depression. This depression lasted only until she decided to follow up the genealogical research with a narrative history of her own and her immediate family's life.

RESOURCES FOR SELF-GENERATED LEARNING

The resources with which people carry out their self-directed learning projects are varied and usually represent their conscious or intuitive perceptions of their own learning styles. Printed materials are basic: books, magazines, newspapers, catalogs, sets of directions, programmed texts. Although the frequently predicted (and lamented) end of reading may be at hand for younger people, the older generation is still print-oriented. Bookstores, libraries, and friends' bookshelves are often the first port of call for a new project, and book sellers and librarians the first resources to be consulted. In the survey, an astonishing 74.7 percent of respondents included reading as one of their primary ways of learning.

Other people—friends, neighbors, experts, teachers, mentors, tutors—are usually involved in self-directed learning projects at some stage. They may be consulted in the early stages to help set the direction, to identify resources, to encourage, or to demonstrate skills and knowledge for the learner to observe. They may advise, instruct, encourage, oversee, or even be asked to evaluate. They may also serve as paid or unpaid tutors or as teachers or consultants. Some learners who enjoy working with others may try to form an informal study or discussion group of like-minded learners with whom they can share their ideas. Others may use a community resource as the starting point for their own learning. For example, they may attend a museum lecture series on impressionist art as a springboard for their own study of late nineteenth-century art; they may sign up for a demonstration of fishing tackle at a local sports store as part of learning how to fly fish.

Television is another familiar resource, especially useful for the physically handicapped or for those who are afraid to drive at night or are otherwise housebound. It is fashionable to deride the television culture; but if one chooses programs carefully, the amount of information and knowledge available is rich in quality of content and presentation. However, such sources as Public Television and the Discovery Channel, good as they are, may be less useful to persons who know precisely what they wish to study; relevant programs may not be available or scheduled exactly when the learner needs them. Even in the age of television, radio also remains an important source of information and is particularly important for people studying politics, community affairs, and music, as well as for the vision-impaired.

THE COMPUTER IN SELF-DIRECTED LEARNING

The omnipresence of computers and computer-spawned information and communication tools in the late twentieth century has provided an interesting case study of a technology that is both a resource for learning and a motivation for learning new skills. The computer can serve brilliantly as teacher or tutor through professionally designed programs that impart a wide variety of skills and information—from basic literacy to animal husbandry to foreign languages to macro-economics. But the computer also demands that you learn its ways. The tool is the subject as well as the resource, a subject with its own language of RAM and ROM, bits and bytes. Learning to use the computer, to exercise its inherent power, is one of the most common learning tasks undertaken by older adults. An astonishing amount of the formal and informal learning detailed in the Elderlearning Survey has to do with learning word processing, spreadsheets, databases, networking, and the Internet. One needs to learn the basics of computers before one can use them to access information and gain skills. Although there is no way of tracking how many older adults took computer classes, 71 respondents reported learning to use the computer as a self-directed learning project, and many more reported using it as a tool for research in other areas, such as genealogy. From November 1995 to mid-February 1996, when the survey data were being received and compiled, the dramatic emergence of the Internet as an elderlearning tool could be tracked. Out of the first 400 respondents, only three said that they were either learning how to use the Internet or using it as a learning resource. By the 860th survey, the number had quadrupled, and 85-year-olds were surfing the Net.

The emergence of a sizeable population of senior hackers is a powerful argument against the shibboleth that older people are afraid to learn new things. Some are becoming avid cyber-granddads and grandmas, putting games on their machines to play with younger grandchildren and using e-mail to keep in touch with the older ones at college. Others are using computers to research their family history, keep up with professional literature, track their finances, or catalog their CDs.

TRAVEL AS A LEARNING RESOURCE

A discussion of whether sponsored study/travel is a formal or informal mode of learning can generate considerable heat among educators, but there is no controversy about the clearly informal learning that individuals or families do on their own. Like the travel experience itself, the processes of preparing itineraries; studying maps; looking up sites of interest; reading about the history, lore, and culture of destinations; and finding suitable accommodations have clear learning components. Whether these components are significant depends upon the methods used and the quality of learning achieved, but such pedagogical concerns are misplaced. The important thing about travel as a mode of learning for Third Agers is that it is stimulating, it enlarges horizons, and it is enjoyable. As we noted in Chapter 6, the overwhelming interest in travel is consistent throughout the ES: 51.6 percent report significant travel-related learning, 55.7 percent name it as a learning style preference, and 55 percent say that they learn on their own through travel. (For further discussion of travel as a learning resource, see Chapter 10.)

WHAT ARE SELF-DIRECTED LEARNERS LEARNING?

The subjects of self-directed learning may be practical or skills-oriented (crafts, income tax preparation, health) or creative and intellectual (music, memoir writing, existential philosophy). Topics may be as earthbound as learning how to build and use a compost pile or as otherworldly as studying the effects of phases of the moon on spiritual awareness (one of the respondents reported this). Our initial research suggests that self-directed learning is far more prevalent and substantial than previously thought and has potential significance for looking at health and life style issues in an aging population.

Molly Dillon is typical of the kind of self-directed learner who continues to grow and learn as she ages.

> Molly is a 72-year-old widow living in a small town in the Midwest. Molly left college to marry Joe, who had just gotten a medical discharge from the Marines for shrapnel wounds received on Guadalcanal. Joe and Molly used his discharge money and cash wedding presents to buy a small feed store in their hometown. While bearing and raising their three children, Molly learned accounting and marketing to help grow the business. Eventually, the couple expanded the store into a discount warehouse, the profits of which sent all three children to college and two of them to graduate school.
>
> When Joe reached 67, they turned the business over to their youngest son, dipped into their savings, and took off on an African safari. Inexperienced travelers, Joe and Molly did a lot of preparation for this trip: reading travel books, attending slide shows sponsored by a local museum, thumbing through old *National Geographics*, and finding out about visas, currency restrictions, required shots, and weather conditions. They bought Joe a new pair of field glasses for bird and animal watching and Molly a video camcorder, which she learned to operate with the help of a friend.
>
> The trip was as wonderful as Joe and Molly had hoped it would be, but on their way home Joe took sick. By the time they got home, Molly had to take him by cab from the airport directly to the hospital. A week later, Joe

died. Before Molly had even unpacked their bags, she was making funeral arrangements and coping with the emotional, financial, and practical effects of her loss.

Molly's grieving was profound, but she had a strong support system of family and friends. As Joe's business partner, she knew that she was not rich; but if she sold her house and moved into a small apartment outside town, she would have enough to live on comfortably.

Fortunately, Molly's energy and civic involvement as well as her long-deferred interests in art and politics quickly took over most of her time. As a member of the League of Women Voters, she now had time to volunteer to work on research to help her chapter decide how they would respond to a referendum on term limits, and also agreed to expand her financial skills to serve as their treasurer. The week at Joe's bedside had also taught her how understaffed the local hospital was, so she signed up for a six-week class for volunteers on how to perform nonmedical patient services, which she now does for one day a week. But the most rewarding of her activities was to take up painting, which she hadn't done since college.

Molly began by taking a class at the local "Y" to get up her artistic courage and to re-learn watercolor technique. Six months later, she joined the local Artists Association and had one of her paintings accepted for their spring exhibition. Over the next few years, using art textbooks and critiques from fellow artists, Molly worked at figure drawing, acrylics, and color theory, began entering regional shows, and had a one-person show at the hospital. She also developed an art history reading list on water color technique in Europe and Asia. Molly's paintings are beginning to sell, which gives her great satisfaction.

When she was asked by a local travel society to talk about her safari to Africa, Molly got up the courage to look at her videos of the trip for the first time since Joe died. She was surprised at how good they were, but not good enough to be shown to strangers. At first she thought she'd just say no, but instead she trotted down to her local photography store to rent editing equipment and get some practical tips. Molly spent three weeks paring down five hours of tape to one and a half hours and writing her script before presenting her "show" to the group. It was a hit.

Recently, feeling a need for ongoing criticism and support as an artist, Molly rented a studio with two other women, a painter and a sculptor. Last year, for the first time, Molly's art "business" showed a slight profit, just enough, she jokes, to keep up with the cost of living. She plans to use the extra money for a trip to the museums and art centers of Europe, combining her love of travel and of art.

Molly's old friends marvel at her energy and good health, which she attributes to keeping mentally active. Her children tease her that with all her activities, they have to make dates just to visit with the grandchildren, but Molly knows that she's made enough brownies and gone to enough Little League games and piano recitals to earn her stripes as a grand-mother. She recounts with glee that last year when the town celebrated "Take Your Daughter to Work Day," 11-year-old Sally elected to spend the day in Molly's studio rather than in her mother's insurance office.

Molly has learned an impressive amount in the five years since Joe died. In a sense, she has invented a new life for herself. Aside from the coping techniques she's devised to keep her life on an even keel without Joe, she's rediscovered old skills and developed new ones through self-initiated and self-directed learning. The significant learning she's accomplished on her own includes

- how to research and present political issues, including term limits, civil rights legislation for gays, anti-pollution measures, and child abuse, all subjects Molly took on for the League of Women Voters
- fiscal management for a nonprofit organization (the League of Women Voters)
- patient services in a hospital setting—needs and modes of delivery
- advanced water color technique, figure drawing, composition, and use of acrylics, oils, and mixed media
- displaying art and managing and publicizing an art business
- art history and the development of water color techniques in Europe and Asia
- editing videotape and preparing a script for presentation

Molly's accomplishments as an elderlearner are remarkable, but not all that unusual. Over the past few years, we have interviewed hundreds of self-motivated learners embarked upon learning projects as diverse as constructing a salt water aquarium, researching family history, learning how to manage money, studying early childhood psychology, and acquiring marketing skills—a list as diverse and creative as the people doing the learning. Each of these learners is achieving an intellectual independence that is a source of joy and pride. Many also report a sense of physical and mental renewal.

It is sometimes difficult to convince self-directed learners that they are indeed really learners. When we questioned one man in his eighties, a Civil War buff who had spent the previous 20 years reading articles and books, visiting battle fields, viewing films and videos, attending meetings of historians, lecturing to groups, and even writing articles for the local newspaper, he at first told us that he hadn't done much learning since high school. His definition of learning was narrowly confined to sitting in classes in a formal school setting. It took a while to persuade him that his self-generated Civil War projects had resulted in genuine, college-level learning.

The broad range of self-generated elderlearning gives the lie to notions of restricted horizons in old age. The last two items on the Elderlearning Survey ask for an estimate of how many hours are spent *per month* on self-generated learning projects and a brief narrative account of what is being learned and how. Out of 865 respondents, 46 percent chose not to answer one or both questions. This is not surprising, given the length and complexity of the survey. The 54 percent response to both questions is thus a tribute to elderlearners' belief in the importance of their learning.

In 1977, P. Penland, in her study of self-planned learning,[4] classified learning projects into three subject matter groups.

- *Formal Topics*—history, languages, science, math, literature, other kinds of formal (academic) learning
- *Practical Topics*—job related, home related, hobbies/crafts, health, sports/games, technologies, travel, civics, etc.
- *Intraself Topics*—religion, psychology, philosophy, sensory awareness, music, art, politics, nature, relationships

Although Penland's subjects were a representative sample of American adults across the board, and ours, almost 20 years later, are confined to Third Agers, over half of whom have some connection with an adult learning organization, we still thought a comparison might prove useful.

	Penland (1977)	Elderlearning Survey (1996)
Formal Topics	6.9 %	27 %
Practical Topics	75.9 %	52 %
Intraself Topics	17.2 %	21 %

The significant gain in the number of formal and intraself learning topics explored at the expense of the number of practical topics was not unexpected. Elderlearners are at an age and stage in which they can indulge their previously submerged interests in the purely abstract and intellectual (formal) or the personal (intraself). They have been relieved of the necessity to keep up with the changing demands of their jobs, and they are less interested in such purely practical functions as car repair and mechanics. They do spend considerable time on health-related topics (medical information, diet, exercise, personal care), and they now have the time to take up hobbies and crafts, and gardening projects.

Elderlearners' specific interests are significantly different from those of Penland's broader group. For one thing, Penland could not have guessed in 1977 that over 15 percent of those in the Elderlearning Survey would report that they are independently studying how to use computers, or using computers to study other subjects. These results challenge any lingering perception of older people as resistant to technology. The most prevalent subjects of independent learning are arts and crafts: music, painting, sculpting, theater, quilting, embroidery, and wood carving. These subjects account for 19.6 percent of self-directed learning. Genealogy or family history, which is vital for understanding one's life and for passing knowledge on to the next generation, accounts for 7 percent of self-directed learning, although in terms of time expended it is probably first. The older adults' search for wisdom and spirituality expresses itself through the 7 percent of self-generated projects relating to Bible study and religion.

The choice of learning that Penland calls "practical" is a further reminder that when people have time to pursue areas of self-expression, they may turn to creative activity[5]; 15.5 percent report self-directed arts and crafts projects, some of them quite extensive. Many more are learning to play an instrument or taking up photography or dance. At a time of life when one's financial resources may be limited, 5 percent have designed projects to learn more about managing their money. For many people, self-directed learning is undertaken to help them in their volunteer activities: putting together a Bible study curriculum, learning Braille to work with the blind, reading child psychology texts, researching a town's architectural history for a restoration project. Other subjects include health-related topics, preparation for travel, sports, gourmet cooking, nautical skills—the list is as inventive and intriguing as the people involved.

Despite the variety and amount of recounted learning in the survey, we know from our in-depth interviews that self-directed learning is still vastly under-reported in a paper-and-pencil questionnaire. Tough needed a two-hour interview for the intensive probing that he did in his original study. Many people still do not take seriously any learning, whether their own or others, that lacks "academic" subject matter, that does not take place in a classroom, that is not designed and led by an "expert," or that does not carry the imprimatur of a recognized institution. In interviews, one can tease out at least double the amount of time and effort that people report for active, independent learning on questionnaires.

A close friend who had volunteered to fill out the Survey reported 20 hours per month of self-directed learning. Because he was not anonymous, we confronted him directly: What about your sustained reading over the past two years about the history of Maine? What about your passionate involvement in local and national politics, for which you read at least two newspapers per day and a number of journals? What about your research for the Foreign Affairs Council? What about preparation for the series of lectures you're giving to the chamber music society on the evolution of the form? What about the recorder lessons you're taking and the hours of practice? What about learning your way around the Internet? The list went on and on. By the time we finished, our friend "admitted" to at least 10 hours per day in active engagement with learning, or 300 hours per month. A true "high learner," his learning is more than equivalent in time to a full-time job, but it took concentrated probing to enable him to recognize and name it.

To get at what we thought might be the other end of the learning spectrum, we interviewed a former housekeeper, a woman who had come to the U.S. as a war bride in the late 1940s. After a divorce, she had supported three children by giving French lessons, working as an aide in a home for retarded children, and running her own home cleaning service. Now retired to Arizona, she professed to be content simply to stay at home and look at the mountains, but upon close questioning we learned that since moving there a year ago she has made a careful study of desert plants so that she can continue her former interest in gardening in a radically different environment. She has also made a deliberate effort to learn about the geology and geography of her new home state, and has embarked on a reading program that she found in an old magazine that includes major works of nineteenth-century fiction from the U.S., Russia, England, and France. She has even begun writing the story of her life as a Belgian war bride. Her total learning time, completely self-generated, was conservatively put at 75 hours per month.

A similar disparity between actual and reported self-generated learning was uncovered in every face-to-face or phone interview we have conducted. People just don't recognize themselves as avid learners, particularly if they have a strong background in formal education. One physician runs a department in a major medical school, does important research, gives papers at conferences around the world, and keeps broadly informed on a number of nonmedical topics. He reported only one self-directed learning activity: learning to make bread. He estimated his informal learning time as 20 hours per month, and when teased about this said he didn't think learning done as part of one's profession counted!

The results of the ES are totally consonant with the earlier work of Tough and Hiemstra in terms of the prevalence of self-directed or informal learning. 78.3 percent of the respondents chose to answer the following question: "How many hours per month do you spend in informal learning?"[6] Their answers ranged from 1 hour to 300 hours, with a mean of 27.86 and a median of 20 hours. The comparable figures for formal learning were a range of 1 to 160 hours with a mean of 17.47 hours and a median of 12 hours. The enormous numerical advantage of self-directed learning over formal learning would have been even greater had the respondents been interviewed face-to-face rather than asked this question in a paper-and-pencil exercise. (For further discussion of the ES data on self-directed learning, see Chapter 6.)

THE SIGNIFICANCE OF SELF-DIRECTED LEARNING

If self-directed learning is ubiquitous, if it is already occurring without outside support among broad segments of the population, and if it seems to be thriving without any academic or legislative help, what does that mean to our society? Is there any point in trying to facilitate or increase such learning?

First, it means that lifelong learning is a reality. Second, it means that the educational establishment, as currently positioned, is largely irrelevant to a hefty chunk of the learning going on among the population. Third, it means that self-directed learning can be a potent force against the possibility of premature decline and dependency in old age.

A narrative response to the ES from a former colleague is a moving example of how self-directed learning can help one cope with a major life crisis. Since his wife was diagnosed with Alzheimer's, Dr. K., a noted educator, has "been in a continual process of trying to keep up with what's known and, given my questioning habits, what *I can learn by observing and working with Ruth and her caregivers.*" In the course of this process, Dr. K. has subscribed to a health letter, used the resources of his health service, consulted with medical experts at Johns Hopkins, facilitated Ruth's participation in research projects, and, most important, used informed observation to study the progress of the disease as it gradually erodes the cognitive processes. He has managed to stay totally engaged at an emotional level with his wife, even as she regresses to childlike behavior: playing with her, feeding her, reading to her, attempting through every possible device to stimulate the brain cells that are still intact. On another level, he has intellectualized what he and she are going through, learning more about learning by noting in meticulous detail the reverse process of unlearning.

> My theory was that if one practiced mental capabilities (such as reading and talking about the reading), one would keep rebuilding capability, etc. Ruth and I, in those early days of her Alzheimer's, would read Winnie the Pooh as well as political news. Initially she preferred to do the reading; later she no longer could. I often wondered during those days whether she *understood* the meaning of the words she was mouthing. One evening I found out: in reading Winnie the Pooh to me, she accidentally substituted an exact synonym for the word that was on the page.

CONCLUSION

Older people come to learning, whether self-generated or formal, with a lifetime of experience in which to ground new data, concepts, and theories. They are uniquely able to question old truths or to test the applicability of those truths to specific situations. The richness of their backgrounds contributes to the richness of their response to unfamiliar constructs, and the results of their learning add immeasurably to their own sense of the meaning of their lives. But the benefits do not stop with the individual learner. The zest and commitment to learning of elderlearners, their continuing growth and development at a time when they might be expected to sit back and let life happen, are modeling a new vision of old age for their children and friends, who are encouraged to face their own aging with more positive attitudes.

If we are agreed that learning at all ages, including older ages, is good for society, then we should look for ways to encourage and support such learning. We can do a few simple, relatively inexpensive things.

- help teachers at all levels learn how to encourage learning as a self-initiated process, so that students of all ages will have the tools to be lifelong independent learners
- encourage libraries to make certain that librarians or aides are available to help older adults identify and find the kinds of information they need
- set up local education information networks, print or computer-based, for older adults, the majority of whom report that they lack knowledge of what resources are available
- set up in schools, libraries, or senior centers a system of learning counselors who are specifically trained to help people plan their own learning projects and find the resources and support they need

These steps would not only give specific assistance to self-directed learning, but would also constitute recognition of the worth of such learning. Such recognition would go a long way toward validating and dignifying the learning experiences in which millions of older Americans are engaged.

NOTES

1. In the Elderlearning Survey, a learning project is defined as taking a minimum of 10 hours. That figure eliminates relatively simple, delimited learning tasks such as learning to program the VCR or mastering a new knitting stitch.

2. "Interests of Adult Learners," in *The Modern American College*, edited by Arthur Chickering and Associates (San Francisco: Jossey-Bass, 1981), p. 297.

3. *Adults' Learning Projects* (Toronto: Ontario Institute for Studies in Education, 1971), p. 28.

4. Discussed by K. Patricia Cross in *Adults as Learners* (San Francisco: Jossey-Bass, 1981), p. 188.

5. Penland classified crafts as "practical" and art and music as "intraself," a distinction that is difficult to maintain. Whether someone is designing new patterns for quilts, learning to play the mandolin, or painting in acrylics, the activity would seem to express a common urge towards "creativity."

6. We assume that the majority of the 21.7 percent who did not answer the question are also self-directed learners. All humans all are, whether we recognize it or not. But the question came at the end of a long and probably tedious survey; the respondents may either have become impatient by then or, as some of their comments indicate, simply found it too difficult to try to figure out how much time they were spending in learning on their own.

CHAPTER 10

Modes of Learning for Older Adults

The young sow wild oats. The old grow sage.

Sir Winston Churchill

I f we take as a given that the phenomenon of elderlearning is a social good, then how Third Agers learn must be of concern both to program administrators and policy makers. These "hows," as they emerged from the Elderlearning Survey, point the way to both traditional and newer, technology-driven modes of learning that older adults are already employing and that would ease the transition to distance learning methodologies capable of reaching all seniors.

The strong preference of many older adults for traditional group learning cannot be ignored. Group learning gives the older person a reason for getting out, an opportunity for social exchange with peers ("meeting people" in ES terms), as well as the mental exercise of testing their cognitive powers in peer group discussion. Group learning *is* learning for most of the older generation, who grew up defining the word in terms of desks lined up in a row in a formal classroom. 68.4 percent of the ES respondents said they preferred classes, workshops, and seminars; only 22.8 percent checked "learning alone" (even though more of their reported learning is self-directed than classroom-based).

However, group learning is not always practical or possible. Some older adults cannot leave an ailing spouse or relative. Some live far from learning centers or have no ready means of transportation, even to a nearby senior center. Some are handicapped or physically unable to leave their homes. Must these older adults forego the intellectual and health benefits of active involvement in the learning process?

Third Agers, through their learning mode preferences, are already pointing the way to new solutions to these problems. In this chapter, we shall deal with both old and new learning modes that can shape the future of elderlearning. We shall also examine the role of travel in Third Age learning.

LIBRARIES

Because the committees that fund U.S. libraries believe libraries are valuable learning resources for their communities, librarians are constantly undertaking demographic studies to support that belief.

In 1948, the Public Library Inquiry (PLI), commissioned from the University of Michigan's Survey Research Center, delivered news librarians didn't want to hear. The survey showed that only 18 percent of adults and less than 50 percent of children had used the public library in the preceding year. Moreover, the users were overwhelmingly white, middle class, and well educated.[1]

In 1991, the National Center for Education Statistics (NCES) conducted a phone survey of a random sample of adults on library usage. The NCES survey showed library use up dramatically. The number of adults reporting library use in the past year had risen to 53 percent, almost three times as many as in the 1948 survey. The majority of these users were young adults (18-24), presumably doing college work or research on occupations; next in frequency were users in their thirties (62 percent) and forties (58 percent). Unfortunately, most of these users were also largely white, middle class, and well educated, although the relative percent of blacks and Hispanics was rising. Only one-third of older adults (over 65) were users,[2] a number well below ES statistics.

The ES responses on library use by older adults are significantly more positive, and the numbers are internally consistent. When asked what resources they use on their own, 47.2 percent of respondents included libraries, the third most popular choice. When asked what community resources they use, 41 percent said libraries, the most popular choice; churches and synagogues (28.5 percent) were a distant second.

The current older generation is a natural consumer of what is still libraries' primary commodity—print-based materials. Older adults were raised in a society in which "literacy" meant books, not computers. Reading ranks first among their preferred learning styles, cited by an impressive 74.7 percent. At this time of life, reading is most often optional, recreational, or curiosity-driven rather than required.

Technology gives libraries the potential to assume an even more important role in elderlearning. They can stock more large print books and pressure publishers to broaden the kinds of material they publish in that format. They can provide computer searches for learning resources and Internet access for those who do not have their own computers. They can, and most already do, lend from a rich store of books on tape, recorded lectures, videos, computer programs, compact disks, and CD-ROMS. They can communicate with older patrons in person or by phone, fax, or e-mail. They can support self-directed learning. They can become the primary university of the Third Age.

To move libraries to a position of centrality in elderlearning would require only a few adjustments to current library practices. Most libraries are already well on the way to diversifying their collections and their lending practices. However, they must add to their high-tech holdings and delivery mechanisms the "high touch" that will support older learners' needs. The allocation of librarians' time must include time spent helping older patrons find their way around what may be to them a whole new universe of resources. Some of us had a hard time mastering the microfiche machines; now we're traveling in cyber space. The intricacies of getting on and off the Web may come easily to 15-year-olds weaned on joy sticks and computer logic; they are bewildering to those who grew up on books and card catalogs in alphabetized drawers.

Libraries will need to "teach" seemingly user-unfriendly technologies to older adults, and librarians must learn how to convey information at times, in language, and at a pace that facilitates older adult learning. Gyms and exercise centers now offer the free services of personal trainers to help novices create exercise programs designed for their unique needs. Libraries should also have personal "learning trainers" to help novices learn how to use their facilities and new machines. Librarians might also support self-generated learning by designating specific personnel, perhaps reference librarians, to work with individuals who need help in defining the scope and direction of an independent learning project or locating appropriate resources to carry it out.

Most important, libraries will have to reach out to elderlearners through announcements in publications that seniors read, through use of targeted mailings, through any and every relevant communications medium. Librarians can offer workshops in local agencies, senior centers, and retirement communities. The message must be that "your" library wants to introduce you to specific offerings and services that can help you do what you want to do. Our librarians will help you learn how to use technologies that will enable you to access books, magazines, tapes, and other sources of information and recreation. You can do this even from your own home, in ways that are adaptable to your own needs. You can't access a learning resource you don't know about or by which you are intimidated.

COMPUTERS AS LEARNING TOOLS

Computers are now indispensable tools for resourcing information. They are not displacing print materials; they are enlarging access to them and enhancing them with audio and visual components. They are also creating new formats, new ways of thinking about knowledge, new skills in information retrieval.

Until recently, the computer's image had three major associations. The first was with business; word processing, databases, spread sheets, and marketing data give corporations and small businesses alike a competitive edge. The second association was with science; computers can do arcane calculations of the size of the universe or the mating habits of houseflies in nano-seconds. The third, and perhaps most pervasive, association of computers is with the young, with computer gamers and hackers, programmers and computer nerds obsessed with new worlds bounded only by the unfettered imagination.

Even mighty IBM, intent on cornering market share in main frames, failed until almost too late to foresee the eventual dominance of personal computers as they became part of domestic life. Today the PC is in over a third of U.S. homes, a repository for recipes and budgets, book lists and income tax information, and letters to Aunt Bessie and the insurance company. Computers can now be bought off the shelf at department stores or discount houses, by phone or mail, at prices lower than ever dreamed of by Thomas J. Watson, the founder of IBM.

Where college freshmen once packed new portable typewriters, they now pack Toshiba "notebooks" complete with modems, CD-ROMS, and more memory than ever dreamed of a mere 20 or even 10 years ago. And their new college address is more often an e-mail station than a postal zip code.

So where does all this leave older adults? Are they too old to learn new technologies? According to the ES, the answer is no. Third Agers' interest in computers—and ability to use them—is matching or exceeding their own middle-aged children's interest and ability. Perhaps retirement gives Third Agers more time to explore computers. Respondents to the ES reported learning about computers "to keep up with changing times," "so I won't feel 'out of it,'" "to understand the world my grandchildren will live in," "because it's fun to try something that's so new," or "so we won't get left behind." (This last comment is from a couple aged 85 and 79.)

13.6 percent of all ES respondents cited the computer as a preferred learning style (19.5 percent of males). When asked what they chose to learn, 32.2 percent of all respondents cited computers (37.9 percent of males). The male-female differences are not surprising given the prevalence of sexual stereotypes about women and technology; the surprise is that so many women are challenging the stereotypes. Moreover, the interest in computers holds fairly steady across all ages from 55 to 95 and is not markedly influenced by previous education or income.

And they *are* learning about computers, in classes at schools, computer stores, senior centers, bookstores, and retirement centers; on their own by trial and error, with books and manuals, with programmed learning texts, and with help from friends, neighbors, and grandchildren. (See Chapter 9 for a discussion of computers in self-directed learning.) We recently attended two classes on the Internet, one in the offices of a company that manages an Internet linking service, one in a public school that is making a deliberate attempt to get an entire community online. Neither was advertised as being for senior citizens, but 70 to 80 percent of the students in both were over 65.

In addition to learning *about* computers, elderlearners are learning *with* computers. Computers have long been touted as powerful learning tools, but for too long computer-generated learning was stuck in a primitive mode. The earliest programs were primarily rote learning drills transferred from old-fashioned workbooks to the electronic screen. Their only advantage over the paper-and-pencil exercises was that young people seemed more motivated by a medium that could be manipulated and gave them direct feedback. More recently, however, with the advent of the CD-ROM, which enables the learner to see, hear, and work with an animated, interactive program, computer learning has become more imaginative and engrossing.

All too often technology is thought of as hard, cold, and unresponsive to human need. The demand for more computers in classrooms is looked upon with undisguised horror by those who feel that the future of books, even of humanistic education, is at stake. If we were ever tempted to think in that way, our experience of what computers can do for elderlearners has changed our minds.

Recently, in preparation for travel, Lois Lamdin's spouse has been learning conversational Italian on a CD-ROM program. The narrator makes a statement, such as "The dog is in the garden." The learner hears the sentence, a dog appears on the screen and begins barking, and the statement is repeated, this time as a question. There is a pause for the learner to answer the question. If he wishes, he can play back his own answer to hear how he sounds. Gradually, his voice takes on the lilt and accent of the teacher. The simple dialogue extends into a conversation, appropriately illustrated and with sound effects. He is introduced to pronoun and verb changes as they occur naturally. He can repeat a section until he's learned it, go back to an earlier section, or go on to the next lesson, all at his own pace. A "help" section offers access to a dictionary, a pronunciation guide, verb construction, etc. There are tests when he wants them, but he doesn't have to take them. There are no time constraints and no competition. The program is completely self-paced, putting the learner in total control. If the sun is shining, he can turn off the computer and go for a walk. If it's raining, he can stay at the computer for hours. It's as though the programmer had designed it expressly for the needs of older adults. What a powerful (and congenial) way to learn—and no worries about bad weather, night driving, parking, or handicap accessibility.

Language study is an especially dramatic example of the computer as a tool for learning, but the ES respondents have found many others. They report using genealogical programs to structure their search for family information, financial programs to learn how to manage their money, online news reports to keep up with politics, geography and encyclopedia programs to plan their travel, and CD-ROMs of great art collections to study Renaissance painting. They dial onto online interest groups in organic gardening, self-help therapies, World War II history, pets, and astronomy. No area of study seems to lack a home on the Web.

The obvious objection, the one we would have made ourselves a few years ago, is that nothing can take the place of human interchange in learning. That is probably true, but the advantages of discussion in a social situation are not always available. Let us take as an example a 75-year-old woman, eager to be able to speak and understand her father's native language before visiting relatives in Berlin. She has a low-to-moderate income and lives in the suburbs, far from mass transportation. How is she to learn German in a classroom setting? Chances are poor that a local college would have a first level course at a convenient time and place, but even if it did, how would she get there, how would she pay for it, and how could she keep up with the 20-year old language majors or the corporate executive preparing for a marketing trip to Munich? Would she want to? How much more convenient for that woman to call the library and ask them to mail her a CD-ROM German program.

But what about the hardware? How can older people afford to buy comput-ers? That may not be a major problem. A 1994 telephone survey by SeniorNet found that 21 percent of older adults already own computers, and 87 percent believe that "older adults should have the same access to advanced services as any other age group."[3] Today, the number of Third-Age computer-owners is growing even more rapidly. Moreover, hardware prices continue to drop. Today a bare bones system, with CD-ROM capacity and a modem, can be had for under $1,000, a price that is within the financial reach of many older persons. Nor is the price beyond the reach of a caring society eager to find ways to lend computers to those unable to afford them. Portable computers, easy for older people to handle, purchased by government or charitable organizations, could be borrowed or rented (through libraries perhaps). The return to society from seniors' improved quality of life, mental and physical health, and con-nectedness to their world would more than repay the investment.

SeniorNet, a nonprofit organization founded in 1986, is one of the "new wave" learning organizations building new rooms in our learning system. Its membership has grown from 22 in 1988 to more than 17,000 today, and it is still rapidly expanding. Members live in all 50 states and several foreign countries. About half the members are students or volunteers at the organization's 75 Learning Centers where they either take or teach computer classes specifically designed for older adults. The others participate through SeniorNet's electronic community, SeniorNet Online.

The SeniorNet Online members are an intriguing example of "high tech, high touch." Here are thousands of people from 55 to over 90, separated by distance but forming a virtual community. Their discussion groups cover everything from bird watching to crossword puzzles, pets, recreational vehicles, and sex, and they come to know each other as individuals in a medium that was nonexistent for the first half to three-quarters of their lives. The following story is a dramatic example of how a caring electronic community can work.

> Ilene Weinberg, a 68-year-old retired social worker confined to a wheelchair by Parkinson's Disease, surfs the world of computer networks up to eight hours a day on SeniorNet. Online, she makes friends, gossips, and exchanges information, using technology to combat the loneliness and isolation of old age. "I'm an old lady, except when I'm online. Then I'm 37, blonde and ready to roll," said Weinberg.
>
> Her computer friends saved her life recently when, disoriented by a bad mix of medication, her normally sunny chatter became garbled on their screens. Knowing she was in trouble, she finally managed to type, PLEASE EVERYBODY LISTEN. Listen they did, and managed to piece together her identity, find her address, and notify her local police department, which sent out a paramedic to help her.[4]

DISTANCE LEARNING

Distance learning is hardly a new concept. It was originally conceived as a way to bring educational opportunities to people in remote communities: women tied to their homes by small children, prisoners, the institutionalized, the sick, the handicapped, those whose jobs involved travel, or those whose learning styles were inimical to conventional classrooms. The original delivery methods included printed course materials that one could order by mail from colleges and universities or from proprietary institutions, or that appeared in newspapers and magazines. Later, radio and television were enlisted as educational media. Contact with instructors was by mail or phone in the beginning, and the courses, especially if they were for credit, came with complete syllabi, reading lists, topics for study, and assignments. Tests and grades were a *sine qua non.*

In the mid-1970s, distance learning entered the mainstream when major institutions like Ohio University and the Regents' College of the University of the State of New York developed highly sophisticated learning packages. Later, as nontraditional education for adults evolved, Thomas A. Edison State College in New Jersey, Maricopa Community Colleges in Arizona, and Empire State College in New York, among others, developed systems whereby distance learners could design their own independent study courses and receive credit for the college-level learning they had already acquired on their own. Eventually, course material was recorded on tapes or carried by television, both public and cable. Mind Extension University, in conjunction with major universities across the country, offers an enormous number of courses for credit across the academic spectrum.

More recently, new technologies have enlarged the scope of distance learning. Faxes, modems, and e-mail have replaced letters and phone calls as means of communication with instructors, and interactive television, CD-ROMs, the Internet, and other still embryonic technologies have significantly increased the range of educational methodologies. We are on the threshold of the virtual classroom.

A recent IBM television advertisement made this point with wit and elegance. It shows an elderly Italian farmer, strolling through his lush vineyard with his granddaughter, speaking in Italian with English subtitles.

> *Grandfather:* Well, I finally finished my doctoral thesis.
>
> *Granddaughter:* Way to go, Gramps.
>
> *Grandfather:* Did my research at Indiana University.
>
> *Granddaughter:* Indiana?
>
> *Grandfather:* Yup. IBM took the school's library and digitized it so I could access it over the Internet. [Closeup of happy face] You know. . . . It's a great time to be alive.[5]

All this background material is prefatory to making the argument that a coherent distance learning network for elderlearners is not only a possibility but a necessity if we are to enable *all* older adults to participate in elderlearning. The new technologies are perfect for older people.

- They are nonpressured, allowing learning to proceed at the learner's own pace.
- They allow a choice of technologies depending on individual learning styles.
- They accommodate handicapping conditions.
- They are interactive, possessing the capacity to give guidance when it is desired or to stay silent when it is not.
- They allow one to learn at one's own convenience for as short or as long a time as desired.
- They are noncompetitive so the individual's learning capacity is not compromised by anxiety.
- They can be shared with friends or used alone. They demand minimal exertion and mobility.

- They are fun.
- They may individually be expensive, but as a shared community resource they are reasonable.

The interest, the educational materials, and the technologies are in place. Books have been published in large type and recorded on tape and CDs; courses have been written; and television, radio, and inventive CD-ROM versions have been produced. History, philosophy, art, music, and travel videos are easily available; taped lectures by famous authors and professors abound. The plethora of learning resources is awe-inspiring. One can learn virtually anything via these media, from ship-building to sheep-shearing, rock 'n roll to chamber music, anthropology to gerontology.

What remains is to catalog these riches and make them available, especially to the growing population of the old-old, whose minds are clear but whose futures are cloudy if disabilities or physical isolation condemn them to a life of cognitive inactivity. This task is neither dauntingly expensive nor administratively complex. Just as interlibrary loan has extended the riches of the great libraries to all libraries, some form of interlearning network loans can make media learning resources accessible to all elderlearners.

The giants of the communications and entertainment industries are already enlarging the definition of telecommunications; fiber optic networks will soon link telephones, televisions, cable, computers, and other electronic sources of services and information. The communications heaven these firms are struggling to create will catapult every household in the country into the twenty-first century, and we must all be ready for the possibilities. Our own designs for the learning society should anticipate, not follow, the fiber optic revolution.

TRAVEL

Take your body on a journey that will exercise your mind.

New Yorker *advertisement for Classic Journeys*

Travel emerged from the Elderlearning Survey as almost everybody's favorite source and mode of learning. Whether it's a community-sponsored trip to a museum in the next town, a family trip to a nearby battlefield, or a major trip abroad, travel is almost universally viewed as an educationally and recreationally significant event, an opportunity to find out more about the culture, history, geography, flora, fauna, people, and foods of another place, and as a way to enlarge one's perspective on the world.

The older people who hit the road in their RVs are an extreme example of this passion for travel, but thousands upon thousands of Third Agers at all income levels view travel as the ultimate high. Letty Cottin Pogrebin calls it "the best revenge against aging since collagen. . . . when we take a trip and enter unfamiliar settings, we reconnect with our childish sense of wonder and discovery, and we discover an unexpected bonus: The clock slows down and life seems to expand."[6]

For many people who have spent their middle years in the service of employers, family, and social obligations, the freedom of retirement unleashes a great lust for seeing the world. If possible, students of genealogy follow their family's trail across the continent and even to its European, African, Asian, or other roots. Those who are interested in art or dance or crafts travel to galleries, performances, and fairs. The study of wildlife, botany, history, geology, and many other subjects can become an impetus for travel, or travel can become an impetus for study. Either way, older Americans are on the move, to the great delight of the travel industry. Chapter 7 discusses study/travel with Elderhostel, but even without Elderhostel, Third Agers have discovered the joys of the road on their own, and have found their own ways to combine learning and travel.

The connections between travel and learning are widely recognized by elderlearners, and their preference for it comes across loud and clear. Travel-related responses in the Elderlearning Survey were consistent no matter the perspective from which we approached the question.

Travel Responses	
Report a significant travel-related learning project in past two years	51.6%
Report travel as a preferred learning style	55.7%
Report travel as a method of learning on their own	55.0%

We had expected income level to define a strong difference in desire to travel, but the numbers remained relatively stable across the economic spectrum. Apparently, a bus ride to a nearby battle field or museum followed by an overnight at Cousin Minnie's satisfies the same needs as a cross-country trip or a full-scale African safari. Nor is wanderlust much affected by age, as we were reminded by a 78-year-old woman who had traveled with Elderhostel in the past two years to the Galapagos, Ecuador, and Antarctica, and hoped to sign up next year for a wilderness trip to Alaska.

Study/travel trips for older adults have become big business, especially for nonprofit organizations. In the U.S., most major museums, arts groups, science organizations, college alumni offices, and professional or affinity groups are using study/travel as an image-promoting way of increasing revenues.

If you are over 60 and have ever taken a study/travel trip or even evinced interest in one, you have probably landed on a multitude of mailing lists. Each day travel opportunities are touted in glossy brochures that subtly hint of special appeal to the older traveler. And why not? Third Agers are the perfect travelers; they have leisure time that is not scheduled by their children's school systems, few pressing responsibilities, and a lifetime of suppressed wanderlust.

On a recent Smithsonian-sponsored nature cruise of the Baja Peninsula, three-quarters of the passengers were over 60. This trip offered long hikes over rocky terrain and across steep sand dunes, adventures in small Zodiac boats that bounced across a rough ocean in pursuit of whales, and snorkeling expeditions to swim with sea lions. Every passenger, regardless of age, participated in every activity, no matter how rugged. Though undoubtedly wearied by all this activity, they still showed up for early morning calls to see the "green flash" on the horizon as the sun rises and late night star watches, and they never missed a meal. The sight of an 83-year-old woman being helped to transfer from the back deck of the ship to a small boat bobbing on a choppy sea was a sight to remember. The crew was skillful; the woman was magnificent.

Like most organized study/travel trips, this cruise *was* a genuine learning experience. A bibliography arrived with the what-to-pack list. A naturalist's book on the Baja Peninsula was sent when the final payment was made, and the list of tour guides sounded like the faculty of a small department in an Ivy League college.

The trip offered at least one lecture each day on some aspect of the terrain to be covered: geology, zoology, botany, history, or culture. Naturalists (5 for 59 passengers) led the expeditions, dispensing wisdom as they went, and after dinner each night there was a debriefing of the day's activities—what had been seen, heard, experienced, learned, as well as an informative preview of the next day's program. The ship's library was stocked with bird, fish, and plant guides, as well as videos and specimens so the intellectually curious, who could still keep their eyes open, could do further research.

Study/travel trips cover an incredible number of countries, continents, modes of travel, special interests, and learning opportunities. One can take a 10-day photographic expedition to Ireland under the tutelage of a professional photographer. The printed suggestion (not requirement) that you pack a range of equipment, including a camera that allows you to change lenses, indicates that this trip is not for the casual point-and-shoot amateur.

One can explore the forests, mountains, and coasts of Costa Rica in search of coatimundis, crocodiles, and boat-billed herons, a trip that is described as "very active." One can fly to the Himalayan kingdoms of Nepal, Bhutan, and Ladakh, a trip that includes "long drives over gravel roads, spartan accommodations, and altitudes ranging up to 11,500 feet . . . a rewarding experience for [Smithsonian] Associates in good health . . . who are fully prepared to meet the challenges of an epic journey."

For the more aesthetically or culturally inclined, there are trips to music and film festivals, a seminar on modern art that traverses the French Riviera, and glimpses of cultures from Zimbabwe to Belize. There are trips to critical Civil War sites, a history of the Manhattan Project at Los Alamos, and an opportunity to join Nobel laureates of literature for a conference at the Carter Center in Atlanta. And these are just the selections from *one* catalog.

Many of these travel/learning trips are physically demanding. A trip that starts with a jet flight may include such less advanced forms of transportation as bicycles, trucks, jeeps, camels, and donkeys. The walking part of the tours can punish the feet of even the best shod traveler. Participants may find themselves hundreds of miles from a physician and thousands of miles from a well-equipped and staffed hospital. They may be eating strange food and may be exposed to exotic bacteria in hostile climates.

Given these hardships, why are these trips marketed so heavily to older adults? Because older adults are the primary consumers of such trips. In today's society, they alone have the necessary leisure, income, and previous education to lust after more learning. Travel is an aphrodisiac to this generation of older Americans, and travel with a reading list, informative guides, and the company of other bright, knowledgeable Third Agers is the ultimate turn-on.

The director of a major museum's travel program says that her organization used to look at people in their sixties as their primary market but have moved the target up to the seventies and now find a significant number of their clients are well into the eighties. She could remember only one trip out of hundreds that was interrupted by a medical emergency, and says she is impressed by the sheer bravery of men and women who cheerfully participate in arduous physical activities and endure with equanimity severe weather, bureaucratic snafus, and local hazards.

But isn't this kind of travel just a diversion for the wealthy, of limited significance to society at large? The answer is not entirely clear. Participants in the Baja trip, who were included in the Elderlearning Survey, were clearly upper income: 69.1 percent of them had an annual income of $60,000 or over. In the actively participating Elderhostel group (207-A), income levels were markedly lower.

Income, Group 207-A	
0 to $19,999	7.3%
$20,000 to $39,999	46.0%
$40,000 to $59,999	26.3%
$60,000+	20.4%

While the amenities are fewer and the prices accordingly lower for Elderhostelers, the impulse for travel, learning, and adventure is the same. Even in the lowest income group (407), where 71.4 percent report incomes less than $39,999, travel rated high among learning choices. The director of an OASIS center told us that trips, no matter how short or how close the destination, are far and away the members' most sought-after activities.

We are not suggesting that travel should be a publicly supported mode of learning. But it should be recognized by program planners as a learning activity that satisfies older people's need for cognitive, social, and physical activity as well as a strong desire to know more about the world before they leave it.

Travel expeditions can be modest—a van ride to hear a band concert or tour a local battlefield, a nature hike in a nearby woods, or a bus trip to a nearby historic site. Relatively low cost travel like this can be distinguished from purely local outings in a number of the following ways.

- a meal or meals in another city or town
- an overnight stay
- some sort of educational preparation for the expedition, whether a handout, maps, or a slide show
- a background talk by a local expert
- a debriefing after the event to discuss what has been learned

For lower income older people, a simple expedition like this can be memorable, brightening their lives in anticipation and, later, in reflection. It is an expanding event in lives that threaten to contract, a way of keeping people connected to each other, to ideas, and to the outside world.

NOTES

1. Jim Scheppke, "Who's Using the Public Library?" *Library Journal* (October 15, 1994), 35-37.

2. Ibid., 36.

3. "SeniorNet Online Electronic Community," seniornet@aol.com.

4. Excerpted from an article by Richard Lorant, "Computer Net Turns into Safety Net for Ailing On-line Senior," *The Times Record*, January 23, 1995, 7, col. 3-4.

5. IBM television advertisement. Reprinted with permission of IBM.

6. "And Miles to Go," *New York Times*, April 21, 1996, section 5, 33.

CHAPTER 11

Socially Constructive Aging

Work, Retirement, Volunteerism, and Leisure Activities

Perhaps with full span lives the norm, people may need to learn how to be aged as they once had to learn to be adults . . . . To fall into purposelessness is to fall out of all real consideration.

Ronald Blythe, The View in Winter

RETIREMENT OR COMMENCEMENT?

Retirement is an event, not a state of being. It means simply that one is giving up the job he or she happens to be doing. What one makes of the event should depend upon individual disposition and circumstance, not on societal injunctions and taboos. We are not minimizing the profound meaning of retirement, but merely cautioning against distortion of that meaning by unexamined assumptions and mandates.

Retirement marks a critical passage in the life course, signalling not only the end of certain kinds of work, but the gift, if one recognizes it as such, of new flexibility in one's social and economic roles, new opportunities for self-expression, and a new concept of time. It is the period of life in which, in Yeats' words, "we are making our souls."

For those whose identity and feelings of self-worth have been completely tied to what they do for a living, retirement can be devastating, casting them adrift in a world to which they no longer feel connected. Old age depression among men, a growing phenomenon, is thought to be connected to their feelings of uselessness and disconnectedness when their structured world of work disappears.[1]

Certainly, the connotations of the word "retire" are overwhelmingly negative; the WordPerfect thesaurus spews out a string of sad synonyms: depart,
leave, retreat, rest, sleep, resign, withdraw. The *Random House Dictionary*
definition is hardly more sanguine: "withdraw, go away or apart to a place of
abode, shelter or seclusion; to fall back, retreat, withdraw, go away or remove
oneself; withdraw permanently from service." "Retirement" is defined as a
withdrawal from or "withdrawal into privacy or seclusion." The emotional
meanings that have accrued to the word "retire" make it difficult for even the
most buoyant of personalities to welcome its approach. No wonder so many
men and women anticipate their retirement with anxiety and depression.

For increasing numbers of men and women, however, these definitions
simply do not match the reality of their experience. The passage from the
Second to the Third Age turns out to be a different "re" word— "release." For
those who have been lucky enough or wise enough to remain closely involved
with their families, friends, and communities throughout their working lives,
who have developed interests not connected with their careers, and who have
nourished a positive vision of retirement, the cessation of work is joyously
positive. The liberation from the nine-to-five routine and the freedom to
follow one's own dreams and desires at one's own pace are things to be
celebrated. We recommend "commencement," defined as "a beginning, a
start," as a more appropriate word to mark the growth possibilities inherent in
this rite of passage.

The History of Retirement

But before we "retire" the word retirement, it would be wise to look at its
historical evolution. Abraham Monk, editor of the recently published *Columbia Book of Retirement*,[2] speaks of the evolution of the concept of retirement as,
next to the changing status of women, the most profound of the cultural
changes that have occurred in the past 100 years in the United States. The
change is relatively recent. In 1861, in the first federal retirement measure,
Congress required naval officers below the rank of vice admiral to resign their
commissions at 62. By 1874, the Canadian Great Trunk Railroad System
established the first corporate retirement plan in North America, and a year
later American Express permitted workers over 60 who had spent at least 20
years with the company to receive some retirement income.[3] In 1920, the first
compulsory old age and disability plan was created for a half million civil
servants. Retirement at a fixed age was becoming, if not a norm, a spot on the
horizon. Still, for a number of years, more than 80 percent of all retirement
payments came from military pensions, and ill health remained the primary
reason for retirement from active work.

Although passage of the Social Security Act of 1935 is seen as the beginning of modern retirement practice in the U.S., retirement as we know it

didn't really begin until after World War II. During the war, few retired because labor was needed for the war effort. In 1974, "The Employee Retirement Income Security Act established minimum vesting and accounting standards and authorized the creation of individual retirement accounts,"[4] thus, fueling the comfortable economic level of many of today's retirees. Ironically, between 1945 and 1979, as the lifespan began to expand, the average age of men's retirement fell from 70 to 64. Present-day policies are caught between the Scylla and Charybdis of keeping the promise of early retirement for a growing population that threatens to outlive the system's ability to pay or raising the retirement age and leaving more people to compete for jobs in a shrinking workforce.

Retirement Today

Prior to 1900, most people worked until they died or became disabled. If they lived long enough and if they were financially able to stop working, they could enjoy retirement for only a few years. At the turn of the century, when men's life expectancy was 46.3 years, those who made it to 65 lived only an average of 1.2 more years, "a comma at the end of life."[5]

Today, a century later, retirement (life after 65) has evolved into a genuine life stage, a full 20 percent or more of the lifespan. In fact, men retiring today can expect to spend more time in this Third Age than they did in their First Age school years. If 65 continues as the conventional retirement age, by the beginning of the twenty-first century retirement for many people will constitute a full third of their lifespan. Already it is not unusual to find men and women living 30 or more years beyond their final paid job, entering a hitherto uncharted territory in which they are the pioneers, making up their life styles as they go. Whether they embrace the time and use it productively or merely endure it, becoming dependent and chronically in need of medical and social services, is of paramount importance to society and to each individual.

Retirement age is, of course, only partially determined by an individual's situations and desires. The policy that mandated 62 as the age for partial Social Security benefits and 65 for full benefits and Medicare is beginning to change in response to the economic conditions and workforce needs of the country. Age 65 has no magic. When Bismarck's Germany legislated the first social security program in 1889, 65 was much older than it is today. The U.S. has retained 65 partly because of tradition and partly because of the implied social contract, but the tradition may be out of date and the contract may need to be rewritten. If we are to retain the mid-sixties as a time when men and women are encouraged to retire, we must be certain of three things:

- that we as a nation can afford it
- that the productivity needs of the workforce will not be compromised

- that we are prepared to transform this lengthening stage of life into a time of renewal and regeneration

We are concerned with the last of these three points when we advocate creating a Third Age of diverse and widespread elderlearning. This transformation may be the key to creating a new and positive societal energy, not only for those who have left paid work but for their families, friends, and neighbors.

New Rites of Retirement—Commencement

Charles Lamb in his essay "The Superannuated Man," wrote as follows about his initial adjustment to retirement:

> . . . for it is a sort of Eternity for a man to have all his Time to himself. It seemed to me that I had more time on my hands than I could ever manage. . . . And here let me caution persons grown old in active business, not lightly nor without weighing their own resources, to forego their customary employment all at once, for their [sic] may be danger in it.

However, when he had grown accustomed to his new leisure, Lamb said, "A man can never have too much Time to himself, nor too little to do."[6]

The respondents to our Elderlearning Survey would agree heartily with at least the first part of that statement. Almost 45 percent of those surveyed, when asked what barriers kept them from learning, checked off "time" as the major barrier. Our discussions and interviews with other Third Agers also provide a picture of lives packed with activity. Not one of our interviewees mentioned boredom or lack of interesting things to do. The reality of life for these elderlearners is totally at odds with gloomy visions of retirement as an abrupt cessation of everything that makes life meaningful. The alternate vision, that this is a wondrous time for renewing old interests and finding new ones, for self-discovery and growth, and for pursuits related to leaving a legacy for one's progeny, is only beginning to be fully appreciated.

If we are to substitute "commencement" for "retirement," marking the event but connoting new beginnings, new horizons, new territory to be explored, then we must invent new rituals to herald the passage. Retirement parties should evolve from the current obligatory occasions for melancholy farewell speeches, poignant jokes, and coworkers' ritualized expressions of regret to genuinely upbeat affairs where the retiree's new life is celebrated. We might jettison the gold watch tradition and mark the occasion with a new laptop computer or a pre-paid Elderhostel trip of the recipient's choice, gifts that look to the future.

Most important, retirement planning programs, which for the past 40 years have been one of the most common forms of organized instruction for older adults, must undergo radical revision. Current models, sponsored by corporations, unions, professional groups, colleges, brokerage houses, and community organizations, tend to focus primarily on financial and estate planning and preparation for THE END. Emphasis is put on the practical aspects of leaving paid work, such as pensions, social security, IRAs, health benefits, and new budgeting strategies, and advice is given about choosing nursing homes, leaving advance directives for terminal health care, and keeping wills and other documents safe for heirs to find. The not-so-subliminal message is that you are going to have less money and need more care as you prepare for death.

All but the best of these retirement preparation programs come too late in one's career to be effective in changing ingrained habits of thinking or even to give one time to make beneficial financial adjustments. They pay minimal attention to the psychological impact of leaving paid work and to the positive educational, recreational, creative, and spiritual opportunities in the life ahead. Program designers, teachers, and trainers in adult education, should be retrained in the new realities of the Third Age. They should create a syllabus of the future for retirement planning seminars that addresses the following issues:

- the complex interconnections between physical and mental health and the importance of continuing to nurture and exercise body and mind
- the bounty of opportunities that leisure bestows
- how to pull selected threads of one's worklife (skills and interests you don't want to relinquish) into one's new life
- self-fulfillment through volunteer work, through giving time and energy to others
- the vital realization that growth and learning need never end

WORK

Where is it written that 65, or any other age, means the cessation of work? Mukunda Rao, an international consultant on social development issues, says "this idea of old age linked to retirement, with a sudden dropping-off from the workforce, is an unfortunate product of the industrial revolution. It needs to be rethought."[7] For many older adults, retirement is either not an option or is a meaningless concept. Writers, painters, musicians, and others in the arts seldom "retire," but go on doing what they love doing until they can do it no more. Picasso painted into his late eighties, Toscanini wielded his baton well into his nineties, and the Delaney sisters published a best seller when they were just short of 100. Scholars may cease teaching classes and receiving a salary, but they seldom give up the pursuit of knowledge that has been the meaning of their lives. The fortunate among them are given on-campus offices so that they may retain access to libraries, laboratories, and the collegiality of the workplace. Professionals, corporate leaders, and the self-employed rarely choose to retire at 65 unless it is to pursue a new interest or life style. They are too engaged in what they are doing. And sometimes, retirement is only temporary. Many retired chief executives and other top managers are finding themselves in demand to run troubled companies that investment banks or boards want to "turn around."[8] Others are plucked out of retirement ("right off the eleventh tee," as one man put it) to take over ailing nonprofit corporations or to consult with entrepreneurial start-ups. Unfortunately, workers at the bottom of the ladder are rarely granted the same opportunities.

In 1993, when "downsizing" entered our vocabulary, Fortune 1000 companies pruned as many as 50,000 positions a month, and in 1994 nearly three million people lost their jobs. Many of these were older workers for whom an unexpected job loss is not only a financial blow but a personal disaster. For those whose concept of self is tied into "what they do," unanticipated job loss (or abruptly enforced retirement) means loss of identity, an event as emotionally devastating as divorce or a death in the family. Those who cope may become stronger in the process. The newspapers are replete with stories like that of the unemployed woman who, at age 77, learned to drive a 12-ton rig and was hired to make the run to El Salvador, or the 69-year-old man who when laid off as a construction engineer went back to school to get his Master of Fine Arts and is now happily teaching and painting on the lower slopes of the Adirondacks. For these people, elderlearning had a pragmatic purpose and an immediate payoff. But not all retirees are so self-directed or so lucky. Some must go through a painful process of withdrawal and creation of a different but meaningful life style.

Some can't retire because their unpaid work never ends. These people are mostly women whose work has been in the home and the community, neither of which gives them a pension or the option of formally calling it quits. Most of those women whose work has been primarily domestic do not want to radically change their habits or their pursuits based on an arbitrary calendar age. For such women (an endangered species since many of their sisters and most of the succeeding generations have already entered the workplace), the trauma of retirement as such is nonexistent, although they must still work through such issues as aging, loss of friends, changes in financial status, and a spouse now permanently home for lunch.

Of the ES respondents, 17.6 percent of the men and women are either working for pay, full- or part-time, or are self-employed. Two groups, at opposite ends of the economic spectrum, are most likely not to retire voluntarily: those who can't afford to and those whose careers are so engrossing that they don't wish to. This phenomenon was dramatically illustrated in the ES groups. Group 107, with an average income below $30,000, reported 22.2 percent still working; groups 807 and 907, with an average income above

$60,000, reported 24.4 percent still working. In the middle income groups, the number of those still working ranged between 6.8 percent to 12.6 percent. The exception to this was in largely female group 407, which reported both low incomes and low numbers still working (9.4 percent).

Working Beyond Retirement Age

For those who want to or must work beyond the conventional retirement age, the current picture is not bright, particularly if they are low skilled. Downsizing and encouraged or mandated early retirement have reduced the number of full-time jobs available. According to data from the Bureau of Labor Statistics, from 1991 to 1992 the unemployment of people 55 and older who wanted to work increased at five times the rate for those under 55.[9] If these trends are not reversed, working full-time may not be a feasible option for those with a need or desire to do so.

A few far-sighted employers have begun to realize that older workers have many advantages over younger. As products of the generations that placed the work ethic next to religion in importance, they are reliable and hard working. Because years of experience have given many of them strong people skills, they are ideal for jobs in service industries. Many are not only willing to work part-time or at irregular hours but frequently prefer it. Most are willing to forego health benefits because they are covered by Medicare, and they have fewer dependents to be covered by insurance. A major study has shown that their productivity is excellent.[10] Contrary to expectations, they lose fewer days to illness than younger workers, and, for most jobs, "the physical demands are well below the capacities of most normal aging workers,"[11] a fact that can only grow in importance with increasing automation of physical tasks.

Whether work is a necessity or a choice for the older person, it should not be an impossibility. However, there are a number of barriers, some intentional, that can make work an impossibility. "The old age security problem is much more fully under control today than is the old age opportunity problem."[12] Current IRS restrictions on the amount one may earn before Social Security is cut back make it difficult for low income retirees to supplement their income. They may also have difficulty finding jobs because of age bias or because their skills have not kept up with the demands of industry or because companies engaged in downsizing simply are not looking for a new source of labor. Moreover, the labor picture is not static but fluctuates in cycles, confounding the efforts of policy makers to respond appropriately. This month's labor shortage is next month's oversupply.

In one of the most provocative books of the late 1980s, *Workforce 2000: Work and Workers for the Twenty-First Century*,[13] William S. Johnston, using the data available at that time, postulated that the nation would soon face a critical shortage of skilled labor. The book spoke of the need to facilitate immigration and use every stratagem to train more women and minorities for the workforce of the future so that we would have enough technical and service workers to survive global competition. A few years later, companies were laying off surplus workers, including thousands upon thousands of managers and technicians who were suddenly redundant. Although some politicians took this opportunity to cry out against the evils of trade agreements, immigration, and the expenditure of public funds to upgrade the technical skills of workers, the layoffs were more likely due to the unpredictable cyclical fluctuations of a free economy.

Retraining for Employment

Although we can't outguess the vagaries of the labor market, we *can* help people of all ages update and upgrade their skills so they can better compete. Programs are springing up around the country to train older adults for jobs that might be considered without futures for young people but which are adequate to give seniors a supplementary income and keep them active and in touch with other people. A 10-week course, co-sponsored by the New York City Department of Aging and a large restaurant chain, is teaching older adults how to operate computerized cash registers, process cash transactions, service customers, and perform other duties that will put them in line for a pay check and personal satisfaction. Almost 73 percent of those who complete the program find jobs. The rapidly growing number of businesses that depend on telephone sales and marketing are also looking to Third Agers for their people skills and dependability.

Other programs are training seniors for paid work in nursing homes, child care centers, and other socially vital agencies that operate on a shoestring budget. Sales, data entry, home care, and clerking are just a few of the many job categories that might be considered. Older workers bring stability, responsibility, and caring to tasks eschewed by younger, more career-oriented workers.

Although low-end jobs may solve some older adults' immediate financial needs, they should not define the limits of retraining. To date, industry has been reluctant to spend money on training older workers whom they choose to replace rather than retrain (unless there are labor shortages in the area). The strength of persisting stereotypes has been a major roadblock. Nor have unions been aggressive about seeking training opportunities for older members, and, unfortunately, Claude Pepper's efforts in Congress notwithstanding, government has failed to take the lead. This generally dismal record has some bright spots. ACS, a computer software company in Florida, has successfully trained retirees for part-time positions as programmers. Graduates work at home at their own pace and on their own schedules for salaries well above minimum wage. Programs also exist to prepare older employees, including engineers, for work in the changing technologies of aerospace electronics systems, for using new methods of handling air freight, and for the production of jet engine components. Older trainees tend to be more likely than younger trainees to complete their training and to remain with their employers.[14]

If, as some predict, the surplus labor of the baby boom generation is succeeded by a shortage as the boomers move towards retirement, then training and retraining of older workers will become a necessity. A major, nation-wide effort could focus on

- late-career planning and job redesign for older workers
- motivation of employers to assume the social responsibility for re-training older workers
- remediation of the lower levels of formal education that are no longer viable in a high-skilled economy
- prevention or reversal of skills obsolescence[15]

VOLUNTEERISM

Service to others is the rent we pay for the privilege of living on this earth.

Pierre Teilhard de Chardin

Maggie Kuhn, that indomitable Gray Panther, had a vision for older people: they were to work for peace and social justice by becoming "mentors, media-tors, monitors, motivators, and mobilizers."[16] This is a tough agenda, but in the Age Age we are moving closer to her ideals.

President Jimmy Carter's mother, Lillian Carter, who served in the Peace Corps in her seventies, was an early role model for the concept of aging as a time of service to society. Vast numbers of Third Agers have found their *raison d'être* not in paid employment, nor in aimless leisure, but in volunteer work of diverse kinds and at many levels. An impressive 72.9 percent of the ES respondents report volunteer activities, 43.1 percent of them volunteer either full-time or at least one to three days per week. These figures are consistent with those reported in other studies across the country and represent an extraordinary wealth of brain and muscle power at the service of society.

These volunteers are not all working in hospital gift shops or planning benefit luncheons or serving on fund-raising committees. Most are engaged in providing vital hands-on services in their communities; these services extend or secure the social safety net because they supplement or complement the services performed by professional or semi-professional workers in perennially understaffed nonprofit agencies and institutions. These volunteers are en-gaged in what Bortz calls "useful aging," what John Rowe calls "successful aging," and what Robert Butler calls "productive aging."

Training for Volunteerism

Like other life transitions, the transitions between work, retirement, and volunteerism are usually preceded or facilitated by learning experiences, formal or informal. (See Exhibit 11.1.) Learning at work or in volunteer activity was reported by 39.3 percent of the ES respondents, and many of them, women in particular, described substantial self-directed learning projects in social service fields, about half in fields similar to those in which they had worked before retirement. These projects typically combined formal classes (mostly noncredit offered by nonprofit agencies or professional organizations) with practical experience and self-directed reading and research. A sampling of the volunteer arenas described includes serving as mental health clinic aides, working with autistic children, dealing with disabled adults, working in drug and alcohol rehabilitation programs, practicing occupational and rehabilitative therapies, and working as aides in hospitals, nursing homes, hospices, child care centers, centers for abused women, soup kitchens, and rape crisis centers. One respondent was being trained "to facilitate the court-ordered transfer of children between their divorced custodial parents in such a way that the children are spared the verbal abuse and violence of the warring couple." There's a new social task for the twenty-first century!

John Lane was an engineer at radio and TV stations for over 40 years before retiring in his seventies. After retirement, he earned a bachelor's degree, and now, at age 80, is a volunteer student teacher at a high school in Portland, Maine.

Toward the end of one class, Lane asks one of the boys to tell him about Napoleon. The boy manages to say, "Napoleon was a French general who tried to conquer a lot of lands," before Lane cuts him off. Smiling from ear to ear, Lane booms, "Boy, that's a lousy answer. Let's give someone else a try." His students like him. "I mess around with him a little, but he messes around with me too," says the Napoleon non-expert.

His supervising teacher, initially worried about whether Lane's energy level would be equal to coping with teenage boys, says that he has had no problem handling either his students or his workload.

Lane cheerfully totes home tests to be graded over the weekend, sometimes using a magnifying glass to decipher the students' writing, but says he's having a wonderful time. When asked if he might go on to take courses for full certification, he laughs and says, "At my age I don't even buy green bananas."[17]

We don't usually think of police work as a job for either older adults or volunteers, but across the country thousands of older adults are training to do unpaid work with law enforcement agencies. In Alexandria, Virginia, 67-year-old Juan Correa rides in patrol cars as a civilian interpreter for the city's

Phase	Learning Needs	Major Components	Major Sources
Work	keeping up with changes in workplace	language skills, technical skills, interpersonal skills, professional knowledge, managerial and supervisory skills	employer-sponsored training, technical schools & colleges, professional organizations and publications, consultants, on-the-job learning, self-directed learning
	preparation for retirement	broadening base of interests, solidifying family and social ties, financial planning, becoming more aware of self as learner	retirement seminars: employers, unions, insurance companies, financial institutions, schools, community colleges, taking courses, reading, increased social activity
Retirement	employing leisure for better quality of life, staying cognitively active, achieving sense of purpose, generativity	re-learning how to learn, expanding range of skills and knowledge, keeping body and mind healthy and active	self-directed learning, schools and colleges, libraries, travel, senior centers, fitness and health centers, book and discussion groups, Elderhostel, ILRs, OASIS, etc.
Volunteerism	achieving sense of purpose and usefulness, finding ways to meld old and new interests in service to others	new professional skills, new interpersonal skills, time management	nonprofit agencies, government agencies, self-directed learning, experiential learning, community colleges

LEARNING NEEDS IN THE THIRD AGE

EXHIBIT 11.1

Hispanic population. In Palm Beach County, Florida, 85-year-old Louis Schiff runs a Citizens Observer Patrol (COP), which wears uniforms, drives specially marked cars, and uses cellular phones and walkie-talkies to patrol the county. A Texas couple, 63- and 73-years-old, accompanies deputies picking up prisoners around Smith County, and a horseback posse in Charleston, South Carolina, includes members up to age 70.[18] These seniors are not about to become victims of crime; they're out to prevent it.

Older adults are also being trained to serve as aides in classrooms, as docents in museums and galleries, and as para-professional librarians. They take on a wide variety of jobs that hard-pressed educational, cultural, and social agencies can no longer afford to staff.

Using Prior Learning and Skills

Older volunteers frequently bring interests and skills out of their working lives into a new *pro bono* context. Those with business experience may offer to manage the finances of the local library or advise a young would-be restaurateur on food purchasing and personnel hiring practices. Teachers volunteer in literacy skills programs or serve as classroom aides in inner city schools or teach English as a Second Language to recent immigrants. A retired hydraulic engineer may consult with an environmental agency on water conservation practices, and a retired dentist may use a former colleague's office space at night to practice his profession for the benefit of poor children or seniors.

A group of physicians, nurses, and other health care workers who retired to Hilton Head, South Carolina, presumably for "golden" years of golf, boating, and bridge, were appalled by the poverty of the workers whose labor undergirded their comfortable life style. They formed a project called Volunteers in Medicine to run a free clinic for the working poor and their children. They even convinced the state to make special arrangements for licensure so that they could continue to practice medicine in this community service mode.

Helen B is a noted graphic artist whose work is in public and private collections across the country. She earned her bachelor's degree from a noted technical arts school, but always felt that her education was deficient in art history.

At age 64, having developed osteoarthritis in both hands as a result of years of pulling prints on a heavy press, Helen cut back her printmaking and enrolled in an Ivy League university's docent program. The program included a demanding series of lectures, classes, and written and oral reports that challenged her to do the things she had previously missed.

Public speaking was the biggest hurdle, but within eight months she was able to organize her own tours, prepare scripts, gauge the level of her audience's interest and knowledge, speak well, and answer questions extemporaneously.

Helen has come to know the collections of the university's many museums and galleries in depth and speaks knowledgeably about the art of a wide range of periods and cultures. She continues to audit art history classes to expand her range.

A valuable asset to the university that invested in her training, Helen leads tours at least one day per week and is frequently asked for by VIP groups to whom she has been recommended. She is also active in the training of successive generations of docents. She says that what she's learned through volunteer work has given her the equivalent of a Ph.D. in art history as well as a new circle of friends in the art world and a welcome substitute for her life's work as an artist.

The possibility of continuing to use their prior learning and skills in a helping rather than a profit-making context is especially appealing to retirees who take pride in what they accomplished during their working lives. Public recognition of what they have accomplished and confirmation of their continued usefulness have energized thousands of older men and women whose lives are enriched by the knowledge that they are of use to others.

A number of associations have sprung up to organize older groups for service roles. R.S.V.P. (Retired Senior Volunteer Program) serves as a conduit between nonprofit organizations and the older adult population to provide services where they are needed. Begun in 1965, R.S.V.P. requires that its members, who are 60 plus, be willing to commit to regular hours without compensation and to accept supervision. SCORE (Senior Corps of Retired Executives) is similarly organized to make the training, skills, and experience of older executives available to small business owners. Both of these programs occasionally lead to jobs as employers realize the abilities of their older consultants. At the high end of business expertise is the Executive Service Corporation started by David Rockefeller 30 years ago. This service has signed up 13,000 former corporate officers who work overseas on short-term business projects, such as increasing the productivity of a sewing machine factory in the Caribbean, advising an Estonian city on solid-waste disposal systems, or privatizing companies in Eastern Europe. While the average age of the volunteers is 67, some are in their late seventies and even eighties.

One volunteer, who said he was sick of bridge and tennis, simply walked unannounced into a nonprofit business training center one day and said, "I'm yours for 20 hours a week. What do you want me to do?" What he ended up doing was designing and managing a "Career Connections" program to serve as a bridge between job seekers and employers, creating a database to hold career information, and setting up financial and marketing strategies that have enabled the organization to make more than 140 corporate job placements per year. The income from this program has enabled the training center to enlarge the scope of its educational activities and offer "scholarships" to those who can't afford the job training they need.

The idea of facilitating their members' entrance into useful volunteer activity has motivated many ancillary programs at Institutes for Learning in Retirement. The Center for Creative Retirement in Asheville, North Carolina, has designed particularly creative ways of promoting community activism among its participants, many of whom have taken on long-term commitments to mentor children in poor school districts.

Political Volunteerism

Older adults are probably the best-informed and most active age group when it comes to politics and current affairs. They are avid readers of newspapers, listeners to public radio, and viewers of CNN and other television news programs. They care passionately, and they vote in such large numbers (70.1 percent of those over 65 voted in 1994) that no politician can afford to ignore them. According to the current stereotype, they vote their own pocketbooks, forming an unassailable bloc where their own narrow interests are concerned. This narrowly age-centered political bias has not been our experience nor has our research borne it out. In fact, in recent elections, Third Agers seem, like the rest of the population, to have split evenly on most controversial social issues: affirmative action, gay rights, welfare reform, education, abortion, and environmental issues. There is no single senior "line" on these issues, but there are some mighty advocates on all sides. Age hasn't stopped Strom Thurmond or Barry Goldwater from political activism. Scott and Helen Nearing were the gurus of environmentally conscious living until their deaths in their late nineties. Only a heart attack silenced Edmund Muskie's democratic voice, and Maggie Kuhn was driving conservatives crazy until her own demise.

Depending on who's talking about him, David Brower is either the grandfather of the modern environmental movement, an inveterate tree hugger, or both. Brower built the Sierra Club from a 2,000-member hiking club in 1956 to a potent, politically powerful organization of 77,000 today. He founded Friends of the Earth, the League of Conservation Voters, and the Earth Island Institute, each of which has had a large role in building the ecological conscience of the latter part of this century.

But the 83-year-old environmentalist still sees problems that he wants to fix and revolutionary solutions that he's eager to try. He envisions a Global CPR Corps for Conservation, Preservation, and Restoration—a sort of volunteer Green Cross to solve problems of deforestation, air pollution, soil erosion, and species extinction. He feels that his age mates, older adults, should be involved. "We need some administrative capability to get it underway. . . . I'm concerned about entitlements—not just for people my age, but for people who haven't been born. We're all entitled to Medicare and a pension and a decent society and a beautiful Earth—and so are those who aren't here yet."[19]

Many of our oldest citizens take to the ramparts to protect the society their grandchildren will inherit. The physically active exhort from platforms and door-to-door, address envelopes, attend meetings and speak out, canvas for charities, or join groups picking up trash on beaches, mountains, and urban playgrounds. Even the physically feeble phone their neighbors, contact their representatives in Congress, and write to the mayor and their state legislators. Older adults teach, counsel, persuade, and are heard.

Non-Organized Volunteerism

The writer of a letter to the editor of a local small town newspaper recently asked plaintively why her contributions and the contributions of people like her were never recognized.

> I walk up and down the roads near my home, picking up bottles and paper and other trash to keep our neighborhood neat. And I watch the children play until their mothers come home from work. And I shop for the man next door who broke his hip, and last week I did his laundry. But no one gives me awards or writes about me in the newspaper. It's as though I'm invisible.
>
> *Sincerely,*
> *Ellen G.*

There are thousands of "invisible" volunteers like Ellen. They used to be primarily women whose work was in the home rather than the office. They were the glue that held neighborhoods together, pitching in wherever they were needed. When these women followed their spouses into the workplace, they left a void. Who was to bring chicken soup to the sick, help the disabled weed their gardens, or read to a youngster while his mother went to the dentist? Those jobs have now fallen mainly to the older neighbors, male and female, who shovel a path around the community mailbox for the mail carrier, water a vacationing friend's plants, pick up a junior high school soccer player when his dad's at work, or coach a chess team. These small acts of kindness, multiplied by millions, make the world a friendlier place and are an eloquent answer to those who equate the graying of the United States with fiscal and social disaster. Third Agers give more than they take.

The Effects of Volunteerism

There is a larger significance to this volunteer activity than merely making Third Agers feel good or look good, larger even than the actual benefits accruing to the recipients of their generosity. These men and women of the Third Age, who are giving so freely of their time and energies, are making possible a new vision of the caring society. They may in fact be President George Bush's elusive "points of light," their individual contributions having the collective potential to transform the way in which we care for the poor, the weak, the sick, and the forgotten. Robert Kahn at the University of Michigan found in his studies of productive activity (defined as "any that might be remunerated under certain circumstances") that "on average, 'retired' people are making more contributions in terms of dollar value than they are receiving in support from society, at least up to age 75."[20]

Perhaps President John F. Kennedy's exhortation, "Ask not what your country can do for you—ask what you can do for your country," continues to pose a challenge for older adults. "Continuing to be useful, having something significant to do with one's life, and providing a service to someone else that otherwise would not be performed might take away some of the fear of growing old."[21]

LEISURE

Beyond issues of work versus retirement or the effects on society of volunteerism, the key to grasping the potential richness of a well-lived old age may lie in a new understanding of the concept of leisure. The word leisure derives from the Latin *licere*, which means "to be permitted." Implicit in this meaning is the notion of personal freedom, the freedom to do what one wants, when one wants. In this context, *leisure* refers to both freedom *from* work, chores, and so on and freedom *to* do as one wishes.

> The Greek word for leisure, *schole*, is the origin of the word for school or scholar in many modern languages. As used by Plato, *schole* referred to the ultimate purpose of education, to liberate one from the toil of work. Once free from unnecessary labor, humans could participate in distinctly human forms of activity such as contemplative thought, creation, or appreciation of the arts. To the Greeks, involvement in these experiences represented leisure.[22]

If leisure is considered in these expanded terms rather than as merely an opportunity for hanging out at the mall, bass fishing, or channel surfing, the concept takes on a resonance that is critical to our understanding of the role learning can play for the older population. But since the Industrial Revolution, leisure has had another meaning—"unobligated" time leftover from working, sleeping, and eating. In this view, life maintenance chores such as knitting and mowing the lawn are still forms of leisure if one performs them during unobligated hours. A third way of viewing leisure uses the *type* of activity rather than time as the defining factor. In other words, if gardening or knitting is *perceived* as a chore, it is one, but if it is perceived as a hobby, then it is a leisure activity. "The underlying assumption is that the enjoyment we associate with leisure is inherent in the activity itself."[23] This definition neatly distinguishes making yet another dinner from gourmet cooking or weeding the vegetable patch from creating a butterfly garden.

The true challenge of retirement is not to find activities that simply fill time but to find activities that are personally fulfilling and lead to a sense of satisfaction. We must get away from the notion that leisure is synonymous with idleness or diversion, a sort of vacation from life. Some retirees, imbued from birth with the work ethic and fearful of leisure, feel compelled to be "busy" in their retirement whether or not this "busyness" accords with their inner needs and desires. They tinker obsessively with household machinery, volunteer for jobs they don't enjoy, or take on unnecessary chores, thus complicating the "maintenance" side of their lives. These people are not using their leisure, they are squandering it.

We suspect that some of the impetus to undertake the kinds of learning activities this book celebrates may originally arise from the demands of an ingrained work ethic, the internal need to keep busy. In fact, 40 percent of the respondents to the ES gave "to fill time productively" as one of their reasons for learning. But while that may be an initial motivation, more seasoned learners say they are learning for the joy it gives them (79.7 percent) and as part of a developmental search "for meaning and wisdom" (37.7 percent). For these older adults, learning is a return to the Greek meaning of leisure as making room in life for contemplation and creative thought.

MacNeill and Teague suggest that instead of conceiving of leisure in terms of time or activity, we might view it as an emotional condition characterized by feelings of mastery, achievement, success, personal worth, and pleasure.[24] Creativity is positively linked to psychological health, to being in control rather than feeling detached and uncommitted.[25] It is a mode by which we can finally come closer to what we have hoped to be, in which we can better understand ourselves and our society and put that understanding to work for society's benefit and for our own. Viewed in this way, leisure time can be as socially constructive as work or volunteer activity. If spent well, it can help us become the wise counselors that our children and grandchildren need, the "mentors, mediators, monitors, motivators, and mobilizers" Maggie Kuhn called for.

NOTES

1. The National Centers for Disease Control and Prevention report that the suicide rate among elderly Americans is the highest of any age group. From 1980 through 1992, 74,675 Americans age 65 and older killed themselves, 19 percent of all the suicides in that period. Men were most at risk, committing 81 percent of suicides among the elderly. See the *New York Times*, January 12, 1996.

2. Abraham Monk, ed., *Columbia Book of Retirement* (New York: Columbia University Press, 1994).

3. W. A. Achenbaum, "Retirement in Historical Context," in *Columbia Retirement Handbook*, edited by Abraham Monk (New York: Columbia University Press, 1994), p. 17.

4. Ibid., p. 21.

5. Janet Belsky, *The Psychology of Aging: Theory, Research, & Interventions*, 2nd ed. (Brooks/Core, 1990), p. 223.

6. Included in *The Art of the Personal Essay*, edited by Phillip Lopate (New York: Anchor Books, 1994), pp. 175, 177.

7. Quoted in Susan Champlin Taylor, "The End of Retirement," *Modern Maturity* (October-November 1993).

8. Barbara Lyne, "Out of Retirement Life, and Back Into the Fire," *New York Times*, August 14, 1994, 3, 21.

9. Eugene I. Lehrmann, "Work and Retirement in the '90s," *Modern Maturity* (September-October 1994), 7.

10. From an AARP-sponsored study by the marketing and social research firm of Yankelovich, Skelly and White, Inc. Described by Horace B. Deets, "No More Stereotypes, Thank You!" *Modern Maturity* (July-August 1994), 4-5.

11. Willard Wirtz, *The Boundless Resource: A Prospectus for an Education Work Policy* (Washington, DC: New Republic Book Company, 1975), p. 142.

12. Ibid.

13. William S. Johnston, *Workforce 2000: Work and Workers for the Twenty-First Century* (Hudson Institute, 1987).

14. Peterson, pp. 201-02.

15. Ibid.

16. Dieter Hessel, "Old and Young in Action Together," *The Older Learner*, 3, 3 (Summer 1955), 3.

17. Ray Routhier, "The Teacher and His Subject Alike: They're Never Too Old," *Maine Telegram* (November 19, 1995), G1-2.

18. These examples are from the *AARP Bulletin*, July-August 1994, p. 5.

19. Excerpted from Beth Baker, "The Art of Being Unreasonable," *AARP Bulletin*, 36,10 (November 1995), 20.

20. Cited in T. Franklin Williams, "A New Scope on Retirement," *Harvard Medical Alumni Bulletin*, 67, 3 (1993–94).

21. Forest J. Berghorn, "Creative Pursuits in Later Life" in *The Dynamics of Aging: Original Essays on the Processes and Experiences of Growing Old*, edited by Forest J. Berghorn et al. (Boulder, CO: Westview Press, 1981), p. 360.

22. Richard D. MacNeill and Michael L. Teague, "Leisure Opportunities, Leisure Resources," *Columbia Book of Retirement* (New York: Columbia University Press, 1994), p. 510.

23. Ibid.

24. Ibid., p. 511.

25. Ibid., pp. 513–14.

CHAPTER 12

An Agenda for the Age Age

We are only now on the threshold of knowing the range of educability of man—the perfectibility of man. We have never addressed ourselves to this problem before.

Jerome Bruner

REVIEW

Before setting out to explore the implications for an action agenda of the major points raised in previous chapters, let's briefly summarize those points.

- As a nation, we are part of a worldwide demographic shift. How we manage this shift, how we rethink our social structures, priorities, and goals will determine whether an aging population turns out to be a blessing or a curse, a source of continued conflict over scarce resources, or a resource in itself.
- The present older adult cohort is healthier, better educated, and more financially secure than any previous generation. They are also engaged in learning to an extent never before seen. This learning strongly enhances the quality of their lives and keeps them firmly attached to their communities in positive ways.
- Growth and development do not stop at the threshold of old age. Human beings have the will *and* the cognitive capacity to continue to grow and learn throughout their lifespan. In fact, the more one learns, the better one learns. "Use it or lose it" is a holistic prescription for body and mind. The concept of the Third Age as part of a continuum

of growth and learning is a useful construct for those who design programs or make policy related to older adults.

- Of older adults engaged in learning activities who responded to the Elderlearning Survey, 87.6 percent describe their health as excellent or good, irrespective of age. Current research indicates a positive correlation between health and continued learning. Elderlearning could substantially reduce the anticipated drain on financial, health care, and nursing home resources heretofore associated with an aging population.

- Self-directed learning is the single most prevalent mode of learning among older adults, growing out of the learner's unique interests and needs and carried on at levels comfortable for the individual. Opportunities for self-directed learning are low cost and readily available to the physically active, the handicapped, and the homebound, irrespective of gender, race, or class.

- The issues of work and retirement in the Third Age have yet to be satisfactorily addressed. Many older adults are still working, and many more would like to be. To the extent that we can make this possible without shutting young people out of jobs, we should continue to tap older workers' knowledge, skills, and productivity. Mentoring roles and part-time or flexible work options are among the potential solutions to be explored.

- The 72.9 percent of older people who reported volunteer activities on the ES represent an enormous untapped resource for this country. Volunteers learn and develop through their service to others; our social and cultural institutions become more effective as the safety net expands; and individuals' lives are substantially improved by the volunteer efforts of their neighbors.

- Intergenerational warfare over scarce resources is neither inevitable nor even likely. Many simple strategies can align older and younger Americans as staunch allies with common goals and interests.

- The expansion of the learning society to include older Americans, which to date has been happenstance, should become a deliberate policy objective, supported by innovative academic, corporate, community, and legislative initiatives. Opening our minds to the potential of elderlearning can help us understand the possibilities inherent in an aging society.

ITEMS ON THE AGENDA

1. Recognition of the Importance of Elderlearning

Our proposed agenda for elderlearning involves no extensive legislative program, no major change in budget allocations, and no new agencies or institutions. The agenda does require a general recognition that adults in the Third Age are still growing and developing, and that this continued growth and development is a plus for society that should be nurtured by significant formal and informal learning opportunities. Learning must be perceived as an integral part of older people's lives, crucial to maintaining their mental and physical health, their involvement in life, and their ability to function independently until claimed by the frailty and disabilities of a brief Fourth Age.

What we are advocating requires attitudinal changes, rethinking of institutional goals, and revised (but not necessarily increased) allocation of resources.

2. The Possibility of Continued Work

In 1900, two-thirds of men 65 and over were in the workforce[1]; by 1950, the number was less than half (46%). In 1993, it had dropped to 16 percent.[2] These statistics dramatically underscore what has become a major economic issue. Current Social Security policies encourage retirement at a time when many men and women are able to work, are not psychologically ready to leave the workplace, and need or want the additional income. Their skills and knowledge constitute an untapped resource.

There are, however, a number of barriers to delayed retirement. Primary among these barriers is the workplace culture itself. Despite abundant evidence to the contrary, older workers are viewed as less able to withstand the rigors of a full work day, less able to adapt to new techniques and technologies, and more liable to illness and absenteeism.

Another major barrier is employers' reluctance to extend training and education opportunities to older workers. Although estimates of what is spent on corporate training and education range "from $40 billion a year upward, approaching the total annual expenditure of all of America's four-year and graduate colleges and universities,"[3] little money is spent on workers over 50 years old. This under-investment in older worker training provides an unintended incentive for economic dependency in retirement on pensions and Social Security.

The financial incentives to retire early, even as early as 62, are a final barrier to delayed retirement. These incentives are compelling but not necessarily in the best interests of society.

At present, the economic potential of the young-old cohort (65-70) goes largely unrecognized, even while legislators are stumbling in their efforts to come to grips with the budgetary consequences of an aging population. The right and left hands of legislation are frequently working at cross purposes. In 1967, the Age Discrimination in Employment Act (ADEA) extended legal protection against discriminatory employer practices based on age and also banned mandatory retirement before age 70. However, until recently, public policy set the normal retirement age at 65, and only now, in response to warnings that the Social Security system may collapse, has a gradual, phased-in rise to age 67 been legislated.[4] This change arises solely from budgetary concerns and does not represent new thinking about work and retirement.

Two major concerns inhibit creative legislative thinking about work and retirement: the worry that enabling people to stay in the workforce longer will penalize the young who are just entering a shrinking labor market, and the perception that a horde of irate older citizens will severely punish any politician who threatens their benefits. These concerns are powerful disincentives to revising current practices and policies.

But these issues are not insoluble. We must recognize that age and experience need not be the "enemy" of youth and ambition. Human resource policy should not regard those approaching or attaining retirement age as impediments to growth and progress, but as potential resources on the employment/productivity continuum to be deployed as needed.

Employers could offer a variety of work options, including flex-time and job sharing, to older workers who have reached conventional retirement age. New permutations of traditional work patterns need to be invented for older adults. Consideration should be given to using older workers or recent retirees to teach or mentor younger workers in basic employability skills or specific technical applications. Older workers or retirees might also be used on a part-time basis to fill in for employees on family or disability leave.

3. Retirement Revisited

For those older adults who have already left the world of work, whether voluntarily or involuntarily, retirement can be a time of fulfillment and personal satisfaction, or a time of irrelevance and depression. Retirement can be a precious gift of time to grow and explore or "a penalty that deprives them of a continuing productive role in society."[5] Many seemingly contradictory ideas are swirling about in print and public conversation about the consequences of retirement for older men and women and for society at large. It is hard to sort out the genuinely creative ideas from the merely expedient.

Some social scientists have called retirement "a roleless role," an uncomfortable thought for a society that gives 30 percent of its potential budget to the 20 percent of its population that is "unproductive" in conventional terms. A more salutory way of looking at retirement is as a time of untapped potential that can be deployed for social good.

Given reasonably good health and sufficient income to satisfy basic needs, the key to a "good" retirement would appear to depend largely upon people's previous histories:

- the quality of their relationships to their families, friends, and communities, their sense of having or being able to create a "support group"

- their commitment to a continued active, healthy life style
- their sense of having accomplished something in their worklife or personal life in which they can take pride, and which they can still offer to society
- the extent of their previous education and their attitudes about learning
- the breadth of their interests
- their expectations about what their retirement will be

The circumstances of personal history are not immutable; if we believe in growth and development at every age, then we must believe that positive interventions can turn a "bad" retirement into a "good" one. For instance, it certainly helps to have gained self-esteem through success in one's career and to have had educational experiences that engendered a thirst for learning. A former secretary, hardly aware of her typing skills as a positive outcome of her career, gains pride in her accomplishments when asked to teach computer keyboarding to her peers. A manual laborer, self-conscious about his lack of formal education, begins to appreciate the learning he has gained on his own when asked to coach high school students at the local youth center. Both the secretary and the laborer are more likely to engage in further learning activities once they have recognized their own accrued learning as well as their ability to pass that learning on.

Given that retirement now accounts for at least a fifth and possibly as much as a third of a person's entire life, it is helpful to look to models of successful retirement to find ways of turning this period to socially and personally desirable ends. Millions of Americans are now redefining retirement as a time

- to contribute one's voluntary labor for the good of the community
- to use one's leisure to engage in contemplation, creation, and appreciation of the arts
- to nurture the young
- to carry on an active creative and intellectual life
- to continue the process of growth and development throughout the lifespan

These retired Americans are models for the future.

This more positive vision of retirement could be reinforced if employers and organizations that provide programs for older adults were to rethink the basic structure of their pre-retirement planning workshops. Taking account of the new realities of healthy, productive aging, these newly designed workshops would recognize retirement as commencement of a new phase of life, a beginning rather than an end to productivity and usefulness. They would stress resourceful use of leisure time along with the current standard issues of financial planning, insurance, wills, and how to choose a retirement community.

4. Breaking Out of the Boxes

Tinkering at the margins between work and retirement is, in the long run, irrelevant. What is needed is a creative rethinking of the present linear life cycle paradigm—education, work, and retirement—and better answers to two questions: "What is retirement a transition *to?*" and "Is retirement a single irreversible event?"

In 1975, Willard Wirtz, who was secretary of labor under Jimmy Carter, became interested in the boundaries between school, work, and retirement and how to create effective policies that would bridge the gaps. His central tenet was that there are currently two worlds, one for youth and the other for maturity, but that we should be developing a lifetime continuum of education and work opportunities.

> The fallacies that "security" is life's ultimate door prize and that retirement is an unskilled occupation are becoming increasingly transparent. . . . New thinking about the relationship between education and work may be as important with respect to the transition of older people from work, as work has traditionally been conceived of, as it is with respect to the transition of young people into it.[6]

Wirtz thinks that in exchange for the "security" of Social Security we have exacted a tradeoff in curtailed opportunity. Ideally, we should extend the opportunities for both learning and contributing to the point at which the spirit as well as the flesh gets tired. He suggests that retirees can play an important guidance and counseling function for young people through developing local work and service training inventories, community intern programs, and service experience opportunities. Thus, the rich work experience of the last generation could be transmitted to the next generation.

At the time, the most startling of Wirtz's ideas was that we might "make a year's free public education available to everybody after he or she reaches age sixty, as an organized series of educational and training opportunities thoughtfully and carefully designed to meet this situation."[7]

In 1986, Harry R. Moody traveled a parallel path, especially in regard to breaking down the rigid boundaries in which education, work, and retirement are assigned sequentially to the life stages of youth, adulthood, and old age.

> What role can learning play in preparing individuals *at every stage of life* for a society where most people can expect to live to old age? These challenges will demand a change in the relation between education and the stages of life, a transformation as far-reaching as the "discovery of childhood" described by Aries.[8]

The beginnings of such flexibility have already been pioneered by the members of the current older generation. World War II interrupted the academic and career progress of many young men and women. Young soldiers and sailors abruptly left their jobs and education to return as more mature, focused students and workers. The GI bill, which enabled hundreds of thousands to get their degrees and even go on to graduate or professional schools, is seen, in retrospect, as one of the most important pieces of social legislation in this century. It enabled a whole generation of men with minimal expectations to get a college education, and it effectively broke the lock step pattern of education as an unbroken continuum in the early stages of life.

Women of the current older generation, especially those now in their seventies, blazed the trail in their "untimely" movements back and forth from work at home, to work out of the home, to school, as economic and biological necessity dictated. These women married early during the war, took "men's" jobs to keep the war machine running and to supplement their GI husband's allotments, and took time after the war to give birth to and nurture the baby boomers. In the late 1960s and early 1970s, as their children needed them less, these women began the unprecedented movement of adults back to school to take up the unfinished business of their educations and to prepare themselves for work outside the home.

These women did not set out to be trailblazers or advance shock troops for feminism. They were simply responding realistically to the changing needs and opportunities of their own lives. Having survived the disruptions of war, they also found stratagems to survive the disruptions of changing economic and family patterns and even divorce. Their demands for a level playing field of opportunity in the workplace and in the classroom went beyond abstractions like justice and fair play; they were instruments for survival. And their recognition that their own learning need never end helped their partners respond to the training and education opportunities that employers, unions, and government agencies made increasingly available. If we take for granted today that further education at any age and in any sequence is a necessity to maintain current job skills, learn new ones, and acquire the tools for a good life, it's partly because women have shown us the way.

Meeting the challenge of retirement requires major shifts in our thinking about the flexibility of life phases so that learning, work, and retirement are not viewed as discrete stages but as states that we enter, leave, and re-enter as our life courses develop. We also need a new appraisal of the economic value of nonpaid (volunteer) work, and an expanded philosophical vision of the meaning of "responsibility" as it applies to generations. It will require recognition of two-way relationships: those who have responsibility (financial or emotional) for older adults and those older adults who must assume greater responsibility for themselves and the welfare of all members of society.

5. The Role of Colleges and Universities in Older Adult Learning

From the early 1980s, when working adults started coming back to colleges and universities, American education has, albeit reluctantly, become more flexible in reaching out to this new constituency. Higher education, especially the community colleges, have gone far in removing the institutional barriers of time and place, and have made a start at adapting the curriculum to the needs of adults. However, adult education has remained a "back door" enterprise, ghettoized in continuing education departments and largely ignored by those engaged primarily in the teaching of full-time traditional-aged students. "The academic mind persists in making status distinctions between regular education and continuing education, between credit and non-credit offerings, distinctions that are reinforced by educational policy and financing patterns."[9]

This "business almost as usual" approach is not working for older adults whose participation in formal higher education for credit is well below 1 percent. There would seem to be a monumental mismatch between the needs and interests of elderlearners and the offerings and methodologies of colleges and universities, a mismatch which the latter are not trying to alter. Colleges seem largely content to keep the three "boxes" of education, work, and retirement separate and intact.

Actually, higher education has no great incentive to change. Unlike the previous influx of working Americans, who were largely supported by government, corporate, and union dollars, older adults presently have no outside sources of support for education. Because their learning is no longer connected to economic incentives, and because they are indifferent to the degrees and credits that are the currency of higher education, older learners are reluctant to pay out of their savings the high cost of taking courses. Some take advantage of the opportunity to audit classes free (although it's poorly publicized in most institutions), but most older adults are unlikely to become paying customers for higher education.

Rather than berating these institutions for not taking on a greater share of responsibility for elderlearning, it would be more productive to look to other roles they can play in this arena. Many of them are already playing host to Elderhostels and Institutes for Learning in Retirement, activities that could be expanded to a larger number of institutions. Many of them are also serving as community resources for elders by providing access to on-campus concerts, plays, and lectures. Perhaps they could open their libraries and athletic facilities to seniors in the community and offer occasional workshops or seminars of special interest to older adults.

The most effective way to motivate the academic community to involve itself conceptually in the issues raised by an aging population might be to declare it politically correct to lavish attention on those over 65 on the basis of prior discrimination. The radicals in the faculty senate could agitate for interdisciplinary departments focusing on studies of older people's art, literature, family status, religion and philosophy, and changing social roles and futures. Textual analysis could uncover previously unrecognized biases. Dissertations could be written on the history of ageism, and studies of such symbols as bifocals and thinning hair could be traced through Norse runes and Mayan artifacts.

More seriously, colleges and universities could play an important role in support of older adults' self-directed learning. As learning specialists, librarians and faculty members could volunteer as mentors to those who know what they want to learn but aren't sure how to go about it.

Higher education, which is still operating on a "youth-oriented, age-decremental model of human resource development"[10] should be leading the new movement, not merely responding to it. Theorists with the universities should be finding ways to adapt to a more comprehensive model of lifespan development, encouraging young students to "stop out" for rich experiential learning, while older students "stop in," structuring the times, methodologies, and content of their offerings to meet the needs of people across the lifespan.

A number of research possibilities should be of interest to those in the health and social sciences as well as to those in education.

- Educators could direct research to the study of older adult learning, to design curricula, methodologies, and educational structures that would motivate older adults of varying educational backgrounds to take advantage of an array of learning opportunities.
- Economists and health professionals could study the relationship between active older learners and their health status. These studies could yield quantitative data on the potential dollar savings to our health care system if more older adults were committed to continued learning.
- Because so much is still to be learned about the cognitive abilities of older adults, graduate departments of education and psychology could play a role in developing and conducting the necessary research on learning and older adults.
- Building on the data from the Elderlearning Survey, researchers could refine and expand the instrument for a larger nationwide study of elderlearners and elderlearning.
- Colleges and universities might serve, along with selected other organizations, as centers for elderlearning resources. They might sponsor elderlearning workshops, collect and organize comprehensive lists of community opportunities for older adult learning, or provide assistance with self-directed learning projects.
- A system of elderlearning awards, *not* credits or degrees, should be devised to recognize older adult learning, whether formal or informal.

- College and university research organizations should track elderlearners and elderlearning activities for planning and institutional research purposes.

Eventually, as the Age Age spawns more fundamental changes in our society, the academic community will perhaps take a more active interest, and then we will see exciting new initiatives springing up in new departments on many campuses.

6. Returning to Learning Workshops[11]

In the early 1980s, a number of major corporations and unions, faced with the rapidity of technological change and recognizing that they could no longer offer job security, set about creating new opportunities for their workers to continue learning not only the skills applicable to their present jobs but skills and competencies that would make them more broadly employable. They had realized that their training efforts would be more effective if the workers understood the environmental context in which training had become a necessity and had a choice in what they would learn.

Over the next few years, corporations like AT&T, Scott Paper, and the Baby Bells, and unions like the UAW, AFSCME, CWA, and IBEW, worked with the nonprofit Council for Adult and Experiential Learning (CAEL) to design and offer "Returning to Learning" workshops especially tailored to workers' needs in an evolving economy. By focusing on the individual's needs, interests, and learning styles, the prospects of employment in a changing workplace, and the availability of learning resources, the workshops enabled tens of thousands of men and women to weather the changes in technology and employment practices in the workplace.

Similar workshops, designed specifically for elderlearners, could cover the following topics:

- the case for continued learning as we age, with evidence that cognitive functions do not necessarily decline
- the connections between learning, health, exercise, nutrition, and vital aging
- self-assessment of learning interests and needs
- formal learning and self-directed learning
- learning styles and strategies
- institution-based and distance learning resources
- the various helping roles older people can play in their communities
- opportunities for community service through volunteerism
- design of an individualized, short-term learning plan

Once the structure of the workshop is in place, selected groups of older adults could be trained to serve as workshop leaders on a volunteer basis. Space could be donated by churches, hospitals, and community centers, and nominal costs for materials and refreshments could be covered by the participants. The only substantial costs would be design and administration, but once the ball got rolling through nominal employer, foundation, or community support, these costs could also be covered by participants.

7. Distance Learning and Self-Directed Learning

Although older adults are already heavily engaged in self-directed learning activities, many could benefit from help in structuring that learning and finding appropriate resources. Distance learning techniques and technologies would also extend the possibility of learning to those older adults who, because of distance or infirmity, cannot access the conventional classes and workshops available to the highly mobile.

Mentoring strategies to assist self-directed learners would be relatively simple to put in place through libraries, colleges, and community centers. However, a distance learning network for elderlearners, although it would have the advantage of building on existing Internet and interactive TV systems, is a more complicated business and would require start-up funding to purchase and distribute the necessary hardware and software. Community-based libraries, which are already in the process of gearing up to handle and disseminate information through new technologies, would be the obvious choice as loci for a distance learning network. This investment would reap huge dividends in extending the reach of learning opportunities for all ages, but especially for older adults. Once the organizational patterns and equipment were in place, elderlearners themselves could manage the enterprise.

8. Intergenerational Activities

Maggie Kuhn made a strong case for proactive intergenerational activities. She did not want her peers to segregate themselves in intellectual or emotional age ghettos, separating themselves from younger generations' concerns and values.

As the lifespan lengthens and resources dwindle, the prophets of gloom have envisioned a struggle between young and old for goods, government dollars, power, and space on a planet that gets smaller all the time. They posit a sort of lifeboat situation in which food and water are in desperately short supply and occupants must be sorted out on the basis of an improvised value system, the losers to be thrown to the sharks.

However, the country is not in a lifeboat, and inter-generational conflict is not inevitable. Many believe just the opposite—an alliance between young and old is not only possible but probable. Alvin Toffler is among the latter.

> We have a system that keeps both age groups out of the job market longer and longer. The young are required to get more and more years of education, while at the other end of the age spectrum, people are being pushed out of the work force at younger and younger ages.[12]

The result is what Toffler calls "middle-age imperialism," a system run by that narrow age band between 35 and 55 who enjoy political and economic power. Ernest Boyer suggests that if young and old could discover their psychological affinity and unite, they "would be a powerful force."[13]

On a less aggressive note, Robert Butler argues that

> We need real mutuality among the generations . . . . We need new contexts, new contracts, and new intergenerational arrangements. We need ways of effectively enabling older persons to mentor and sponsor the young.[14]

Margaret Mead argued that "the continuity of all cultures depends on the living presence of at least three generations."[15] She saw older people as giving children perspective on the past and a vision of the future." This can happen informally in families, or it can happen deliberately in learning situations designed to build connections between the generations.

However, few of our modern institutions are structured to foster intergenerativity. At a time when more children have living grandparents, they are much less likely than in the past to know them well. Families move across the country. Education across the spectrum is largely structured by age groups. Retirement villages are deliberately designed to keep older people segregated, for whose benefit we are not sure. Beyond the family, social groups tend to emerge on age lines, and even mass media programming focuses on separate age cohorts. Neither MTV nor Sesame Street extends an invitation to grandparents.

However, there are welcome harbingers of change. In many communities, older people are being trained to work in nursery schools and teenagers are working in nursing homes. A 1987 study found that 25 percent of the staff in child care centers and 7 percent of preschool teachers are seniors over 55.[16] The public library system in Los Angeles has 200 senior volunteers who come to local libraries to read to children and give them a "grandlap."

A different kind of intergenerational day-care center is appearing across the country. In some corporate parks, working men and women can drop off their preschool children *or* aging parents who can't be left alone. Under the supervision of professionals, the older people read stories to the children, hand out cookies at meal time, help them go to the bathroom, and provide an attentive audience for their high jinks. The children pick up dropped articles for the older people, fetch glasses, or stop by for a cuddle. The mutual benefits of this proximity are boundless.

For young children, the benefits of intergenerational relationships, whether with their own grandparents or with surrogates, include the love and attention that induces a special bonding, the diminution of loneliness, values and new perspectives, a sense of history, and cultural continuity.

Young people who come into contact with older people in classrooms may be profoundly affected by studying alongside people who don't *have* to be there, who are committed to learning for learning's sake, and who bring their rich experience of life to the service of abstract theory.

There are many possibilities for common ground. Elderhostel now has intergenerational programs, and many travel companies are promoting grandparent/grandchild tours. Sixth graders are teaching computer skills to older people, and they, in turn, are teaching crafts and skills to younger children. Some Institutes for Learning in Retirement are actively involved in intergenerational programming.

The most compelling issue for uniting the generations is preservation of the environment. In many communities, the most active volunteers, those who clean up the beaches, count the birds, gather water samples, and lick the envelopes are predominantly the old and the young—those who are working to preserve the planet for their grandchildren and those who hope to inherit a livable earth.

The real answer, the ethical and practical answer, to those who prophesy intergenerational war is to mobilize the older generation's potential contributions to the educational and emotional nourishment of the young in what Maggie Kuhn called "transgenerational" bonding. In mutual educational and voluntary activities, young and old can work as partners for peace and social justice.

ACTION ITEMS—WHAT SHOULD BE DONE AND BY WHOM?

The Role of Government

National and state governments must lead the effort to encourage and support elderlearning. At the federal level, the president must use the bully pulpit to raise the national consciousness about the potential benefits accruing to the nation from recognition of the positive roles older citizens can play.

Although reversal of stereotyped thinking is among the most difficult tasks we face, federal and state governments can do a number of things of symbolic importance. Because language is critical in signalling attitude, the term "older adult," instead of senior, senior citizen, retiree, and similar patronizing appellations with end-of-the-road connotations, should be the language of choice when talking about the 65 plus population. Uniform use of this term would help us break out of the mutually exclusive boxes of school, work, and retirement. If the federal government viewed older adults as positive contributors to society rather than as drains on scarce resources, a trickle-down effect would be inevitable.

First on the congressional agenda should be a creative, bipartisan rethinking of the whole issue of work and retirement. The paradoxical situation in which we have a plethora of older, healthier individuals who wish to continue working and new, young workers who need access to scarce jobs must be resolved, as must the seeming conflict between the present and projected costs of Social Security and the potential social injustices that will occur if radical changes are made to the current system. There are difficult policy implications in all this and conceivably even new legislation, but we must leave the details for those who are more adept at social engineering.

The Bureau of the Census, the National Center for Education Statistics, and other data-gathering organizations should devise more precise ways of tracking elderlearning and other older adult activities. They must begin using more discrete age categories, e.g., 60-64, 65-69, 70-74, 75-79, etc., rather than the all-too-prevalent 55 or 65 plus to denote all older citizens.

Funding for aging research should be reprioritized to give greater prominence to wellness and the positive role that elderlearning can play on health and quality of life, along with obvious and needed research on disease prevention and the decrements of old age. A shift from an illness to a wellness model is well under way in some gerontological circles but should be encouraged by more generous resource allocation.

A system of tax incentives might be devised for companies and organizations that sponsor elderlearning programs, that include older workers in a full range of employee training programs, or that offer a pre-retirement program that includes information on elderlearning. In order to qualify, such programs would have to meet strict quality standards.

Finally, by removing the age restrictions on educational loans and grants, the message would be sent out loud and clear that lifelong learning is a reality and a social good.

State governments should also include elderlearning on their agendas and reconsider it among their priorities. Governors and state legislatures have a strong role to play in encouraging state colleges and institutions to take on some of the tasks of elderlearning, and they should include elderlearning initiatives and activities in their education reporting requirements.

The Role of Employers

Employers should recognize the need for more flexible boundaries between work and retirement in the Age Age. Among the strategies they might use to ease the transitions between full-time employment and cessation of work are options for a variety of flex-time and job-sharing opportunities. These strategies would provide additional benefit to the company by retaining the knowledge and skills of experienced workers. Older workers or recent retirees might also teach or mentor younger workers, especially in workshops that address basic employability skills. Moreover, older workers or retirees can be used on a part-time basis to fill in for employees on parental or disability leave.

In light of what is now known about the learning capacities of older adults, companies might rethink their training policies. By extending training opportunities to their older as well as to their younger employees, they may find that their productivity is significantly increased.

Companies should develop new and innovative ways of celebrating retirement as a commencement of a new phase of life rather than as an end to productivity and usefulness. This new awareness should not only be incorporated into the design of pre-retirement workshops, it should become part of the company culture.

Just as businesses and organizations have become sensitized to the use of inappropriate sexist language comparable attention should be paid to the elimination of ageist language and stereotyped thinking regarding older adults. By offering training to employees throughout the lifespan, business could signal the attitude that everyone is a continuous learner regardless of age.

The Role of Organizations and Foundations

Funding sources currently available through organizations such as AARP or through private foundations should be adjusted to include support for the positive effects of elderlearning and the expanded roles for older adults in our society. One activity of immediate importance in shifting the learning paradigm would be support for the design of Elderlearning workshops and for training the volunteers who will offer them. Another priority would be support for outcomes research on the connections between learning and health, learning and longevity, and learning and quality of life.

The role of libraries in elderlearning can be expanded to include help for individuals in their self-directed learning projects, on-site training in computerized search and retrieval strategies, and development of a system of distance learning opportunities.

The Role of Schools, Colleges, and Universities

The learning "establishment" could play a critical role in helping us break out of the boxes. By emphasizing learning as a continuous lifelong process, which includes both formal and informal elements, schools, colleges, and universities can underscore the idea that learning is neither synonymous with education nor co-terminus with youth. This idea could be further underscored by encouraging a variety of intergenerational learning activities with the under-standing that learners of all ages have much to learn from each other.

CONCLUSION

Although the items on the new agenda for the Age Age may seem a daunting set of tasks calling for enormous new expenditures and the creation of multiple new bureaucracies, that is emphatically *not* the case. The modest sums envisioned to set the wheels in motion can largely be handled by a modest redistribution of resources. If, for instance, by opening up new avenues of learning we can reduce the amount of money spent on home care and nursing homes by even a modest one-half to one percent, that sum could more than cover start-up costs for the effort to give a national imprimatur to elderlearning.

As for the threat of new bureaucracies, that need not and must not happen. The major work connected with bringing the new agenda into being can be done by elderlearners themselves. They are capable and they are motivated; they just need to be mobilized, encouraged, and, in some cases, trained to work with local institutions and agencies to build the infrastructure of the elderlearning system.

The key to building a strong system of elderlearning lies with these new, healthier, smarter, and physically able older Americans who are confounding the direst predictions of the prophets of doom. They have the experience and the ability to set up training for volunteers in social service fields; to organize a distance learning system; to serve as advisors to self-directed learners; to run learning workshops; and to gather, write up, and disseminate information about local learning resources. They are fully capable of doing the majority of the tasks we have outlined. In fact, they are already doing many of them.

The more than 300 Institutes for Learning in Retirement across the country provide a model for this self-actualizing work. Most of the Institutes had their inception in the vision of groups of elderlearners who wanted to create a learning environment for themselves and came together to make it happen. The Institutes are directed by their members, and the various tasks that keep them going—fiscal management, billing, record keeping, membership out-reach, programming, course selection, teaching, mailing, and phoning—are carried out by them through a series of volunteer committees and individual efforts.

Most older adults, unless seriously ill or disabled, do not need extensive helping services. The difference in mental attitude between those who remain autonomous and independent and those who have succumbed to being "taken care of" by well-meaning family members or social agencies is frequently the difference between perceiving themselves as healthy or sick. By encouraging older adults to take on the tasks connected to their own physical and mental well-being, and by opening up the concept of this new volunteer "work" that will keep them vitally connected to their communities, we are not imposing on them, we are empowering them. By recognizing the worth of their experience, skills, and knowledge, we can help assure their continued functioning as full-fledged "responsible" members of society until the inevitable encroachments of aging curtail their productivity. Harry Sky, a retired rabbi, but non-retired intellectual, reminded us that

> . . . we are a society consisting of the old and the young, teachers and learners. Society is a chain with many links. If one link is weakened then the entire chain is in danger of unraveling. Each link has to be examined and strengthened so that the chain may continue to function—as the symbol of unity of our entire society.[17]

Old age must not be viewed as "left over life to kill." It is, like youth and early maturity, a time of opportunity, of growth, of learning. The current explorers of the uncharted territory of aging, blazing the trail for their children and grandchildren, are engaged in a dynamic learning process, the outcome of which will define whether the country sinks under the burden of the Age Age or arrives at a new flowering of caring, compassion, and wisdom from which all generations must benefit.

NOTES

1. Matilda White Riley and John W. Riley, Jr., "Longevity and Social Structure: The Added Years," *Daedalus*, 115, 1 (Winter 1986), 58.

2. Hobbes and Damon, p. 4-1.

3. Ernest L. Boyer, "Foreword," in Nell P. Eurich, *Corporate Classrooms: The Learning Business* (Princeton, NJ: The Carnegie Foundation for the Advancement of Teaching, 1985), p. ix.

4. If the same ratio of years left to live were applied to today's retirement age as applied when Social Security age was set at 65, today's retirement age would be closer to 78.

5. Malcolm H. Morrison, "Work and Retirement in an Aging Society," *Daedalus*, 115, 1 (Winter 1986), 271.

6. *The Boundless Resource: A Prospectus for an Education Work Policy* (Washington, DC: New Republic Book Co., 1975), pp. 12, 128.

7. Ibid., p. 145.

8. "Education in an Aging Society," *Daedalus*, 115, 1 (Winter 1986), 191–192.

9. Moody, p. 201.

10. Ibid., p. 197.

11. This term has been copyrighted by the Council for Adult and Experiential Learning, 243 South Wabash Ave., Suite 800, Chicago, IL 60604. Unauthorized use of the term is prohibited.

12. Quoted in Elliot Carson, "The 'Revolution' Hits Midlife," *AARP Bulletin*, 36,11 (December 1995), 15.

13. Ernest L. Boyer, *Ready to Learn* (Princeton, NJ: Carnegie Foundation for the Advancement of Teaching, 1991), p. 15.

14. Butler and Kiikuni, p. xxv.

15. Ibid., p. 109.

16. "Wanted: Child-Care Workers, Age 55 and Up," *New York Times*, December 15, 1987, A1.

17. Quoted by George Neavoll, "They Have No Time for Rockers," *Maine Sunday Telegram*, June 12, 1996, 3G.

APPENDIX A

Elderlearning Survey Questionnaire

Reproduced here is the questionnaire filled out by respondents to the Elderlearning Survey.

Survey of Formal and Informal Learning

Part I: WHO YOU ARE *(all answers are kept confidential)*

1. **SEX:** ❑ Male ❑ Female

2. **STATUS:** ❑ Single ❑ Married ❑ Divorced ❑ Widowed

3. **AGE:** ❑ Below 55 ❑ 55 to 59 ❑ 60 to 64 ❑ 65 to 69 ❑ 70 to 74
   ❑ 75 to 79 ❑ 80 to 84 ❑ 85 to 89 ❑ 90 to 95 ❑ 96+

4. **DO YOU LIVE:** ❑ alone ❑ with spouse/partner ❑ with friends
   ❑ with children or relatives ❑ in a retirement community

5. **INCOME CATEGORY:** ❑ 0 to $19,999 ❑ $20,000 to $39,999
   ❑ $40,000 to $59,999 ❑ $60,000+

6. **EMPLOYMENT STATUS:**
   ❑ Do you work for pay? ❑ full-time ❑ part-time
   ❑ Self-employed or own your own business ❑ retired

7. **WORK AS A VOLUNTEER:** ❑ yes ❑ full-time ❑ part-time ❑ 1-3 days per week
   ❑ once a month ❑ occasionally ❑ no

8. **HIGHEST LEVEL OF EDUCATION:** ❑ grade school ❑ high school ❑ 2 years college
   ❑ 4 years college ❑ grad./prof. school

9. **RACE OR ETHNIC BACKGROUND:** ❑ African-American ❑ Asian-American Caucasian ❑
   ❑ Hispanic ❑ Native American ❑ Other

10. **HEALTH STATUS:** Please check (✓) the term that most accurately describes your current health status.
    ❑ excellent ❑ good ❑ fair ❑ poor

PART II. WHAT YOU CHOOSE TO LEARN

Please check (✓) ALL of the areas that describe your significant learning projects, *both formal and informal,* during the past two years. **A significant learning project is defined as one that takes 10 or more hours.**

- ❑ music, art, dance, photography, arts-related, crafts
- ❑ literature, drama, or humanities
- ❑ languages or multicultural learning
- ❑ physical sciences (astronomy, geology, etc.)
- ❑ learning for a new career
- ❑ politics, foreign affairs, current events
- ❑ computers, computer programs, new technologies
- ❑ environment or environment-related
- ❑ health and nutrition
- ❑ community development or community building
- ❑ other (please specify) _____

- ❑ building, construction, home repair
- ❑ writing, journalism, journal keeping
- ❑ nature, biological sciences
- ❑ philosophy, religion, self-actualization
- ❑ learning in field of current or previous career
- ❑ history, family history, genealogy
- ❑ finances, financial planning, investing
- ❑ gardening or agriculture
- ❑ travel or travel-related
- ❑ sports, leisure, or recreation

PART III. WHY YOU ARE LEARNING

Please check (✓) your **top five (5)** reasons for learning.

- ❑ to help me in my present job
- ❑ to prepare for a new job or career
- ❑ to pursue a new interest or hobby
- ❑ for the joy of learning
- ❑ as part of a search for meaning and wisdom in my life
- ❑ to engage in a creative activity

- ❑ to meet people and socialize
- ❑ to pursue a long-standing interest or hobby
- ❑ to fill in the blanks in my previous education
- ❑ to fulfill a community service purpose
- ❑ to fill time productively
- ❑ other (specify) _____

PART IV. HOW YOU PREFER LEARNING

All of us have different learning styles. Some prefer the stimulation of a formal class. Others prefer to learn on their own in a variety of ways. Please check (✓) the **learning resources with which you are personally most comfortable.**

- ❑ reading
- ❑ discussion
- ❑ hands-on activities
- ❑ experimenting
- ❑ travel

- ❑ group meetings
- ❑ observation of experts
- ❑ computer programs
- ❑ field work
- ❑ learning alone

- ❑ television
- ❑ classes, workshops, seminars
- ❑ self-generated learning projects
- ❑ internet and other computer networks
- ❑ learning with a friend or colleague

PART V. WHERE YOU ARE LEARNING

Check (✓) all that apply.

1. **On your own:**
- ❑ at home
- ❑ outdoors (nature)
- ❑ museums, galleries, etc.

- ❑ libraries
- ❑ travel
- ❑ at work or volunteer activity

- ❑ nature centers
- ❑ other (specify)_____

2. In **community-based learning resources:**
- ❑ senior centers
- ❑ community centers
- ❑ YMCA/YWCA
- ❑ other (specify)_____

- ❑ churches, synagogues
- ❑ local or city agencies
- ❑ hospitals, health facilities

- ❑ libraries
- ❑ parks
- ❑ social clubs

3. Please check (✓) all of the **learning programs for seniors** that you have used in the past two years.
- ❑ Elderhostel
- ❑ Alumni Organizations
- ❑ 55 Plus
- ❑ other (specify)_____

- ❑ College Learning in Retirement Programs
- ❑ OASIS
- ❑ Shepherd's Centers

- ❑ Church study groups
- ❑ Local or city agencies

4. Please check (✓) the **educational institutions** in which you have taken courses, workshops or seminars during the past two years.
- ❑ local public schools
- ❑ 4-year public colleges

- ❑ community colleges
- ❑ 4-year private colleges

- ❑ universities
- ❑ other (specify)_____

5. In the past two years, how many formal courses have you taken:
- ❑ for credit _____
- ❑ not for credit _____
- ❑ audited _____

PART VI. BARRIERS TO LEARNING

Check (✓) the **three** most important barriers which prevent you from participating in learning activities.

☐ time
☐ money
☐ lack of information about what is available

☐ distance
☐ insufficient offerings
☐ lack of motivation

☐ fear of new technologies
☐ physical handicap
☐ lack of confidence in my learning ability

☐ other (specify)_____

PART VII. TIME SPENT IN LEARNING

Please estimate the average amount of time you spend in **formal or sponsored** learning activities during an average month: _____ hours per month

Please estimate the average amount of time you spend in **informal or self-planned** learning projects or activities each month: _____ hours per month

PART VII. YOUR INFORMAL OR SELF-PLANNED LEARNING

Please describe briefly a learning activity that you have undertaken on your own in the past two years. WHAT did you set out to learn? WHY did you want to learn it? What RESOURCES did you use? How much TIME did this activity take? What MEANING does it have for you? (You may append another sheet of paper if you wish.)

_____
_____
_____

_____ Signature (optional)

Thank you for participating in this survey.

APPENDIX B

Resources for Elderlearners

NATIONAL ELDERLEARNING PROGRAMS

Elderhostel
75 Federal St.
Boston, MA 02110
Phone: (617) 426-8056
Internet: http://www.elderhostel.org

Institutes for Learning in Retirement
Elderhostel Institute Network
56 Dover Rd.
Durham, NH 03824
Phone: (603) 862-0725
Fax: (603) 868-1528

OASIS
7710 Carondelet, Ste 125
St. Louis, MO 63105
Phone: (314) 862-2933
Fax: (314) 862-2149
E-Mail: oasisinst@aol.com

Shepherds Centers of America
6700 Troost, #616
Kansas City, MO 64131
Phone: (816) 523-1080
Fax: (816) 523-5790
E-mail: shepherd@qni.com
Internet: http://www.qni.com/shepherd

STUDY/TRAVEL PROGRAMS

Discovery Tours
American Museum of Natural History
Central Park West at 79th St.
New York, NY 10024-5192
Phone: (800) 462-8687 or
(212) 769-5700
Internet: discovery@amnh.org

Elderhostel (see above)

Interhostel
University of New Hampshire
6 Garrison Ave.
Durham, NH 03824-3529
Phone: (800) 733-9753 or
(603) 862-1147

Smithsonian Study Tours and Seminars
1100 Jefferson Dr., SW
MRC 702
Washington, DC 20560
Phone: (202) 357-4700
Fax: (202) 633-9250
Internet: http://www.si.edu/tsa/sst

University Vacations
North American Headquarters
International Building
9602 NW 13 St.
Miami, FL 33172
Phone: (800) 792-0100 or
      (305) 591-1736
Fax: (305) 591-9102
E-Mail: univac@icanect.net

INDEPENDENT LEARNING OPPORTUNITIES

American Open University of New York
Institute of Technology
Building 66, Office 227
Central Islip, NY 11722
Phone: (516) 348-3000

Center for Distance Learning
Empire State College
2 Union Ave.
Saratoga Springs, NY 12866
Phone: (518) 587-2100
Internet: http://www.esc.edu

Governor's State University at Western Illinois University
Educational Broadcasting and Extended Learning
Phone: (309) 298-1864
Internet: http://www.ecnet.net/users/miebis

Knowledge TV
(Knowledge TV is a national cable network dedicated to educational programming, delivering college-level classes in universities. Knowledge TV is available through local cable programming, satellite television, and VHS tapes.)
Phone: (800) 777-MIND
E-mail: meu.edu
Internet: http://www.jec.edu

Ohio University External Student Program
309 Tupper Hall
Athens, OH 45701
Phone: (800) 444-2420

Regents College of the University of the State of New York
Cultural Education Center
Albany, NY 12230
Phone: (518) 474-3703

Thomas A. Edison State College
1010 West State St.
Trenton, NJ 08625
Phone: (609) 984-1100

INTERNET WEBSITES

Age of Reason
Sponsored by Seniors on Line, this website has extensive information on all sorts of topics of interest to seniors in Canada and the U.S.
Internet: http://www.ageofreason.com

SeniorNet
International community of computer-using seniors.
Internet: http://www.seniornet.org

University Continuing Education Association (UCEA)
[Formerly the National University Continuing Education Association (NUCEA)] Though aimed at continuing education providers, the UCEA continuing education website offers information about college and university programs, distance learning opportunities, professional development, a UCEA fact file, and "What's Happening" for news and events.
Internet: http://www.nucea.edu/

NOTE: Many state and local museums and arts organizations and various alumni, professional, and affinity groups also provide study/travel opportunities for their members.

PRINT MATERIALS

Directory of Accredited Home Study Schools.
   A brochure giving school names,
   subject areas, a description of each
   program and contact information. For
   a copy of the directory, call CAEL at
   (800) 327-2235

How to Study Independently,
   Regents College (free).
   Phone: (518) 474-3703

BIBLIOGRAPHY

AARP Bulletin, 36,10 (July-August 1994).

Achenbaum, W.A. "America as an Aging Society: Myths and Images." *Daedalus*, 115, 1 (Winter 1986), 13-30.

————. *Images of Old Age in America, 1790 to Present.* Ann Arbor, MI: Institute of Gerontology, University of Michigan, Wayne State University, 1978.

————. "Retirement in Historical Context." *Columbia Book of Retirement*, Abraham Monk, ed. New York: Columbia University Press, 1994, 12-28.

Aging Society, Daedalus, 115, 1 (Winter 1986).

Allen, Robert E. "The Anxiety Epidemic." *Newsweek*, April 8, 1996, 15.

"Alumni Notes." *Harvard Medical Alumni Bulletin*, 67, 3 (Winter 1993-94), 15–18.

American Society on Aging. *Serving Elders of Color: Challenge to Providers and the Aging Network*. American Society on Aging, 1990.

Anstey, Kaarin, Lazar Stankov, and Stephen Lord. "Primary Aging, Secondary Aging, and Intelligence." *Psychology and Aging*, 8, 4 (1993), 562-70.

Bacon, Carrie L. *Celebrating Diversity: A Learning Tool for Working with People of Different Cultures*. AARP, 1990.

Baker, Beth. "The Art of Being Unreasonable." *AARP Bulletin*, 36, 10 (November 1995), 20.

Baltes, Paul, and K. Warner Schaie. "Aging and IQ: The Myth of the Twilight Years." *Psychology Today* (March 1974), 35-40.

Bashore, Theodore. "Age, Physical Fitness and Mental Processing Speed." *Annual Review of Gerontology and Geriatrics*, M.P. Lawton, ed. *Clinical and Applied Gerontology*. (Spring, 1989).

Bateson, Mary Catherine. *With a Daughter's Eye*. New York: Washington Square Press, 1985.

Beauvoir, Simone de. *The Coming of Age*. New York: G.P. Putnam's Sons, 1972.

Beckman, Brenda Marshall, and Catherine Ventura-Merkel. *Community College Programs for Older Adults: A Resource Directory of Guidelines, Comprehensive Programming Models, and Selected Programs*. League for Innovation in the Community College, 1993.

Belsky, Janet. *The Psychology of Aging: Theory, Research, & Interventions*, 2nd ed. Brooks/Cole, 1990.

Berghorn, Forest J., Donna E. Schafer, and Associates. *The Dynamics of Aging: Original Essays on the Processes and Experiences of Growing Old*. Boulder, CO: Westview Press, 1981.

Berman, Phillip L., ed. *The Courage to Grow Old*. New York: Ballantine Books, 1989.

Bianchi, Eugene C. *Aging as a Spiritual Journey*. New York: The Crossroad Publishing Company, 1982.

Birren, James E., and Betty A. Birren. "The Concepts, Models, and History of the Psychology of Aging," *Handbook of the Psychology of Aging*, James E. Birren and K. Warner Schaie, eds. 3rd ed. San Diego: Academic Press, 1990, 3-20.

Birren, James E. and K. Warner Schaie, eds. *Handbook of the Psychology of Aging*, James E. Birren and K. Warner Schaie, eds. 3rd ed. San Diego, CA: Academic Press, 1990.

Booth, Wayne, ed. *The Art of Growing Older: Writers on Living and Aging*. New York: Poseidon Press, 1992.

Bortz, Walter M. *We Live Too Short and Die Too Long*. New York: Bantam Press, 1991.

Bowen, Catherine Drinker. *Yankee from Olympus: Justice Holmes and His Family*. Boston: Little Brown & Co., 1949.

Boyer, Ernest L. *Ready to Learn*. Princeton, NJ: Carnegie Foundation for the Advancement of Teaching, 1991.

Brademas, John. "Universities Must Treat Adult Education as a Fundamental Part of Their Mission," *CHE*, 36, 33 (1990), B1, 2.

Brody, Jane E. "Good Habits Outweigh Genes as Key to a Healthy Old Age." *New York Times*, February 28, 1996, C9.

Bronte, Lydia. *The Longevity Factor: The New Reality of Long Careers and How It Can Lead to Richer Lives*. New York: HarperCollins, 1993.

Burke, Deborah M., and Gary D. Laver. "Aging and Word Retrieval: Selective Age Deficits in Language," *Aging and Cognition: Mental Processes, Self-Awareness and Interventions*, Eugene A. Lovelace, ed. Amsterdam: North-Holland Press, 1990, 281–300.

Butler, Robert N. "Cycles, Clocks, and Power Plants," *Geriatric Curriculum Development Conference and Initiative. AJA Proceedings*, 97, 4A (October 17, 1994), 4A-35S, 4A-39S.

―――. "The Facade of Chronological Age: An Interpretative Summary," *Middle Age and Aging*, Bernice L. Neugarten, ed. Chicago: University of Chicago Press, 1968, 235–42.

―――. "The Life Review: An Interpretation of Reminiscence in the Aged." *Psychiatry*, 26, (1963), 65–76.

―――. "On Behalf of Older Women: Another Reason to Protect Medicare and Medicaid." *New England Journal of Medicine*, 334, 12 (March 21, 1996), 794-96.

―――. *The Tragedy of Old Age in America*. New York: Harper & Row, 1975.

Butler, Robert N., and Kenzo Kiikuni, eds. *Who is Responsible for My Old Age?* New York: Springer Publishing Co., 1993.

Butler, R., and M. Lewis. *Aging and Mental Health: Positive Psychological Approaches*. St. Louis: C.V. Mosby, 1973.

Bynum, Louise L. *Motivations of Third-Age Students in Learning in Retirement Institutes*. Dissertation, University of South Carolina, 1992.

Callahan, Daniel. *Setting Limits: Medical Goals in an Aging Society*. New York: Simon & Schuster, 1987.

Carlson, Elliot. "The 'Revolution' Hits Midlife." *AARP Bulletin*, 36, 11 (December 1995), 15, 16.

Chickering, Arthur W. and Associates. *The Modern American College*. San Francisco: Jossey-Bass, 1981.

Clarkson-Smith, L., and A.A. Hartley. "Relationships Between Physical Exercise and Cognitive Abilities in Older Adults. *Psychological Aging*, 4, 2 (June 1989), 183-89.

"Colleges of the Third Age." *TAFE Newsletter*, 22 (September 1986), 7.

Comfort, Alex. "Age Prejudice in America." *Social Policy*, 7 (1976), 3-8.

―――. *A Good Age*. New York: Crown Publishers, 1976.

Cowdry, E.V. *Problems of Aging*. Baltimore: Williams & Williams, 1939.

Cox, Harold. *Later Life: The Realities of Aging*. Upper Saddle River, NJ: Prentice-Hall, 1984.

Cross, K. Patricia. *Adults as Learners*. San Francisco: Jossey-Bass, 1981.

Cumming, Elaine, and William F. Henry. *Growing Old: The Process of Disengagement*. New York: Basic Books, 1961.

Day, Jennifer Cheeseman. "Population Projections of the United States by Age, Sex, Race, and Hispanic Origin: 1992-2050." *Current Population Reports*. U.S. Department of Commerce, Bureau of the Census, 1992, P 25-1092.

Deets, Horace B. "No More Stereotypes, Thank You!" *Modern Maturity* (July-August 1994), 4-5.

DeGenova, Mary Kay. "If You Had Your Life to Live over Again: What Would You Do Differently?" *International Journal of Aging and Human Development*, 34, 21 (1992), 135-43.

Dennis, Wayne, "Creative Productivity between the Ages of 20 and 80 Years," *Middle Age and Aging*, Bernice L. Neugarten, ed. Chicago: University of Chicago Press, 1968, 106-14.

Dillman, Don A., James A. Christenson, Priscilla Salant, and Paul D. Warner. "What the Public Wants from Higher Education: Work Force Implications from a 1995 National Survey." Economic Sciences Research Center (SESRC), Washington State University, technical report number 95-52, 1995.

Doucette, Don, and Catherine Ventura-Merkel. *Community College Programs for Older Adults: A Status Report*. League for Innovation in the Community College and AARP, March 1991.

Dustman, Robert, et al. "Aerobic Exercise Training and Improved Neuropsychologic Function of Older Individuals." *Neurobiology of Aging*, 5 (1984), 35-42.

Eurich, Nell P. *Corporate Classrooms: The Learning Business*. Princeton, NJ: Carnegie Foundation for the Advancement of Teaching, 1985.

Evans, William, and Irwin M. Rosenberg. *Biomarkers: The Ten Keys to Prolonging Vitality*. New York: Simon and Schuster, 1991.

Fischer, Richard, Mark Blazey, and Henry Lipman, *Students of the Third Age*. New York: MacMillan, 1992.

Friedan, Betty. *The Fountain of Age*. New York: Simon and Schuster, 1993.

Fries, James. *Vitality and Aging: Implications of the Rectangular Curve*. W.H. Freeman & Co., 1981.

Gerzon, Mark. *Coming Into Our Own*. New York: Delacorte Press, 1992.

Goggin, Noreen L., and George E. Stelmach. "Age-related Deficits in Cognitive-Motor Skills," *Aging and Cognition: Mental Process, Self-Awareness and Interventions*, Eugene A. Lovelace, ed. Amsterdam: North-Holland Press, 1990, 135-55.

Gose, Kathleen, and Gloria Levi. *Dealing with Memory Changes as You Grow Older*. New York: Bantam Books, 1988.

Greenberg, Reva. *Education for Older Adult Learning*. Westport, CT: Greenwood Press, 1993.

Hagestad, Gunhild O. "The Aging Society as a Context for Family Life." *Daedalus*, 115, 1 (Winter 1986), 119-39.

Harris, L. and Associates. *The Myth and Reality of Aging in America*. Washington, DC: The National Council on the Aging, Inc., 1975.

Henry, Sherrye. "Keep Your Brain Fit for Life." *Parade* (March 17, 1996), 8-11.

Herzog, A., N. Regula, J.S. House, and J.N. Moran. "Relation of Work and Retirement to Health and Well-being in Older Age." *Psychology and Aging*, June 1991, 6, 2, 202-11.

Hess, Beth B. "Postword: Where We Are and Where We Might Go." *Aging in Society: Selected Reviews of Recent Research*, Matilda White Riley, Beth B. Hess, and Kathleen Bond, eds. Mahwah, NJ: Lawrence Erlbaum Associates, 1983, pp. 253-66.

Hessel, Dieter. "Old and Young in Action Together." *The Older Learner*, 3, 3 (Summer 1995), 1, 3.

Hiemstra, R.P. *The Older Adult and Learning*. Lincoln: University of Nebraska Press, 1975.

Hobbs, Frank B., and Bonnie L. Damon. *65+ in the United States*. Washington, DC: Bureau of the Census, 1996.

Hutchison, Frank. *Aging Comes of Age*. Louisville, KY: Westminster/John Knox Press, 1991.

Jackson, James S., Linda M. Chatters, and Robert Joseph Taylor. "Roles and Resources of the Black Elderly." *Aging in Black America*. Thousand Oaks, CA: Sage Publications, 1993, 1-18.

Jacques, Paul J., and Karen M. Riggs. "B Vitamins as Risk Factors for Age-Related Diseases." *Nutritional Assessment of Elderly Populations: Measure and Function*, Irwin H. Rosenberg, ed. New York: Raven Press, 1995, 234-51.

Johnston, Priscilla W., ed. *Perspectives on Aging: Exploding the Myths*. Ballinger Publishing Co., 1981.

Johnston, William S. *Workforce 2000: Work and Workers for the Twenty-First Century*. New York: Hudson Institute, 1987.

Kidder, Tracy. *Old Friends*. Boston: Houghton Mifflin, 1993.

Kolata, Gina. "New Era of Robust Elderly Belies the Fears of Scientists." *New York Times*, February 27, 1996, A1, C3.

Kolb, David, "A Conversation with David Kolb." *CAEL Forum and News*, 17, 1 (Spring 1994), 8-9.

Lamb, Charles, "The Superannuated Man," *The Art of the Personal Essay*, Phillip Lopate, ed. New York: Anchor Books, 1994, 172-78.

Lamdin, Lois. *Earn College Credit for What You Know*, 2nd. ed. Chicago: CAEL, 1992.

Langer, Ellen. *Mindfulness*. Reading, MA: Addison-Wesley, 1989.

Lapp, Danielle. *Don't Forget: Easy Exercises for a Better Memory at Any Age*. New York: McGraw-Hill, 1987.

Laslett, Peter. *A Fresh Map of Life: The Emergence of the Third Age*. London: Weidenfeld and Nicolson, 1989.

Leaf, Rose. "University of the Third Age: Stretching the Boundaries—A Self-Resourced Coalition for Learning." *Stretching the Boundaries: A Quarterly Experience*. Australian Consortium on Experiential Education, Inc., 32 (1994), 25-27.

Leas, Richard, et al. *How to Avoid Charges of Age Discrimination in the Workplace*. New York: Executive Enterprises Publications Co., Inc., 1989.

Lehrmann, Eugene I. "Work and Retirement in the '90's." *Modern Maturity* (September-October 1994), 6-7.

Lewis, Robert. "Here Come the Boomers." *AARP Bulletin*, 36, 11 (December 1995), 1, 10-12.

Lifelong Learning Trends: A Profile of Continuing Education. Washington, DC: NUCEA, 1990.

Lonergan, Edmund T., ed. *Extending Life: A National Research Agenda on Aging.* Institute of Medicine, Division of Health Promotion and Disease Prevention. Washington, DC: National Academy Press, 1991.

Lopate, Phillip, ed. *The Art of the Personal Essay.* New York: Anchor Books, 1994.

Lorant, Richard. "Computer Net Turns into Safety Net for Ailing Online Senior." *The Times Record*, January 28, 1995, 7, cols. 3-4.

Lovelace, Eugene A., ed. *Aging and Cognition: Mental Processes, Self-Awareness and Interventions.* Amsterdam: North-Holland Press, 1990.

―――. "Basic Concepts in Cognition and Aging." *Aging and Cognition: Mental Process, Self-Awareness and Interventions*, Eugene A. Lovelace, ed. Amsterdam: North-Holland Press, 1990, 1-28.

―――. "Cognitive Aging: A Summary Overview." *Aging and Cognition: Mental Process, Self-Awareness and Interventions*, Eugene A. Lovelace, ed. Amsterdam: North-Holland Press, 1990, 407-34.

Lyne, Barbara. "Out of Retirement Life and Back into the Fire." *New York Times*, August 14, 1994, 3, 21.

MacNeill, Richard D., and Michael L. Teague. "Leisure Opportunities, Leisure Resources." *Columbia Book of Retirement*, Abraham Monk, ed. New York: Columbia University Press, 1994, 509-24.

Manheimer, Ronald J. and Denise Snodgrass. "New Roles and Norms for Older Adults through Higher Education," *Educational Gerontology*, 19 (1993), 585-95.

McDonnell, Tessa. "A Conversation with David Kolb." *CAEL Forum and News*, 17, 1 (Spring 1994), 8-9.

McLeish, John A.B. *The Ulyssean Adult: Creativity in the Middle and Later Years.* Toronto: McGraw-Hill Ryerson, Ltd., 1976.

Mills, Eugene S. *The Story of Elderhostel.* Hanover, NH: University of New Hampshire Press, 1993.

Molloy, D.W., D.A. Beerschoten, M.J. Borrie, R.G. Crilly, and R.D. Cape. "Acute Effects of Exercise on Neuropsychological Function in Elderly Subjects." *Journal of the American Geriatric Society*, 36, 1 (January 1988), 29-33.

Monk, Abraham, ed. *Columbia Retirement Handbook.* New York: Columbia University Press, 1994.

Moody, Harry R. "Education in an Aging Society." *Daedalus*, 115, 1 (Winter 1986), 191-210.

Morrison, Malcolm H. "Work and Retirement in the Aging Society." *Daedalus*, 115, 1 (Winter 1986), 269-93.

Morse, Claire K. "Does Variability Increase with Age? An Archival Study of Cognitive Measures." *Psychology and Aging*, 8, 2 (June 1993), 156-64.

Moses, Campbell. "Doctors Learning from Retirement," 1994 (unpublished paper).

National Center for Health Statistics. *The Longitudinal Study of Aging 1984-1990*. USHHS, 1991.

National University Continuing Education Association. *Lifelong Learning Trends: A Profile of Continuing Higher Education*. Washington, DC: NUCEA, 1990.

Neavoll, George. "They Have No Time for Rockers." *Maine Sunday Telegram*, June 12, 1996, 3 G.

Nemy, Enid. "World of Opportunities for Tirelessly Retired." *New York Times*, August 11, 1984, C1, 8.

Neugarten, Bernice L., ed., *Middle Age and Aging: A Reader in Social Psychology*. Chicago: University of Chicago Press, 1968.

Neugarten, Bernice L., and Joan W. Moore, "The Changing Age-Status System." *Middle Age and Aging*, Bernice L. Neugarten, ed. Chicago: University of Chicago Press, 1968, 5-21.

Neugarten, Bernice L., and Dail A. Neugarten. "Age in the Aging Society." *Daedalus*, 115, 1 (Winter 1986), 31-49.

Newman, Maria. "Elderly Angered by Changes for Courses at New School." *New York Times*, February 7, 1994, A1, B7.

Norton, Dianne. "A Brief History of U3A." *Third Age News*, supplement, 1.

Nuessel, Frank. *The Image of Older Adults in the Media: An Annotated Bibliography*. Westport, CT: Greenwood Press, 1992.

Palmer, John L., and Stephanie G. Gould. "The Economic Consequences of an Aging Society." *Daedalus*, 15, 1 (Winter 1986), 295-323.

Pearce, Sandra D. "Toward Understanding the Participation of Older Adults in Continuing Education." *Educational Gerontology*, XVII, 5 (September-October 1991). 451–464.

Peck, Robert C., "Developments in the Second Half of Life." *Middle Age and Aging*, Bernice L. Neugarten, ed. Chicago: University of Chicago Press, 1968, 88-92.

Peterson, David A. *Facilitating Education for Older Learners*. San Francisco: Jossey-Bass, 1983.

Philibert, Michel. "A Philosophy of Aging from a World Perspective." *Perspectives on Aging*, Priscilla W. Johnston, ed. Ballinger Publishing Co., 1981, 237–256.

Pifer, Alan, and D. Lydia Bronte. "Introduction: Squaring the Pyramid." *Daedalus*, 115, 1 (Winter 1986), 1-11.

Pollner, Fran. "Being President Can Be Hazardous to One's Health." *U.S. Medicine*, 32, 5, 6 (March 1996), 1, 23.

Quinn, Joseph F. "The Future of Retirement." *Columbia Retirement Handbook*, Abraham Monk, ed. New York: Columbia University Press, 1994, 570–590.

Reynolds, Sharon M. "Aging with Grace: The School Sisters of Notre Dame Study," *Odyssey* (Winter-Spring 1993) 2-7.

Riley, Matilda White, Beth B. Hess, and Kathleen Bond, eds. *Aging in Society: Selected Reviews of Recent Research*. Mahwah, NJ: Lawrence Erlbaum Associates, 1983.

Riley, Matilda, White and John W. Riley, Jr. "Longevity and Social Structure: The Added Years." *Daedalus*, 115, 1 (Winter 1986), 51-75.

Routher, Ray. "The Teacher and His Subject Alike: They're Never Too Old." *Maine Telegram*, November 19, 1995, G1-2.

Rowe, J.W., and R.L. Kahn. "Human Aging: Usual and Successful." *Science*, 237 (1987), 143-49.

Salthouse, Timothy, A. "Cognitive Competence and Expertise in Aging." *Handbook of the Psychology of Aging*, James E. Birren and R. Warner Schaie, eds. San Diego: Academic Press, 1990, 310-19.

Salvia, John, and James E. Ysseldyke. *Assessment*. Boston: Houghton Mifflin, 1991.

Sarton, May. "A Literary Perspective." *Perspectives on Aging*, Priscilla W. Johnston, ed. Ballinger Publishing Co., 1981, 117–50.

Schaie, K. Warner, "Age Changes and Age Differences." *Middle Age and Aging*, Bernice L. Neugarten, ed. Chicago: University of Chicago Press, 558-70.

Schaie, K. Warner. "Intellectual Development in Adulthood." *Handbook of the Psychology of Aging*, James E. Birren and K. Warner Schaie, eds. San Diego: Academic Press, 1990, 291-309.

Scheppke, Jim. "Who's Using the Public Library?" *Library Journal*, October 15, 1994, 35–37.

Schooler, Carmi. "Psychosocial Factors and Effective Cognitive Functioning in Adulthood." *Handbook of the Psychology of Aging*, James E. Birren and K. Warner Schaie, eds. San Diego: Academic Press, 1990, 347-58.

Seccombe, K., and M. Ishii-Kuntz. "Perception of Problems Associated with Aging: Comparisons Among Four Older Age Cohorts." *The Gerontologist*, 31, August 1991, 527-33.

Sheckley, Barry G., Lois Lamdin, and Morris T. Keeton. *Employability in a High Performance Economy*. Chicago: CAEL, 1993.

Sheehy, Gail. *New Passages: Mapping Your Life across Time*. New York: Random House, 1995.

Simonton, Dean Keith. "Creativity and Wisdom in Aging." *Columbia Retirement Handbook*, Abraham Monk, ed. New York: Columbia University Press, 1994, 320-29.

Singer, Henry W. "A World of Centenarians." *Med Ad News*, 15, 3 (March 1996), 1, 19-24.

Smith, Anderson D., and Denise C. Park. "Adult Age Differences in Memory for Pictures and Images." *Aging and Cognition: Mental Processes, Self-Awareness and Interventions,* Eugene A. Lovelace, ed. Amsterdam: North-Holland Press, 1990, 69-96.

Snowdon, David A., Sharon K. Ostwald, and Robert L. Kane. "Education, Survival and Independence in Elderly Catholic Sisters 1936-1988." *American Journal of Epidemiology,* 130 (1989), 999-1012. (http://www.coa.uky.edu/nunnet)

Sontag, Susan. "The Double Standard of Aging." *Saturday Review,* September 23, 1972, 28-29, 31-38.

Staudinger, U.M., J. Smith, and P.B. Baltes. "Wisdom-related Knowledge in a Life Review Task: Age Differences and the Role of Professional Specialization." *Psychology and Aging,* 7, 2, June 1991, 271-81.

Stones, M.J., and D. Dawe. "Acute Exercise Facilitates Semantically-Cued Memory in Nursing Home Residents." *Journal of the American Geriatric Society,* 41 (1993), 531-34.

Strange, John H. "A Cultural Revolution: From Books to Silver Discs." Unpublished article, 1995.

Swift, Jonathan. "Gulliver's Travels." *The Portable Swift.* New York: Viking Press, 1948, 432-35.

Taylor, Susan Champlin. "The End of Retirement." *Modern Maturity* (October-November 1993), 32-39.

Thurow, Lester C. "The Birth of a Revolutionary Class." *New York Times Magazine,* May 19, 1996, 46-47.

Tough, A. *The Adult's Learning Projects: A Fresh Approach to Theory and Practice in Adult Learning.* Toronto: Ontario Institute for Studies in Education, 1971.

————. "Interests of Adult Learners." *The Modern American College,* Arthur W. Chickering and Associates, eds. San Francisco: Jossey-Bass, 1981, 296-305.

————. "Major Learning Efforts: Recent Research and Future Directions." In *The Adult Learner: Current Issues in Higher Education.* Washington, DC: American Association for Higher Education, 1978.

U.S. Department of Commerce. *Statistical Abstract of the United States.* Washington, DC: Bureau of the Census, 1994.

Von Mering, Otto, "Societies in Transition: The Impact of Longevity on Generations." *Educational Gerontology.* XVIII, 1 (March 1992). From a talk at Aging Annual Conference, Plenary Session, Symposium on "International Aging. An Opportunity for Exchange." May 20, 1991, Miami Beach, FL.

Watkins, Beverly T. "With More Adult Students on Campuses, Some Colleges Are Adjusting Their Curricula and Teaching Methods." *Chronicle of Higher Education*, 35, 19 (January 18, 1989), A27, 32.

Weinstock, Ruth. *The Graying of the Campus*. New York: Educational Facilities Laboratory, 1978.

"Where's the Vitamin E?" *U.S. News and World Report*, June 10, 1996, 102.

Williams, T. Franklin. "A New Scope on Retirement." *Harvard Medical Alumni Bulletin*, 67, 3 (Winter 1993-94), 13-15.

Willis, Sherry L. "Current Issues in Cognitive Training Research." *Aging and Cognition: Mental Processes, Self-Awareness and Interventions*, Eugene A. Lovelace, ed. Amsterdam: North-Holland Press, 1990, 263-80.

Wirtz, Willard. *The Boundless Resource: A Prospectus for an Education Work Policy*. Washington, DC: New Republic Book Co., 1975.

INDEX

AARP. *See* American Association of Retired Persons
ACE. *See* American Council on Education
ACS, 150
ADEA. *See* Age Discrimination in Employment Act
adult life cycle tasks, 28
African Americans, 70–71, 131
AFSCME, 170
age bias, 149. *See also* ageism, stereotypes
Age Discrimination in Employment Act (ADEA), 163
age irrelevant curriculum, 102
Age of Learning, 12–13
Age of Reason, 183
ageism, 1–5, 8, 22. *See also* stereotypes
language of, 175
Agenda for the Age Age, 161–78
agenda action items, 173–76
"boxes" of education, work, learning, 166–67, 168, 174
aging, 15–25
of brain, 39–41
chronological, 15–17
creativity in, viii, 29, 61–64, 76, 126, 159
cultural, 20–21
definitions of, 17, 18
developmental, 15, 29–30

economic uncertainty of, 11
four ages theory of, 30–32
gathering data on, 2, 17, 174
growth and development in, viii, x, 2, 29–30, 32, 39, 62, 148, 161, 163, 177
issues raised by aging U.S. population, 8–12
life stage theory of, 27–29, 176
medical definition of, 17–18
negative attitudes toward, 4, 20–21
nonphysiological, 41–43
physiological, 18–20, 39–41
positive aspects of, 9–10
primary and secondary, 41
problems of, 5
research on, 174
social and cultural factors in, 42
socially constructive, 143–60
sociogenic, 20
stage theory of, 27–29
state of mind, 21–22
stereotypes of, 3, 4–5, 9, 21, 36, 38, 102, 156
successful, 22
theory of, 30–32
time of opportunity, 177
of U.S., 5–8
useful views of, 21–22
wellness model of, 174

Aging in Black America (Jackson et al.),
        71
altruism of older population, 105–06
alumni organizations, 79
Alzheimer's disease, 41, 56, 128
American Association of Retired Persons
        (AARP), xi, 3, 66–67, 175
American Council on Education (ACE),
        xi, 89
American Express, 144
American Medical Association, 18
American Museum of Natural History,
        182
American Open University of New York,
        183
Aristotle, 37, 58
AT&T, 170

Baltes, Paul, 39
Barchas, Jack, 40
barriers to learning, 81–83, 92–94, 168
Berens, Michael, xi
Berkeley, Bill, xi, 103, 104
Birren, James, 24
Bismarck, Otto Von, 11, 16, 145
Blacks. *See* African-Americans
Blazey, Mark, 98
Blythe, Ronald, 15, 143
Bortz, Walter, xii, 1, 6, 7, 18, 19, 52, 53,
        65, 151
Bowdoin College, xi, 97
Brademas, John, 90–91
brain
        aging of, 39–41
        as computer, 49
        exercise of, 52–57
        maintenance of function, 52–58
Bronte, Lydia, 20
Brooklyn Institute for Retired Profession-
        als and Executives, 107, 108
Brooks, Christine, xi
Brower, David, 156
Bruner, Jerome, 161
Brunswick, Maine, xi, 97
Bureau of the Census, 6
Bureau of Labor Statistics, 149
Burke, Deborah M., 49
Burns, George, 1
Butler, Robert N., 6, 7, 8, 19, 54, 151

CAEL. *See* Council for Adult and
        Experiential Learning
Callahan, Daniel, 10
Canadian Great Trunk Railroad System,
        144
Career Connections, 155
Carnegie-Mellon University, 108
Carter, Lillian, 151
CCR. *See* Center for Creative Retirement
CD-ROM, use of by elderlearners, 133–
        35, 137, 138
Center for Creative Retirement (CCR),
        xi, 96, 156
Center for Distance Learning, 183
Chandler Medical Center, 56
churches and synagogues as learning
        resources, 78–79, 81, 115, 131
Churchill, Sir Winston, 130
Citizens Observer Patrol (COP), 154
CNN, 22
cognitive abilities of older learners, 36–
        51, 52–59
        connections to physical health, 52–57
        cross sectional vs. longitudinal studies,
                45–47
        crystallized and fluid intelligence, 38,
                47–48, 50
        diet and, 59
        effects of training on, 59–61
        further research in, 169
        measuring, 43–45
        maintenance of, 39, 41–3,
        mind-body connections, 52–59
        noncognitive factors, 45
        nonphysiological factors, 41–43
        physical exercise and, 52, 53, 57–58
        physiological aging of, 39–41
        skills retention and loss, 47–50
        social involvement and, 52–57
cognitive competence, 43–49
College for Seniors, 96
college towns, as attractions for retirees,
        95–97
colleges and universities. *See also* higher
        education
        accommodating older students, 88–89
        barriers to older students, 82–83, 92–
                94, 168

courses taken, 80–81
credentialling function, 92, 168, 169
credits, 80–81, 92, 168, 169
data tracking, 17, 90–91
grades, 93
graying of campus, 88–90
lack of interest in older adults, 90, 93
irrelevance of, 128
non-classroom strategies for elder-
    learning at, 94–98
non-credit programs, 81, 97
older adult enrollment at, 90–92
older adult learning in, 88–100
possibilities for research, 169–70
potential roles and functions, 94, 98–
    99, 168–70, 175–76
reasons for lack of enrollment at, 92–
    93
resistance to change, 94, 168
responsibility to Third Agers, 98
roles to be played by, 98–99, 168–70,
    175–76
steps to be taken by, 99
tuition, 93
Colleges of the Third Age (Australia),
    33–34
Comfort, Alex, 17, 20
commencement, 143–44, 146–47. See also
    retirement
community colleges, 80, 91, 97–98. See
    also colleges and universities
community learning resources, 78–79, 81,
    86, 114–15
computers
    as language tutors, 134–35
    as learning resource, 74, 77, 119, 121,
        125
    as learning tools, 125, 132–36
continuing education, learning, 1, 13, 15,
    79, 90, 175
Council for Adult and Experiential
    Learning (CAEL), 89, 90, 170, 183
creativity in aging, viii, 29, 61–64, 76,
    126, 159
Cross, K. Patricia, 82
cross-section vs. longitudinal studies of
    cognitive aging, 45–47
cross-sectional testing, 45–47

crystallized intelligence, 38, 47–48, 50
Cumming, Elaine, 23
CWA, 170

Dartmouth College, 95–96
degrees. See colleges and universities,
    credentialling function
Delaney, Elizabeth, 63, 147
Delaney, Sara, 63, 147
demographics
    age in England, 7
    age pyramid, 6–7
    of aging population, 5-8, 11, 90, 161
    continued growth projections, 6–7
    decline in disability rates, 10
    decline in mortality rates, 5–6
    function of social and technological
        change, 7–8
    need for change in policies and
        institutions, 8
    rising life expectancy, 5
    worldwide growth in older population,
        6, 161
Department of Labor, 17
Dewey, John, 39
diet, 59
Directory of Accredited Home Study
    Schools, 184
Discovery Tours, 182
disengagement theory, 22–25, 31, 101
    life enhancing, 21
    male oriented, 23
    as opposed to engagement, 23
    questions about, 23–24
    for women, 23
distance learning, 136–38, 170, 171, 175,
    176
    advantages of for older learners, 137–
        38
    mentoring for, 171
    network for, 171
diversity, 70–71, 103, 112, 113
Doerr, Harriet, 63
Duke University, 96, 107
Dustman, Robert, 57

Educational Exchange Program, 114
Einstein, Albert, 52, 62

Elderhostel, vii, viii, xi, 2, 22, 24, 53, 66–
    67, 79, 80, 92, 93, 95, 101–05, 111,
    117, 139, 141–42, 146, 168, 173, 182
Elderhostel Institutional Network, vi,
    107, 108, 109
Elderhostel Service Programs, 105–06
elderlearners, See also Elderlearning
    Survey
    age of, 68
    by group, 67
    gender of, 67–68
    income of, 69, 141–42
    level of education, 70
    living arrangements of, 69
    marital status of, 68
    race or ethnic origin of, 70
    self-rated health status of, 9–10, 19,
        72–74, 162
    volunteer status of, 69–70, 162
    work and retirement, 9, 69, 148–49,
        162
    years of formal education, 71, 93
Elderlearning Questionnaire, 179–81
Elderlearning Survey, ix, xi, 9–10, 15, 17,
    19, 30, 62, 63, 66–87, 118, 120, 121,
    151, 162. See also elderlearners
    age of participants, 68
    barriers to learning, 81–83, 93, 146
    correlations between time spent
        learning and other factors, 85–6
    courses taken, 80, 81, 90–92
    educational level of participants, 70–
        71, 93
    expansion of, 169
    formal and informal learning, 83–86,
        91, 121
    groups surveyed, 66–67
    health status, self-rated, 9–10, 19, 72–
        74, 162
    high learners, 85–86
    how they learn, 76–77, 120, 130, 131,
        133, 138–39
    income of learners, 141–42
    learning styles and preferences, 76–77,
        120, 125–26
    meanings to be derived from study,
        66–87, 85-86
    time spent in learning, 83–86, 124–25
    what they're learning, 30, 42, 43, 74–
        75, 76, 125

    where they're learning, 77–81, 120,
        152
    who the learners are, 67–74, 148–49
    why they're learning, 75–76
Eliot, T.S., 52
Empire State College, 37, 136
employment, 9, 12, 69, 86, 147–51
England, demographics of aging, 7
Erikson, Erik, 29–30
exercise and intelligence, 52, 53–54, 57–
    58

Federal Council on Aging, 71
55 Plus, 79, 115
Fischer, Richard, 98
flexibility of life phases, 166–67, 174–75
fluid intelligence, 38, 47–48, 50
formal and informal learning, 80–81, 83–
    86, 88–100
    defined, 84
    non-college-based, 111–115
    relative time spent in, 83–86
    services of formal learning, 101–16
foundations
    funding for aging, 18
    roles for, 175
four ages theory, 30–32
A Fresh Map of Life: The Emergence of the
    Third Age (Laslett), 30
Friedan, Betty, 20

genealogy, 29–30, 74, 125, 139
generations, relations between. See
    intergenerational issues
generativity, 29
Gerberding, John, viii
Glasgow, Ellen, 101
Godel's Theorem, 43
Goggin, Noreen L., 57
Gordon, Barry, 49
government, role of, 173–74
Governor's State University, 183
Gray Panthers, 151

Harvard Medical School Bulletin, 43
Harvard University, Institute for Learning
    in Retirement, 107
Having Our Say (Delaney and Delaney),
    63

health
    correlation with learning, 82, 162, 169,
        175
    health care costs, 10–11
    health care system, 10, 11, 12
    male and female, 19
    of older adults, 9, 19, 72–74, 82, 161
    self-rated, 9–10, 19, 72–74, 82, 162
Henry, William F., 23
Hiemstra, R.P., 85, 127
higher education, 88–100. See also
    colleges and universities
    accommodation to older students, 88–
        89
    barriers to older adult participation,
        81–83, 92–94, 146, 168
    credentialling, 92, 168, 169
    older adult participation in, 80, 90-92
    reluctance to change, 94, 168
    research possibilities, 169–70
    response to older adults, 168
    roles to be played, 168–70, 175–76
Hispanics, 70, 131, 154
Holmes, Oliver Wendell, 37, 38, 39, 62
Horizons 60, xi
hospitals and health facilities as learning
    resources, 78, 123, 124
How to Study Independently, 184
Howe, Reuel L., 66

IBEW, 170
IBM, 134, 137
independent learning. See informal
    learning, learning, self-directed
    learning
informal learning. See also learning, self-
    directed learning
    defined, 84
    time spent in, 83–86
    under-reporting of, 84–85
Institutes for Learning in Retirement, xi,
    33, 34, 43, 66–67, 79, 80, 86, 92, 93,
    95, 96, 101, 106–11, 117, 156, 168,
    173, 182
    as model, 111, 176
    differences among, 107, 116 (f.n.8)
    governance of, 109
    issues raised by, 107–08
    quality of, 108–10, 116 (f.n.9)

institutionalization of elderly, 54–56
intelligence in older adults. See cognitive
    abilities of older learners
intelligence quotient (IQ), 43–47
intelligence testing, 43–47
    limitations of, 44–45
    social, cultural, and environmental
        factors in, 46
intergenerational issues
    activities, 171–73, 176
    competition, 12, 171–72
    cooperation, 12, 13, 95, 162, 172
    day care center, 172
    learning, 95, 96, 99, 111, 114
    tensions, 12, 162
    travel, 173
Internet, 77, 121, 126, 131, 133, 137, 171,
    182–3
I.Q. See intelligence quotient
Ishii-Kuntz, M., 20

Jackson, James, 71
Johns Hopkins University School of
    Medicine, 49, 128
Johnson, William S., 149
journal keeping, 30

Kahn, Robert, 158
Keeton, Morris T., xi
Kendal at Hanover retirement commu-
    nity, 95, 96
Knowledge TV, 183
Kuhn, Maggie, 151, 156, 159, 171, 172

LaFarge Lifelong Learning Institute, 114
Langer, Ellen, 36
Laslett, Peter, 7, 27, 30–32, 98
Laver, Gary D., 49
Leadership Asheville Seniors (LAS), 96
League of Women Voters, 41, 123, 124
learning. See also cognitive abilities of
    older learners, informal learning,
    self-directed learning
    counselors, mentors, trainers and, 129,
        132
    education and, 56–57
    effects of on elder learners, 13
    formal and informal, 83–86
    high learners, 85–86, 119

learning (continued)
    how older adults learn, 76–81, 120,
        130, 131, 133, 138–39
    importance of to older learners, ix, 13,
        128, 162–63
    independent learning opportunities,
        183
    institutional barriers to, 82, 168
    joy of, 75
    key to strong system of, 176–77
    lifelong, 12, 13, 90, 111, 128, 163
    and memory in the aged, 36–50, 58,
        59–60
    needs of older adults, 153 (chart)
    outcomes in Elderhostel Service
        programs, 106
    prevalence of among older learners,
        161
    resources for, 77–80, 101–16, 120–22,
        130–42, 170, 182–84
    society and, 162, 163
    styles and preferences, 76–77, 170
    subjects of, 30, 74–75, 76–77, 125–26
    tax incentives for elderlearning, 174
    value of to older learners, ix, 13, 128–
        29, 162
    at work or volunteer activities, 152
leisure, 2, 16, 158–59
    challenge of, 159
    concept of, 158
    learning and, 159
    links to psychological health, 159
libraries, xi, 78–79, 99, 129, 131–32, 171,
    172, 175
life expectancy, 1, 19, 24, 145
    biological potential for, 7, 19
    education and, 56–57
    in England, 7
    increase in, 5–8
life stage theory, 27–35
    breaking out of the boxes, 166–67
lifespan. See life expectancy
Linnehan, Mary, xii
Lipman, Henry, 98
longitudinal studies, 38, 46–47,
longevity. See life expectancy
Lopatin, Anita, xi, 112–13

MacArthur Foundation Consortium on
    Successful Aging, 60
MacNeill, Richard D., 159
Manheimer, Ronald, xi, 96
Mann, Marylen, 111
Manton, Kenneth, 5, 10
Maricopa Community Colleges, 136
Maslow, Abraham, 53
Maugham, Somerset, 36
May Foundation, 111
McClearn, Gerald E., 60
McCoy, Vivian Rogers, 28
McMaster University, 58
Medicaid, 4
Medicare, 4, 10, 16, 145, 149, 156
memory, 39–50, 58–60
    long-term, 49
    overload, 49
    short-term, 40, 47–49, 58, 59–60
    tip-of-the-tongue phenomenon, 49
    training, 59–60
mentoring, 129, 132, 162, 171, 175
mind-body connections, 52–61
Mind Extension University, 137. See also
    Knowledge TV
Mindfulness (Langer), 36–37
mindlessness, 36–37
Monk, Abraham, 144
Moody, Harry R., 101, 166
Museum of Natural History, 22
museums, 77, 81
myths of aging, deconstruction of, 38–39

National Center for Education Statistics
    (NCES), 68, 80, 131, 174
National Institute of Aging, 6, 56
National Institutes of Health, 18
National Research Institute, 90
Nearing, Helen, 156
Nearing, Scott, 156
Neugarten, Bernice, 23, 29
New School for Social Research, 34, 107–
    08
New York City Department of Aging, 150
North Carolina Center for Creative
    Retirement, xi, 96
North Carolina State University, 96
"nun study" of aging, 56, 64 (f.n.9)

OASIS, xi, 58, 66–67, 71, 79, 111–13, 142, 182
   in Pittsburgh, 112–13
Ohio University, 136, 183
old, definitions of, 1–2, 15–25. *See also* aging, definitions of
older adult learning, ix
   crystallized intelligence, 38, 47–48
   early studies, 38.
   longitudinal studies, 38
   terminal drop, 39
older adults. *See also* Third Age, Agers
   economic potential of, 163
   inclusion in learning community, 2, 162, 163
   level of previous education, 93
   new life roles for, 13
   preferred terminology, 173–74
   responsibility for change, 167, 176–77
   resource for society, 32
organizations, roles for, 175

Park, Denise C., 49
Peace Corps, 151
Penland, P., 125–26
Penn State University, 59
pension systems, 9
Pepper, Claude, 52, 150
Peterson, David A., 43–44, 102, 115
physical exercise. *See* exercise and intelligence
PLATO Society (UCLA), 107
Pogrebin, Letty Cottin, 138–39
Princeton University, 96–97
prior learning assessment (PLA), 89
Public Library Inquiry (PLI), 131
public schools as elderlearning resource, 80, 91–92, 134

quality of life issues, 13

Rao, Mukunda, 147
reading by elderlearners, 76–77, 120, 128, 131
Regents' College, New York, 136, 183
removing institutional barriers, 168
research on aging, 17–18, 174, 175
Research Triangle Park, 96

resources for elderlearning, 77–81, 120–22, 130–42, 182-4, 88–142
   allocation of, 4, 12, 176
retirement, 2, 8, 22, 92, 143–47
   age of, 11, 65, 145, 148, 149
   challenge of, 159, 166–67
   "commencement," 146–47, 175
   definition of, 143–44
   downsizing and, 148, 149
   economic potential of elder workers, 163
   flexibility in, 166–67, 174–75
   history of, 11, 16, 144–45
   keys to "good," 164–65
   life stage and, 145
   planning for, 146–47, 164–65
   policies for, 11, 16, 145, 163–64
   rites of, 146
   voluntary and involuntary, 16, 148–49, 163
   of women, 23, 148
   work and, 69, 174
retraining programs for older adults, 17, 150–51
"Returning to Learning" workshops, 170–71, 176
Riegel, Klaus, 38–39
Riegel, Ruth, 38–39
Robichaud, Anne, 104–05
Rockefeller, David, 155
Rosenberg, Irwin, xii
Rowe, John W., 19, 60, 151
R.S.V.P. (Retired Senior Volunteer Program), 155

Salthouse, Timothy A., 44–45, 57
Sarton, May, 62
Schaie, K. Warner, 39, 42, 46, 53, 57
schools, roles for, 175–76
Schopenhauer, Arthur, 88
SCORE (Senior Corps of Retired Executives), 155
Scott Paper Company, 170
Scripps College, 58
Seccombe, K., 20
self-directed learning, 13, 76–77, 83–85, 117–29, 162, 170–71 *See also* informal learning, learning

self-directed learning (continued)
    computers and, 121, 125
    learners, 118–19
    learning skills for, 99
    prevalence of, 76–77, 83–85, 162, 170,
        171
    resources for, 120–22, 132–142
    significance of, 127–29
    structure of, 119–20
    subjects of, 122–27
    time spent in, 83–86, 126–27
self-generated learning. See informal
        learning, learning, self-directed
        learning
Senior Academy for Intergenerational
        Learning (SAIL), 96
SeniorNet, 22, 135–36, 183
Seniors in the Schools, 96
Shakespeare, William, 27–28, 61
Sheehy, Gail, 1, 28, 29
Shepherd's Centers, 79, 115, 182
Sierra Club, 156
Simonton, Dean, 61
Sky, Harry, 177
Smith, Anderson D., 49
Smithsonian Institution, 22, 66–67, 140–
        41, 182
Snowdon, David, 56
social activity and mental health, 52–57
Social Security, 4, 9, 11, 16, 149, 163–64,
        166, 174
    age of benefits eligibility, 11, 16, 145
    history of, 144–45
    policies, 11, 149, 163–64, 174
stereotyped thinking and mindlessness,
        36–37
stereotypes of age and aging, 3–4, 21, 36–
        38, 102, 156
    countering of, 4–5, 38, 175
    deconstructing myths of aging, 38–39
    penalties and costs, 16
    reversal of, 173–74
    social effects of, 4
standardized testing, 43–45
statistics, aging population See also
        demographics
    in civilian labor force, 9
    disability rates, 10

in Elderlearning Survey, 66–87, passim
in schools, colleges and universities,
        90–92
St. Louis University, xi
Stelmach, George E., 57
Stones for Ibarra (Doerr), 63
Students of the Third Age (Lipman), 98
study/travel. See travel and learning
Suzman, Richard, 56
Swift, Jonathan, 19
Syracuse University, 107

tax incentives for elderlearning programs,
        174
Teague, Michael L., 159
Teilhard de Chardin, Pierre, 151
telecommunications and learning, 132–38
television, 47, 76, 119, 120–21
Tennyson, Alfred Lord, 61
terminal drop, 32, 39
Third Age, Agers. See also older adults
    defined, 31, 32, 33, 109
    learning and, 96, 111, 117, 122, 146
    as life stage, 145
    preparation for, 98
    as time of development, 62, 109
    travel and, 138–39
    as volunteers, 99
Thomas A. Edison State College, 136, 183
Thurmond, Strom, 52, 156
Thurow, Lester C., 8
Tiger in the Grass (Doerr), 63
time, as barrier to learning, 146
tip-of-the-tongue phenomenon, 49
Tough, Allen, 84, 85, 118–19, 126, 127
travel and learning, viii, 22, 74, 76, 101–
        06, 115, 121–22, 138–42, 182–83
Trevelyan, Humphrey, 63
Triangle area (North Carolina), 96
Tufts University Human Nutrition
        Research Center on Aging, 59
two-year colleges. See community colleges

UCEA. See University Continuing
        Education Association
United Auto Workers (UAW), 170
Université du Troisième Age, 33, 34
universities. See colleges and universities

Universities of the Third Age, 33–34, 98, 107
  libraries as, 132
University Continuing Education Association (UCEA), 183
University of Michigan, 38, 131, 158
University of North Carolina, 96
University Vacations, 183
U.S. Census Bureau, 91
U.S. Special Committee on Aging, 10

Vaupel, James, 5
Verscheuren, Jim, xi
vitamins, 59
volunteer activity of older adults, 9,10, 67–70, 86, 99, 111, 151–57, 162, 176, 177
  at Center for Creative Retirement, 96
  correlation with learning, 86, 106
  effects of, 157–58
  Elderhostel Service Programs, 105–06
  nonorganized, 157
  political, 156–57
  relative participation of men and women, 70
  in service of social goals, 10, 105–06, 162, 170
  training for, 152–54
  using prior learning and skills, 154–56
volunteerism, 151–59. See also volunteer activity of older adults
Volunteers in Medicine, 154
voter turnout of older adults, 10, 156

Watson, Thomas J., 133
Wechsler, David, 43
Wechsler Adult Intelligence Scale (WAIS), 43–5. See also intelligence quotient
wellness model of aging, 174

What the Public Wants from Higher Education (1995), 94
Willis, Sherry, 60
Wirtz, Willard, 166
wisdom in aging, 35 (f.n.9), 61–64, 177
  in ancient and Eastern societies, 61
Wolfe, Stewart, 19
women, 34 (f.n.4), 67–8, 69, 70, 75–76, 88, 91, 113
  blazing a trail, 167
  computers and, 133
  disengagement and retirement, 23, 34 (f.n.4), 167
  participation in formal education, 67–68, 88, 91, 113
work, 9, 147–50
  barriers for older adults, 149–50, 163
  beyond retirement age, 148, 149–50, 163–64
  downsizing, 148, 149
  economic potential of elder workers, 163
  education and, 166
  flexible options, 162, 164, 166–67, 175
  number of older adults employed, 9, 163
  productivity of older workers, 149, 158, 162
  retirement and, 9, 69, 162–63, 166, 174–75
  retraining for, 150–51, 163
  under-investment in training for, 163
workforce, seniors in, 9, 13, 69
Workforce 2000, 149–50
World War II, 166–67

Yeats, William Butler, 117, 143
YMWCAs, YMWHAs, 78, 115, 123

ISBN 0-89774-959-6

9 0 0 0 0

9 780897 749596